Family-Friendly Policies and Practices in Academe

Family-Friendly Policies and Practices in Academe

Edited by Erin K. Anderson
and Catherine Richards Solomon

LEXINGTON BOOKS
Lanham • Boulder • New York • London

Published by Lexington Books
An imprint of The Rowman & Littlefield Publishing Group, Inc.
4501 Forbes Boulevard, Suite 200, Lanham, Maryland 20706
www.rowman.com

Unit A, Whitacre Mews, 26-34 Stannary Street, London SE11 4AB

British Library Cataloguing in Publication Information Available

Library of Congress Cataloging-in-Publication Data

Family-friendly policies and practices in academe / edited by Erin K. Anderson and Catherine
Richards Solomon.
  p. cm.
Includes bibliographical references and index.
ISBN 978-0-7391-9439-3 (cloth : alk. paper) – ISBN 978-0-7391-9440-9 (ebook)
1. College personnel management–United States. 2. College teachers–Family relationships–United
States. 3. College teachers–United States–Leaves of absence. 4. College personnel management–United States–Case studies. 5. College teachers–Family relationships–United States–Case
studies. 6. College teachers–United States–Leaves of absence–Case studies. I. Anderson, Erin K.,
1974- editor of compilation, author. II. Solomon, Catherine Richards, 1974- editor of compilation,
author.
LB2331.68.F36 2015
378.1'1–dc23
2015002891

Printed in the United States of America

Dedicated to my parents, Bill and Sharyn Anderson, who always put family first. And to my husband, Jonathan Schultz, whose support in our family enables me to succeed in the workplace.
—Erin K. Anderson

* * *

Dedicated to my husband, John, for encouragement in every stage of my career, to my daughters, Natalie and Ellie, as the inspiration for this book, and to my parents and sister, who gave me roots to grow and wings to fly.
—Catherine Richards Solomon

Contents

Part I

Inspecting the Ivory Tower:
What We Know about Work/Life
Policies in the Academy

Chapter One

Introduction to Volume

Erin K. Anderson and Catherine Richards Solomon

Academe has experienced rapid and profound changes in the composition and characteristics of faculty since the mid-1900s. Given these changes, many universities have begun to offer family-friendly policies to address the varied work/family concerns of their faculty bodies. In this book, we present research studies about varied dimensions of faculty's work/family management as well as innovative case studies by faculty who have developed policies and programs at their respective universities. Thus, this edited volume showcases cutting-edge research about work/family issues at academic institutions and provides concrete guidance for faculty and administrators looking to act as agents of change at their universities.

CHANGING LANDSCAPE OF ACADEME

In the last forty years, the composition and characteristics of faculty at universities and colleges in the United States has drastically changed. In particular, academe has seen a surge in women in graduate programs and tenure-track faculty positions. About half of all doctoral degrees awarded at the beginning of the twenty-first century were earned by women (Mason, Wolfinger, and Goulden 2013; National Center for Education Statistics 2011). Despite the high number of women PhDs, faculty positions remain mostly populated by men as women continue to disproportionately occupy non-tenure track and adjunct teaching positions (August 2006; West and Curtis 2006; Wolfinger, Mason, and Goulden 2009). Women comprise only a third of full-time faculty—including both tenure and non-tenure track (West and Curtis 2006). A recent study of graduate students shows that many, both women and men, are hesitant to work in academe because they view it as hostile to faculty with family responsibilities (Mason, Goulden, and Frasch 2009). These graduate students are perhaps familiar with standards of success in academia that are rooted in a gendered model of sole devotion to work and a lack of family responsibilities (Solomon 2011). Once in a tenure-track position, however, there appears to be further attrition of women faculty. They move up faculty ranks slower than faculty who are men and continue to be underrepresented in tenured associate and tenured full faculty positions (Mason and Goulden 2002). Long faculty workweeks and women's responsibility for family work could account for this attrition (Kotila, Schoppe-Sullivan, and Dush 2013; Misra, Lundquist, and Templer 2012; O'Laughlin and Bischoff 2005). Faculty members of all ranks work, on average, close to sixty hours a week (Jacobs and Winslow 2004). And women, regardless of education, occupation, or professional rank, still tend to perform the greatest proportion of the second shift (Bureau of Labor Statistics 2014; Hochschild 1989; Tichenor 2005). Thus, because of the lack of congruency between women faculty's home life and their work responsibilities, many women faculty never attain tenure-track positions, and when they do, they face obstacles to moving up the tenure ladder. Thus, many work/family researchers and feminist scholars examine the experiences of women in academe in an effort to transform academia into a more gender inclusive institution.

In this introductory chapter, we provide a short overview of the literature on work/family conflict for women in academe. In addition, we examine the growing literature of work/family conflict for men in academe, as their experiences managing work and family responsibilities appear to be evolving (Solomon 2010). Indeed, despite the benefits of working in academe (e.g., flexible schedules, autonomous work), many faculty, both men and women, experience high levels of work/family conflict and dissatisfaction with their work hours (Misra, Lundquist, and Templer 2012; O'Laughlin and Bischoff 2005; Ward and Wolf-Wendel 2012).

WORK/FAMILY CONFLICT FOR WOMEN FACULTY

As increasing numbers of women complete advanced degrees and pursue careers in academia, many more faculty must find a balance between their research and teaching demands and family care. Women disproportionately perform this balancing act, as much research documents (Misra, Lundquist, and Templer 2012; O'Laughlin and Bischoff 2005). Scholars also find that there seems to be a negative effect on women for attending to their family's needs. Having a baby pre-tenure reduces the chance that women will earn tenure by 25 percent (Mason and Goulden 2004b). Implicit discrimination seems to occur in the other direction as well: women who advance into tenured positions are less likely to get married and have children than men who occupy tenured positions (Mason and Goulden 2004a). When they are married, women faculty are more likely than men to be married to a spouse who works full-time (Mason, Wolfinger, and Goulden 2013) and they are less likely to have children, or the number of children they want, than are men (Mason and Goulden 2004a).

Women at both research universities and liberal arts colleges report conflict between work and family responsibilities (Ward and Wolf-Wendel 2012). Women at research universities experienced conflict between their research and family responsibilities whereas women at liberal arts colleges describe experiencing conflict between teaching and service and family responsibilities.

WORK/FAMILY CONFLICT FOR MEN FACULTY

According to a small, but growing, body of recent research about men faculty, men in academe increasingly feel that they too deal with the challenges of combining careers and family (Solomon 2010). Similar to women, some men now report delaying having children until they earn tenure (Solomon 2011). Planning children around professional demands has long been a strategy employed by women; there is now greater evidence men are organizing their personal and professional lives in similar fashion (Solomon 2010). Both male and female professors also report experiencing work/family stress at comparable levels (O'Laughlin and Bischoff 2005; Solomon 2010). These changes could be in part because faculty men are more likely than in previous generations to have spouses who work for pay or to be single parents (Jacobs and Gerson 2004). In addition, societal expectations of fathers' involvement with their children have evolved to expect more hands-on, engaged fathering (Bianchi, Robinson, and Milkie 2006; Sandberg and Hofferth 2001; Solomon 2014; Yeung, Sandberg, Davis-Kean, and Hofferth 2001). Thus, men faculty are likely to be dealing with an increased expectation for home involvement, which leaves less time to devote to their professional lives.

FAMILY-FRIENDLY POLICIES IN ACADEME

In response to the increase of women doctoral recipients and to the increase in work/family conflict experienced by men and women faculty, many universities have developed family-friendly policies and programs to recruit and retain the best faculty by helping them manage their work and family responsibilities. It appears that elite research universities offer the most cutting-edge policies and programs, perhaps in an effort to attract the "best and brightest" of doctoral recipients (Hollenshead, Sullivan, Smith, August, and

Hamilton 2005). The policies most commonly offered by universities are paid maternity leave, paid parental leave, and an extension on the tenure clock.

CONTRIBUTIONS IN THIS BOOK

In part one, we focus on empirical studies that demonstrate the need for innovative programs and policies for faculty at colleges and universities. These pieces explore issues such as the influence of workplace culture on the use of existing policies, the value of work/life programs for employee retention, men's experiences with leave-taking, and the need for a variety of family-support policies, including elder care.

In "University Family-Friendly Policies: Professors' Experiences and Perceptions," Catherine Richards Solomon presents research about faculty's experiences with family-friendly policies, such as paid maternity leave, paid parental leave, and tenure extension. Very few studies examine the experiences of professors using such policies or how the use of these policies shape work/family management of professors with children. These issues are explored through in-depth interviews with mothers and fathers who worked as untenured tenure-track assistant professors. She concludes that faculty with children found the policies to be useful for the immediate period following the birth or adoption of a child, but more help is needed for long-term work/family management. Thus, although such policies seemed important to faculty in managing their work and family responsibilities, a shift in the culture of academe is necessary for university culture to be more accommodating to family life.

In chapter three, "Do Work/Life Policies Matter?: The Importance of Work/Life Policies for Reducing Faculty Intention to Quit," Catherine White Berheide and Rena Linden consider the value faculty place on work/family policies as a way to help them manage competing demands in their lives. Academic institutions are expanding the numbers and types of work/family policies they offer in part to decrease turnover among their faculty. But do such policies accomplish this function? Berheide and Linden emphasize that department and workplace culture are arguably more influential in faculty retention than the mere existence of polices. If faculty do not feel they are able to use such policies, then the policies themselves have little impact. Grounded in a new institutionalism perspective, these findings highlight the role of institutional culture in policy utilization.

In chapter four, "'Could I be THAT Guy?': The Influence of Policy and Climate on Men's Paternity Leave Use," Erin K. Anderson looks at men on the faculty and staff at the same institution who have the same paid parental leave available to them, but use this policy at different rates. The norms and the logistics of leave use vary significantly between these two types of academic employees. Interviews with fathers who have been eligible for fifteen weeks of paid leave reveal that men seem to be more concerned with the consequences of their absence from the workplace on their colleagues and their own careers than they are with contributing to childcare and household labor. In contrast to much research that finds men unlikely to use the Family and Medical Leave Act (FMLA) because they would lose important income, Anderson finds that even when income is not at stake, coworkers, careers, and workplace climate are powerful factors that influence men's decisions whether or not to utilize parental leave.

Rona J. Karasik, Debra L. Berke, and Scott D. Scheer examine faculty thoughts about a work/family issue that hasn't received much attention in the research: elder care. Chapter five, "Caring for Aging Parents: Managing the Personal and Professional in Academia," utilizes a life course perspective to identify and investigate the practices and concerns a growing number of workers have with helping to manage the needs of aging parents. While "stop the clock" and parental leave policies are increasingly common in the academy, few policies exist to assist faculty in the performance of elder care or allow for bereavement time. Policies that would allow a faculty member to accomplish this kind of care work are particularly relevant to women, who are more likely to provide assistance for activities of daily living for older family members. This issue, like many other work/family issues, is likely to arise at the time of one's professional career in which they are trying to achieve tenure or promotion. The fact that few policies exist that address the issues related to elder care means caregivers may be more likely to face limitations in their professional pursuits.

In chapter six and subsequent chapters we address in greater depth the prevalence and types of policies and programs universities and colleges provide as well as offer procedural information on how such policies have been developed and assessed at a variety of institutions.

REFERENCES

August, Louise. 2006. "It Isn't Over: The Continuing Under-Representation of Women Faculty." Center for the Education of Women. Retrieved August 1, 2012 (http://www.cew.umich.edu/sites/default/files/augustfemrep06_0.pdf).

Bianchi, Suzanne M., John P. Robinson, and Melissa A. Milkie. 2006. *Changing Rhythms of American Family Life*. New York: Russell Sage.

Bureau of Labor Statistics. 2014. "Economic News Release: American Time Use Survey—2013 Results." Retrieved December 10, 2014 (http://www.bls.gov/news.release/atus.nr0.htm).

Hochschild, Arlie, and Anne Machung. 1989. *The Second Shift: Working Parents and the Revolution at Home*. New York: Viking.

Hollenshead, Carol S., Beth Sullivan, Gilia C. Smith, Louise August, and Susan Hamilton. 2005. "Work/Family Policies in Higher Education: Survey Data and Case Studies of Policy Implementation." *New Directions for Higher Education* 130:41–65.

Jacobs, Jerry A., and Kathleen Gerson. 2004. *The Time Divide: Work, Family, and Gender Inequality.* Cambridge, MA: Harvard University Press.

Jacobs, Jerry A., and Sarah E. Winslow. 2004. "Overworked Faculty: Job Stresses and Family Demands." *Annals of the American Academy of Political and Social Science* 596:104–29.

Kotila, Letitia E., Sarah J. Schoppe-Sullivan, and Claire M. Kamp Dush. 2013. "Time in Parenting Activities in Dual-Earner Families at the Transition to Parenthood." *Family Relations* 62:795–807.

Mason, Mary Ann, and Marc Goulden. 2002. "Do Babies Matter?" *Academe* 88:21.

———. 2004a. "Do Babies Matter (Part II)? Closing the Baby Gap." *Academe* 90.

———. 2004b. "Marriage and Baby Blues: Redefining Gender Equity in the Academy." *Annals of the American Academy of Social and Political Science* 596: 86–103.

Mason, Mary Ann, Marc Goulden, and Karie Frasch. 2009. "Why Graduate Students Reject the Fast Track." *Academe* 65.

Mason, Mary Ann, Nicholas H. Wolfinger, and Marc Goulden. 2013. *Do Babies Matter? Gender and Family in the Ivory Tower.* New Brunswick, NJ: Rutgers University Press.

Misra, Joya, Jennifer H. Lundquist, and Abby Templer. 2012. "Gender, Work Time, and Care Responsibilities among Faculty." *Sociological Forum* 27:300–23.

National Center for Education Statistics (U.S. Department of Education). 2011. *National Survey of Postsecondary Faculty: Digest of Educational Statistics, Table 197.* Retrieved December 1, 2012 (http://nces.ed.gov/programs/digest/2011menu_tables.asp).

O'Laughlin, Elizabeth M., and Lisa G. Bischoff. 2005. "Balancing Parenthood and Academia: Work/family Stress as Influenced by Gender and Tenure Status." *Journal of Family Issues* 26:79–106.

Sandberg, John F., and Sandra L. Hofferth. 2001. "Changes in Children's Time with Parents: United States 1981–1997." *Demography* 38:423–36.

Solomon, Catherine Richards. 2014. "'I Feel Like a Rock Star': Fatherhood for Stay-at-Home Fathers." *Fathering* 12:52–70.

———. 2011. "'Sacrificing at the Altar of Tenure': Assistant Professors' Work/Life Management." *The Social Science Journal* 48:335–44.

———. 2010. "'The Very Highest Thing Is Family': Male Untenured Assistant Professors' Construction of Work and Family." Pp. 233–55 in *Advances in Gender Research: Interactions and Intersections of Gendered Bodies at Work, at Home, and at Play*, edited by V. P. Demos and M. T. Segal. Bingley, UK: Emerald Group Publishing Limited.

Tichenor, Veronica. 2005. *Earning More and Getting Less: Why Successful Wives Can't Buy Equality.* New Brunswick, NJ: Rutgers University Press.

Ward, Kelly, and Lisa Wolf-Wendel. 2012. *Academic Motherhood: How Faculty Manage Work and Family.* New Brunswick, NJ: Rutgers University Press.

West, Martha S., and John W. Curtis. 2006. "AAUP faculty gender equity indicators 2006." Retrieved January 15, 2014 (http://www.aaup.org/reports-publications/publications/see-all/aaup-faculty-gender-equity-indicators-2006).

Wolfinger, Nicholas H., Mary Ann Mason, and Marc Goulden. 2009. "Stay in the Game: Gender, Family Formation, and Alternative Trajectories in the Academic Life Course." *Social Forces* 87:1591–621.

Yeung, W. Jean, John F. Sandberg, Pamela E. Davis-Kean, and Sandra L. Hofferth. 2001. "Children's Time with Fathers in Intact Families." *Journal of Marriage and Family* 63:136–54.

Chapter Two

University Family-Friendly Policies

Professors' Experiences and Perceptions

Catherine Richards Solomon

In 2001, the American Association of University Professors (AAUP) issued a "Statement on principles of family responsibilities and academic work." In this statement, the AAUP urged universities to be more accommodating to professors' family responsibilities. In part, this accommodation should occur because of the growing number of women in faculty ranks. Even though the number of women faculty has greatly increased since the 1960s, women still comprise less than half of all faculty (National Center for Education Statistics 2011). According to West and Curtis (2006), women make up only a third of full-time faculty. Many women struggle in academe because of work and family responsibilities (as women continue to shoulder the majority of family work) and the lack of family-friendly policies[1] (Ward and Wolf-Wendel 2004; Young and Wright 2001). Partly because of these issues, women tend to be disproportionately represented in non-tenure track positions (August 2006; Wolfinger, Mason, and Goulden 2009). Instituting family-friendly policies may enable universities to move toward gender equity by increasing the presence of women among tenured faculty.

Some research has indicated that men experience work/family conflict in academia, too. Both male and female professors report experiencing work/family stress at a comparable level (O'Laughlin and Bischoff 2005; Solomon 2010, 2011). There is also some indication that men plan children around their professional demands (Solomon 2010, 2011). Thus, there seems to be a need to develop family-friendly policies for women, but perhaps also to meet the work/family needs of the current cohort of men in academe.

In addition to gender equity, another reason for offering family-friendly policies is to attract faculty, particularly at research universities where the

9

expectations for scholarship can be quite rigorous. A study of graduate students demonstrated that many young scholars, men and women, are choosing to work outside academia because they do not perceive it as family-friendly (Mason, Goulden, and Frasch 2009). Thus, the lack of family-friendly policies seems to be detrimental to academe both in terms of gender equity and attracting bright faculty. When policies are in place, what role do they play in professors' work/family management? I address this question in this exploratory study. Understanding how professors experience such policies is crucial to stemming the flow of talented scholars, particularly women, out of academe.

WORK/FAMILY ISSUES AND FAMILY-FRIENDLY POLICIES

Businesses have increasingly offered some type of family-friendly policy as many workers in the United States experience work/family conflict (Bianchi and Milkie 2010; Matos and Galinsky 2012). There are more mothers than fathers who report conflict between work and family responsibilities (Bryon 2005), but the number of men experiencing work/family conflict has grown in the past fifteen years (Aumann, Galinsky, and Matos 2011; Bellavia and Frone 2005). Work/family conflict is especially prevalent among professionals, who report higher levels of conflict than non-professional workers (Jacobs and Gerson 2004; Matos and Galinsky 2011). These higher levels seem due to high expectations for the work hours, face time, overtime, and an exclusive devotion to work (Blair-Loy 2003).

In general, it seems that employees are interested in policies that allow them to work flexible hours, that allow for part-time work, that allow for working from home, and that provide help with childcare (Blair-Loy and Wharton 2002; Galinsky, Bond, and Friedman 1993). Employees who work in settings that allow for a certain degree of control over their work schedules and that focus on output instead of work hours report lower levels of work/family spillover (Kelly, Moen, and Tranby 2011; Matos and Galinsky 2011). When available, family-friendly policies are generally used more often by women with young or school-aged children than other groups (Blair-Loy and Wharton 2002). These women tend to report high levels of satisfaction with such policies (Glass and Riley 1998).

Workers' perceptions and experience of these policies are not always positive, however. Taking a parental leave or reducing work hours can be perceived as hurting one's chances for career advancement because it supposedly signals a weak devotion to work (Blair-Loy and Wharton 2002). In addition, policies that allow for flexible hours can actually increase the number of hours employees work and increase work/family conflict for workers in employment sectors with unclear boundaries between home and work

(Blair-Loy 2009; Galinsky, Bond, and Friedman 1996; Hill, Hawkins, Ferris, and Weitzman 2001). Supportive supervisors can protect employees from potential repercussions for using policies (Allen, Shockley, and Poteat 2008; Blair-Loy and Wharton 2002). Employees with supportive supervisors are more likely to use such policies (Allen, Shockley, and Poteat 2008; Blair-Loy and Wharton 2002) and are less likely to report work/family conflict (Bryon 2005; Matos and Galinsky 2011). These results illustrate how climate can be more important for work/family management, as climate can affect whether individuals use policies and how such use is perceived by others (Behson 2005; Blair-Loy and Wharton 2002; Jacobs and Gerson 2004).

UNIVERSITY FAMILY-FRIENDLY POLICIES

The availability of family-friendly policies varies widely across universities (AAUP 2001; CEW 2007; Norrell and Norrell, 1996). Policies can range from six weeks of paid maternity leave to a full semester of paid leave for both men and women (CEW 2007; Norrell and Norrell 1996). This leave can include offering reduced teaching duties following the birth or adoption of a child for professors who provide at least half of the caregiving duties (CEW 2007; Hollenshead, Sullivan, Smith, August, and Hamilton 2005; UC Faculty Family Friendly Edge 2003; WorkLifeLaw 2009). Many universities also have an explicit tenure extension policy, which is normally the addition of a full year to the tenure clock (CEW 2007; Hollenshead et al. 2005; Norrell and Norrell 1996). This policy is sometimes automatically applied to a faculty member's tenure clock and can be used separately or in conjunction with parental leave (CEW 2007; WorkLifeLaw 2009).

In a comprehensive review of institutions, the Center for the Education of Women (CEW) found that only about 30 percent of universities and colleges offered paid parental leave for women in addition to paid maternity leave through a formal, written, institution-wide policy (2007). Eighty percent of colleges and universities offered paid maternity leave for six weeks (CEW 2007). About 21 percent offered a period of modified duties (a reduction in teaching, for example) (CEW 2007). Finally, about two-thirds of academic institutions allowed faculty to stop the tenure clock for a year (CEW 2007).

Very few research studies exist in which there is an in-depth examination of professors' perceptions of and experiences with university family-friendly policies. One focus group study has shown that formal policies help parents as they care for newborns or newly adopted children and can make faculty feel more positive about their institutions (Drago and Colbeck 2003; Lundquist, Misra, and O'Meara 2012). However, policies are underused, particularly by men (Drago, Crouter, Wardell, and Willits 2001; Lundquist, Misra, and O'Meara 2012). This underuse seems to stem from a fear of negative repercussions for taking family leave (Armenti 2004; Drago, Crouter, Wardell, and Willits 2001; Finkel and Olswang 1996; Norrell and Norrell 1996). However, the support of colleagues after having children seems important for professors' feelings about work and family, regardless of the availability of policies (Drago and Colbeck 2003; Young and Wright 2001).

Almost all studies that have examined faculty's use of policies are based on survey data (Drago, Crouter, Wardell, and Willits 2001; Finkel and Olswang 1996; Mason and Goulden 2004; Young and Wright 2001), but see Drago and Colbeck (2003) and Lundquist, Misra, and O'Meara (2012). Thus, there is very little detailed information about individuals' experiences with such policies. Norrell and Norrell (1996), who conducted a review of university policies, called for in-depth research that examined professors' experiences. As Kossek, Lautsch, and Eaton (2006) also argued, it is not sufficient to simply determine whether policies are available and the number and type of professors who have used policies because doing so only produces partial knowledge about the efficacy of such policies. To address these gaps, I conducted an exploratory study of professors' perceptions of and experiences with their universities' family-friendly policies.

METHODS

Given that relatively little is known about professors' experiences with university work/family policies, I chose a qualitative research design for this exploratory study. A qualitative design was especially appropriate for this study as such a method allowed me to explore participants' "interior experience[s]" (Weiss 1994, 1). To approach a rich understanding of people's work experiences, interviewers seek "deep" information and understanding of participants' experiences (Johnson 2002).

I conducted in-depth face-to-face semi-structured interviews with untenured tenure-track assistant professors. I recruited participants from two large research universities, both located in a Northeastern state. One university, Hilltop (a pseudonym) was private, and the other, Valley (also a pseudonym) was public. The selection of these specific universities was based on the similarity in size, similarity in faculty composition, and similarity in type of university. The universities offered different formal family leave policies for faculty, which I describe below. I used systematic random sampling to gather a diverse sample and minimize selection bias. Systematic random sampling involves selecting a random starting point and then choosing every *k*th item after that on the list of items (participants) (Schutt 2001). To select my sample, I used university and department listings of faculty. From these listings, I selected small samples of faculty to email about my project.

I recruited both men and women as I wanted to examine how gender was related to perceptions of and experiences with these policies. As this was an exploratory study, I wanted to get a range of perceptions of the policies. Therefore, I recruited professors with and without children and professors who had not used a family-friendly policy. Additionally, I hoped to include enough participants from racial-ethnic minority groups to reflect the demographics of these universities (between 15–20 percent of the sample).

I interviewed thirty-seven assistant professors. Sixteen of these participants worked at Valley (eight women and eight men) and twenty-one participants worked at Hilltop (eleven women and ten men). Twenty-one participants were parents. Participants who were from racial and ethnic minorities comprised 19 percent of the sample. The ages of participants ranged from twenty-eight to forty-nine years old. Every participant with children was married and/or in a long-term committed relationship (one participant) (for simplicity's sake, I will refer to all of these individuals as spouses). Participants had between one and four children, ranging from infants to teenagers, but the majority of participants' children were infants or toddlers. Marital status of participants without children varied: seven were married, six were single but had a partner, and three were single and not in a relationship. Participants' disciplines included sciences, humanities, social sciences, fine arts, education, and business.

I used a semi-structured interview guide when interviewing participants. Topics included career trajectories, work responsibilities, tenure expectations, family and living situations, daily schedules, leisure activities, childcare situations (when relevant), and family-friendly policies. Interviews lasted between one hour and three hours, with the majority running one and a half hours. I tape-recorded the interviews and transcribed each verbatim for analysis. Bogdan and Biklen's (1998) approach guided data analysis. I looked for patterns and topics in the data that related to family-friendly policies. I then grouped these patterns and topics into codes which comprised the key themes. These codes were grouped into larger themes which reflected the different aspects of participants' experiences.

Hilltop's family leave policies. Hilltop University had three policies to specifically address professors' family responsibilities: extension of the tenure probationary period, parental leave upon the request of parents, and maternity leave. Hilltop University allowed for two one-year extensions during the five pre-tenure years for any tenure-track professor, male or female, who became a parent through birth or adoption of children less than seven years of age. The parental leave policy allowed for a semester of half duty with full pay: either a reduction of one course *or* up to one-half of a semester without any duties. This leave was available to both men and women, and had to be taken within twelve months of a birth or an adoption. The maternity leave policy (considered part of the medical disability policy) allowed for a woman to take between six and eight weeks of paid leave due to medical disability as prescribed by her doctor or midwife. A woman could combine the maternity and parental leaves if her maternity leave extended at least four weeks into a semester. By combining these policies, a woman could receive a full semester off from teaching duties at full pay. By offering these polices, Hilltop University offered among the most progressive and generous policies at colleges and universities (CEW 2007; Norrell and Norrell 1996).

Valley's family leave policies. Valley University's paid family leave policies were similar to many other universities in the United States (CEW 2007; Norrell and Norrell 1996). Valley University had the same maternity leave policy as Hilltop, but considered maternity leave as sick leave with pay. Valley offered six to eight weeks of paid maternity leave policy, five days of paid paternity leave, and up to seven months of unpaid leave to women or men for childcare purposes. The paid maternity leave could begin no more than four weeks before the delivery and allowed for six weeks off after the birth of a child for a normal delivery or eight weeks for a cesarean section. Men were eligible to take five days of paid sick leave following the birth of a child. Faculty could also request seven months of unpaid leave for childcare purposes. If both parents worked for the university and both wanted to take this seven-month leave, they would have to split the leave. For cases of adoption, employees could take six months of unpaid leave for those adoptions that required a child to live with the adoptive parents six months prior to the official adoption. Valley did not have a specific tenure extension policy, like Hilltop. Any leave taken from work with full pay was counted toward years of service. Any leave from work taken without full pay was not counted toward years in service. This means that for untenured assistant professors, if they took any leave with full pay, their tenure clock did not stop. If they took any leave without full pay, their tenure clock stopped for the amount of time taken off from work. For example, if an untenured assistant professor took three months off from work without full pay, the tenure clock stopped for three months.

RESULTS

Knowledge of Policies: Parental Leave and Tenure Extension

Participants' knowledge levels about their universities' policies varied. Several knew very little, a few had some knowledge but were unclear on the details, and several had a more complete understanding of what the policies offered. More participants with children, those who had used a policy, and those who were women more accurately described the policies than did participants without children, those who hadn't used a policy, or those who were men. For example, Amy, a married thirty-one-year-old white woman at Valley with a son, described the maternity leave policy at Valley to me. She said, "From what I understand, you automatically get six weeks but you have to use your accrued sick leave for that . . . and that's paid because it's sick leave."

David, a single thirty-eight-year-old white man, and Elizabeth, a married thirty-year-old white woman, had differing levels of knowledge about the Hilltop policies. Neither professor had children.

> From what I understand of them, one can basically get either a full-course reduction or teach no courses the semester after they've had a child, depending on if they're the primary caregiver. I think if both parents in a couple [are] academics [at the university], both of them can take this reduction. (David)

> I know if you have a child and you're the primary caregiver, you can have a year off your tenure clock and you get a reduced teaching load as well, instead of teaching two classes you teach one class. (Elizabeth)

Whereas David was aware of only the parental leave policy, Elizabeth described both the parental leave and tenure extension policies. This might be because Elizabeth planned on having children in the near future, whereas David had no definite plans to do so. David and Elizabeth were exceptions in that the majority of participants without children seemed to know the least about the policies. Many participants without children mentioned learning about such policies if necessary. One such example was Charles, a single thirty-six-year-old white man at Hilltop, who said, "I suppose I would become more familiar with them [university policies] if this [having a baby] were to happen . . . I think there are some [policies] but I can't be too specific about [them because] really I don't know much about it. If it were to happen, I would certainly research it."

Other participants knew nothing about their universities' policies because they said they required no time off, given the flexible nature of their work. These participants were men who worked at Valley, where only a short paid paternity leave existed. Peter and Jin were examples of such participants. Peter was an engaged thirty-year-old white man at Valley. He shared his thoughts,

> Let's say [my fiancée] gets pregnant [and] has a baby. I can put things on cruise control for a month or two and not really have it affect [things]. I could come to campus to teach and be at the meetings and spend the rest of my time at home. I can just take a little research hiatus. Again with this type of position I don't think it's really that big of a deal to have [a leave].

Jin also was unaware of the paternity leave policy. He was a married forty-five-year-old Asian man whose wife did not work for pay. When I asked,

"When your son was born, did you take any kind of leave or time off?" he replied after a long pause, "I don't think there was a leave or I can ask for a leave. Maybe there is a policy [or] you can ask for those things. But as I'm not required [to be] sitting [here] eight hours a day, I don't think I need to do that." These responses represent a gendered perspective on balancing work and family as these men did not see themselves as primary caregivers for their children, because their spouse would (or did, as in the case of Jin) provide the majority of care for a baby. These quotes illustrate the influence of gender on individuals' perspectives on policies.

Almost all participants at Hilltop who knew about the parental leave policy lauded it. Both men and women, with and without children, felt good about working at Hilltop in part because of the policies. Participants felt lucky because they knew of other universities' less generous policies. Elizabeth, described above, shared her opinion,

> So the university seems to be pretty good in terms of supporting [family responsibilities], especially compared to other places. Other places give you nothing. It's like, oh you have a kid, that's too bad. Your tenure clock is still ticking and you still have to teach full-time, so it doesn't give you [anything] . . .
> I: Do you know people who are in that position?
> Yeah, I sure do and other places I interviewed that was the [norm]. Hilltop seems to me to be the exception in terms of how enlightened they are rather than the rule . . . I don't have any complaints about their family policy because it's a lot better than a lot of places.

Experience of Parental Leave Policies: Hilltop

Parental leave helped parents meet both work and family responsibilities and to create desirable care situations for their children. Several parents mentioned that aside from practical concerns, parental leave lessened occupational pressures to work during the early stages of parenthood. This was true for both men and women. For example, Todd, a thirty-eight-year-old married white man with a son, shared, "Yeah, I took advantage of the parental policy leave for a course reduction. I did that, which was good and freed up some time. I also took advantage of an offer that they have to stop the tenure clock for a year. That lessened the pressure."

How participants at Hilltop experienced their use of the parental leave policy was influenced by the culture of their individual department. One such example was Meg, a married thirty-two-year-old white woman. She shared how her department chair seemed very supportive while she was on leave, "The person who was the chair of the department at the time, he made it really clear that parental leave was intended to be *that* and I wasn't coming back so I could make up for all the stuff that I had missed when I was away."

Despite Meg's perception of a supportive chair, she made sure to come to the office several times while on leave so she didn't fall behind in her research. Thus, she still experienced some occupational pressure to work while on parental leave.

Mick's work situation affected when he took his parental leave. Mick delayed taking parental leave because he worried about how his colleagues might react to his withdrawal from teaching a certain class, even though it would have been easier for his family. Mick was a married thirty-three-year-old white man. He said,

> [My wife's] serious work period hit [after my son was born] and I had arranged for parental leave but didn't—well the parental leave happened in the spring and not the fall. . . . It would have been much better to have done the parental leave that fall because he was a really little baby and she was working a whole lot. But I guess by the time she got pregnant and it occurred to me to ask for parental leave . . . by then I had also signed up to teach this interdisciplinary [course] . . . I had committed to that a little before she got pregnant and if I had pulled out of that all hell would have broken loose. So anyway, I ended up taking my parental leave in the spring, which made the fall pretty crazy . . . [because] between the two of us we couldn't really cover taking care of the baby as we liked to.

Mick's case represents a gendered experience of taking leave. He took leave when it would be least disruptive to his work life, even though it was challenging for his family life. Instead of work fitting around family demands, family demands had to fit around his work responsibilities. Fitting family around work demands illustrates hegemonic masculinity in which breadwinning is a central component of masculinity and fatherhood (Connell 1995).

For the most part, faculty felt Hilltop's administration supported the parental leave policies. Nevertheless, there were still some underlying aspects of academia that encouraged participants to make various concessions in their family lives for work. Participants worried about falling behind in research or about losing status in their departments while on parental leave. These reactions to leave-taking point to a need for change in occupational expectations toward professors taking leave.

Experience of Parental Leave Policies: Valley

Only one participant at Valley had experience with the leave policy. Jamie was a married thirty-two-year-old white woman who was in her second trimester of pregnancy during our interview. She reacted to the paid maternity leave policy at Valley,

> But the maternity leave [policy] doesn't really work for faculty because they give you six weeks so it's just the normal regular policy, right? It's six weeks

off and [because] I'm due in August, I'm not going to be able to take six weeks off [because] then it would be eight weeks into the semester [when I'd come back] and then resume professional responsibilities. . . . So I was searching around for what to do and I went to my chair with solutions, rather than going to her [asking what to do] . . . and she was like, "Fabulous. Let's do it.' She doesn't have to worry about it but she's also very supportive.

This lack of a semester of leave meant that professors have to create their own individual solutions for parental leave. Other participants felt that additional parental leave was needed. For example, Amy shared her thoughts, "[I] definitely [would like] paid maternity and paternity leave. Twelve weeks, I think, would be wonderful."

Tenure Extension Policies

Many participants at both universities thought their universities should offer some kind of extension in the tenure clock for the birth of a child. Professors thought that doing so would ease work-related stress as parents adjusted to their new family responsibilities.

> I think they're wonderful policies. The other thing [they allow for] is that when you have a baby you can get a year off your tenure clock. For two babies, you can actually get two additional years for tenure. That's really helpful. (Kendra, Hilltop)

> Well, the only thing I can think of is maybe, if somebody wanted to have a kid and they were a new professor [and] they didn't have tenure yet . . . if they would allow you a tenure free year off or something like that where you could just have maybe a leave of absence or that you could teach but your research could be suspended for that year, [it] doesn't count towards your tenure. So that could be something that would be helpful. If you had a year where you didn't have to, not that you wouldn't do any research work, but where you wouldn't worry that that's counting towards tenure and that might be something that could really help. (April, Valley)

April's comment that one would still do research work even with an extension illustrates how professors face expectations that their scholarship productivity be continuous, despite policies that allow for interruptions or a year "off."

Whereas most participants were in favor of a paid parental leave longer than six weeks, there was some disagreement over whether universities should offer a tenure extension policy. A couple of participants at Valley thought an explicit tenure extension policy might be problematic. Their thoughts about such a policy were tied to concerns about hurting their careers by receiving "special" treatment. Two were men without children and one, Amy, had one child. Amy shared,

> The whole tenure clock thing, I don't know if it would be a stop the clock kind of policy that I would advocate for but maybe [chuckles] for every kid you have you should have to do two fewer publications. [Laughs] I think there has to be some way to say, "Look this person has all these things going on." I don't know if a hard and fast policy is the best way to do that. I mean definitely maternity and paternity leave. There's no question in my mind that, that every place should have paid maternity and paternity leave. At this point I struggle with the whole tenure and child thing. Should that give people extra leverage or more flexibility or shouldn't it? I really struggle with it. . . . My reason for not thinking we should is that we need to have some standard. We need to have some consistent criteria and then if you're going to say, "Oh well she has a kid," should you say, "Oh well she got divorced and he had a car accident and his father died?" How do you decide what is more important than something else? I think that gets kind of messy and so it's just easier to say, "These are our criteria, you meet it or you don't." . . . If you get special treatment because you have children is that somehow saying you can't do as good of a job as somebody who doesn't? [There] could be kind of the negative repercussions of that.

Department Climate

Department climate had a profound effect on how participants felt about their family responsibilities and using their universities' policies. Even though many participants felt pressured to meet a very high standard of success, some felt that their department colleagues understood that they had responsibilities outside of work. This support somewhat mitigated occupational pressures.

> My colleagues do realize [that] I have a family, a very young family [with] four kids under eight . . . They recognize that and there'll be some times [when] they'll say, "Well can anyone go to this? No, Skip why don't you stay with your family." (Skip, Hilltop)

> I have a very supportive department. It's very supportive of its junior faculty especially.
> I: So, can you give me some examples of how they're supportive?
> Oh, they let me show off the pictures, they let me complain about being jet lagged [from visiting my family in [other state]]. They just don't make any snide comments about "Well if you'd been around." I never have heard any comments like that. If I have to miss a meeting, I don't [get] rebuked for it. People ask about how my partner is doing or how my daughter is doing. (Sydney, Hilltop)

> Faculty functions, things like opening of the school year receptions at the dean's house, kids are welcome to come to that. The holiday party at wintertime where all the alumni and all these people are invited, kids are welcome to come. . . . In some places, you could be looked down upon because [when] your kid is sick and you got to take care of them [it's like] you should have an alternate arrangement. . . . The kind of [supportive] culture [in my department] makes parenting on the tenure track incredibly easier. (Jenny, Hilltop)

One of the commonly mentioned factors related to a supportive department climate was having colleagues with children. Such participants felt a lot of support, more so than participants with colleagues who did not have children. Amy shared her experience during her interview at Valley, "They took me and my husband and [my son] out to dinner and some of the professors brought their kids and it was just very family friendly and just not at all what my image of academia was like."

These professors also spoke of how colleagues and administrators, whom they considered to be "supportive" of their personal life responsibilities, did not bother them about their other responsibilities or activities as long as they finish their work. This belief can create an understanding environment about family responsibilities because it also assumes that professors can manage their work responsibilities with little oversight. April, a white married thirty-three-year-old woman without children who worked at Valley said,

> There's no pressure to be here exactly at any time as long as you are covering your responsibilities. I think the climate is fairly family-friendly actually, more so than when I worked in the corporate world. 'Cause there, there is really an emphasis on hours and you should be there a lot of hours and whatnot, even if you're not being any more productive [than if you were working fewer hours].

Other participants perceived their colleagues as not supportive. They felt a high expectation for face time. For example, Shane, a white married thirty-two-year-old man who worked at Hilltop, said this about his colleagues:

> I'm the one junior faculty member and their expectation is I'm going to be here 8:00 to 5:00 Monday through Friday. My God, I can't tell you how many times [at] 2:00 in the afternoon I'm just staring at my computer hoping that I'll find something to keep me interested and then that night at home, I'll sit down at 7:00 after dinner [and] write two chapters. But here I'm just sort of twiddling my thumbs saying "God I want to be home with my family, with my kids."

Almost all participants, however, wanted their colleagues to be supportive of their non-work responsibilities. They felt this was an important part of managing work/life issues. Amy perhaps put it best when she said, "But I think life is different if you have these competing priorities and particularly, if I get on my soapbox I say . . . 'If these aren't the people supportive of family life and raising kids, then who the heck are?' So I feel like there needs to be a consideration of that."

CONCLUSION

In general, participants' preferences for parental leave and tenure extension policies support the American Association of University Professors' (2001) call for universities' increased receptiveness to and support for faculty's family responsibilities. The policies at Hilltop greatly aided participants' transition to parenthood by relieving the stress of individually arranging for time off, worrying about missing classes, and concerns about maintaining productivity for tenure. Valley's six weeks of paid maternity leave was viewed as inadequate by those who knew about it, because it did not allow for leave that meshed conveniently with faculty's work schedules (i.e., the semester system). This mismatch meant that professors would be responsible for organizing individual solutions, as illustrated in Jamie's case. There was a desire for more paid policies and a need to have those policies work in sync with the academic calendar.

It is questionable whether professors would have been inclined to use the childcare or implicit tenure extension policies at Valley because they were unpaid. Unpaid family leave policies, like the FMLA, are not widely used because many people cannot afford time off from work without pay (Gerstel and McGonagle 1999; Hudson and Gonyea 2000; Norrell and Norrell 1996). Like other workers, professors might be unlikely to take this unpaid childcare leave because of economic constraints. The Valley tenure extension policy (adjusted time to meet scholarship expectations) was based on the length of time professors could go without pay. Compared with the Hilltop policy, which allowed professors to get a tenure extension even if they were working full-time, the Valley policy only really benefited professors with sufficient finances. Professors have to have enough accumulated financial resources or partners' salaries to support them if they take such a leave. Thus there seems to be differential access to these leaves which creates inequalities among faculty.

In addition, the paid paternity leave at Valley only allowed for five days off from work. As I was told by the Human Resources officer in charge of this leave, this is because the father was "really only helping the mother recover from the delivery." Such assumptions that underlie these official policies discourage men's family involvement and their opportunities to be full-time caregivers. They also reify the idea that providing intense caregiving is a woman's responsibility and men only help out with these duties (Thompson 1991; Williams 2000). However, as other research on men in academe has shown (Solomon 2010), men want to be and are more involved with the hands-on care of their children and often arrange their work lives around their family demands.

As others have written (Solomon 2008, 2011; Wilson 1999), the lack of adequate policy could be hard for untenured faculty as they may be hesitant to push for parental leave policies. Pushing for such policies could jeopardize their career by being portrayed as "bad departmental citizens" or wanting special treatment (Wilson 1999). Assistant professors' fears might not be related so much to the *actual* reactions of department colleagues or administrators, but to their untenured status and what this kind of behavior *can* mean to others. That is, even though administrators might seem supportive, individuals may fear that they might be pushing the limits by asking for a policy that is not formally stated. The backlash against parents is not simply a figment of these professors' imaginations. Professors with children are often criticized for receiving "special treatment" through paid parental leave policies (Williams, Alon, and Bornstein 2006), although the majority of universities do not even offer such policies.

The efficacy of family-friendly policies is limited, then, given department culture in academe toward work/family issues. My research demonstrates how department climate and colleagues' attitudes influence the use of parental leave policies. Participants spoke at length about how department climate and colleagues' attitudes toward their family responsibilities had a major effect on their work/life management. Women and men in supportive departments felt that they did not have to disavow their family responsibilities, especially while at work. Other participants worked in departments where they felt an expectation of exclusive devotion to work. These professors spoke of giving in to that expectation because they feared being perceived in a negative light and maybe damaging their chances for tenure. Attitudes of colleagues and administrators affected how participants felt about parental leave policies. Prior research has shown chairs to be especially instrumental in whether faculty use such policies (Frasch, Mason, Stacy, Goulden, and Hoffman 2007).

Thus it seems that the climate of academia is still not conducive to integrating work and family responsibilities. It is a gendered institution (Acker 1990) in which women and men are expected to be disembodied or ideal workers—workers who have no responsibilities outside of work (Acker 1990; Williams 2000). The experiences of these professors are not exclusive to academia. Many other research studies have demonstrated that professionals feel expected to be solely devoted to their career (e.g., Blair-Loy 2003; Jacobs and Gerson 2004). Indeed, the very nature of professionalism requires professionals to exhibit a high level of commitment to their careers, to have an uninterrupted career path, to hold themselves to a high standard of success, to be self-directed and autonomous, and to be willing to sacrifice for delayed occupational rewards (Evetts 2003; Hertz 1986; Leicht and Fennell 2001).

In addition to the institution of policies like those at Hilltop, what might be needed are broad changes to our societal definition of a "successful (work) life." This rethinking of the successful work life would allow for interrupted or a slower engagement with one's career. Rethinking what it means to be successful professionally at the societal level would involve changing the meaning individuals make of their work involvement. Such a redefinition of professional success would require changes at the occupational level and in the definition of professionalism. Instead of an exclusive devotion being the standard in professionalism, an integration of work and personal life would be considered the norm. The reward structure of the occupation would have to change to reflect this new model. Instead of formally and informally rewarding only super-productivity or exclusive devotion, additional opportunities for reward or recognition would be in place. Workplaces would reduce the amount of work expected of employees, shorten workweeks, and provide time during the workweek for employees' involvement with their community, for caregiving responsibilities, and for involvement with children's schools or day cares. Changes are needed not just at universities, but in societal attitudes about and practices of work as well.

NOTES

1. For the sake of simplicity I use the term "family-friendly" to include policies that in some way accommodate professors' family responsibilities. Under this heading, I include parental/childcare leave, maternity leave, paternity leave, and tenure extension policies.

REFERENCES

Acker, Joan. 1990. "Hierarchies, Jobs, and Bodies: A Theory of Gendered Organizations." *Gender and Society* 4:139–58.

Allen, Tammy D., Kristen M. Shockley, and Laura F. Poteat. 2008. "Workplace Factors Associated with Family Dinner Behaviors." *Journal of Vocational Behaviors* 73:336–42.

American Association of University Professors (AAUP). 2001. "Statement on Principles of Family Responsibilities and Academic Work." *Academe* 87:55–61.

Armenti, Carmen. 2004. "May Babies and Posttenure Babies: Maternal Decisions of Women Professors." *The Review of Higher Education* 27:211–31.

August, Louise. 2006. "It Isn't Over: The Continuing Under-Representation of Women Faculty." Center for the Education of Women. Retrieved August 1, 2012 (http://www.cew.umich.edu/sites/default/files/augustfemrep06_0.pdf).

Aumann, Kerstin, Ellen Galinsky, and Kenneth Matos. 2011. "The New Male Mystique: The National Study of the Changing Workforce." New York: Families and Work Institute.

Behson, Scott J. 2005. "The Relative Contribution of Formal and Informal Organizational Work-Family Support." *Journal of Vocational Behavior* 66:487–500.

Bellavia, Gina M., and Michael R. Frone. 2005. "Work-family Conflict." Pp. 113–47 in *Handbook of work stress*, edited by J. Barling, E. K. Kelloway, and M. E. Frone. Thousand Oaks, CA: Sage Publications.

Bianchi, Suzanne M., and Melissa A. Milkie. 2010. "Work and Family Research in the First Decade of the 21st Century." *Journal of Marriage and Family* 72:705–25.

Blair-Loy, Mary. 2003. *Competing Devotions: Career and Family among Women Executives.* Cambridge, MA: Harvard University Press.

———. 2009. "Work without End?: Scheduling Flexibility and Work-to-Family Conflict among Stockbrokers." *Work and Occupations* 36:279–317.

Blair-Loy, Mary, and Amy S. Wharton. 2002. "Employee's Use of Work-family Policies and the Workplace Social Context." *Social Forces* 80:813–45.

Bogdan, Robert, and Sari Knopp Biklen. 1998. *Qualitative Research for Education: An Introduction to Theory and Method.* 3d ed. Boston: Allyn and Bacon.

Bryon, Kristin. 2005. "A Meta-analytic Review of Work-family Conflict and its Antecedents." *Journal of Vocational Behavior* 67:40–45.

Center for the Education of Women (CEW). 2007. "Family-friendly Policies in Higher Education: A Five-year Report." University of Michigan Research Brief.

Connell, R.W. 1995. *Masculinities.* Berkeley: University of California Press.

Drago, Robert, and Carol Colbeck. 2003. "Final Report from The Mapping Project: Exploring the Terrain of U.S. Colleges and Universities for Faculty and Families for the Alfred P. Sloan Foundation." The Pennsylvania State University, December 31.

Drago, Robert, Ann C. Crouter, Mark Wardell, and Billie S. Willits. 2001. "Final Report to the Alfred P. Sloan Foundation for the Faculty and Families Project." The Pennsylvania State University, March 14.

Frasch, Karie, Mary Ann Mason, Angy Stacy, Marc Goulden, and Carol Hoffman. 2007. "Creating a Family Friendly Department: Chairs and Deans Toolkit." Retrieved August 1, 2012 (http://ucfamilyedge.berkeley.edu).

Evetts, Julia. 2003. "The Sociological Analysis of Professionalism: Occupation Change in the Modern World." *International Sociology* 18:395–415.

Finkel, Susan Kolker, and Steven G. Olswang. 1996. "Child Rearing as a Career Impediment to Women Assistant Professors." *The Review of Higher Education* 19:123–39.

Galinsky, Ellen, James T. Bond, and Dana E. Friedman. 1993. *The Changing Workforce: Highlights of the National Study.* New York: Families and Work Institute.

———. 1996. "The Role of Employers in Addressing the Needs of Employed Parents." *Journal of Social Issues* 52:111–36.

Gerstel, Naomi, and Katherine McGonagle. 1999. "Job Leaves and the Limits of the Family and Medical Leave Act: The Effects of Gender, Race, and Family." *Work and Occupations* 26:510–34.

Glass, Jennifer L., and Lisa Riley. 1998. "Family Responsive Policies and Employee Retention Following Childbirth." *Social Forces* 76:1401–35.

Hertz, Rosanna. 1986. *More Equal than Others: Women and Men in Dual-career Marriages.* Berkeley: University of California Press.

Hill, E. Jeffrey, Alan J. Hawkins, Maria Ferris, and Michelle Weitzman. 2001. "Finding an Extra Day a Week: The Positive Influence of Perceived Job Flexibility on Work and Family Life Balance." *Family Relations* 50:49–58.

Hollenshead, Carol S., Beth Sullivan, Gilia C. Smith, Louise August, and Susan Hamilton. 2005. "Work/Family Policies in Higher Education: Survey Data and Case Studies of Policy Implementation." *New Directions for Higher Education* 130:41-65.

Hudson, Robert B., and Judith G. Gonyea. 2000. "Time yet not Money: The Politics and Promise of the Family and Medical Leave Act." *Journal of Aging and Social Policy* 11:189–200.

Jacobs, Jerry A., and Kathleen Gerson. 2004. *The Time Divide: Work, Family, and Gender Inequality.* Cambridge, MA: Harvard University Press.

Johnson, John M. 2002. "In-Depth Interviewing." Pp. 103–20 in *Handbook of Interview Research: Context and Method,* edited by J. F. Gubrium and J. A. Holstein. Thousand Oaks, CA: Sage Publications.

Kelly, Erin L., Phyllis Moen, and Eric Tranby. 2011. "Changing Workplaces to Reduce Work-Family Conflict: Schedule Control in a White-collar Organization." *American Sociological Review* 76:265–90.

Kossek, Ellen Ernst, Brenda A. Lautsch, and Susan C. Eaton. 2006. "Telecommuting, Control and Boundary Management: Correlates of Policy Use and Practice, Job Control, and Work-Family Effectiveness." *Journal of Vocational Behavior* 68:347–67.

Leicht, Kevin T., and Mary L. Fennell. 2001. *Professional Work: A Sociological Approach.* Malden, MA: Blackwell Publishers.

Lundquist, Jennifer H., Joya Misra, and KerryAnn O'Meara. 2012. "Parental Leave Usage by Fathers and Mothers at an American University." *Fathering* 10:337-63.

Mason, Mary Ann, and Marc Goulden. 2004. "Do Babies Matter (Part II)? Closing the Baby Gap." *Academe* 90.

Mason, Mary Ann, Marc Goulden, and Karie Frasch. 2009. "Why Graduate Students Reject the Fast Track." *Academe* 65.

Matos, Kenneth, and Ellen Galinsky. 2012. *National Study of the Changing Workforce: 2012 National Study of Employers.* New York: Families and Work Institute.

———. 2011. *National Study of the Changing Workforce: Workplace Flexibility among Professional Employees.* New York: Families and Work Institute.

National Center for Education Statistics (U.S. Department of Education). 2011. *National Survey of Postsecondary Faculty: Digest of Educational Statistics, Table 197.* Retrieved December 1, 2012 (http://nces.ed.gov/programs/digest/2011menu_tables.asp).

Norrell, J. Elizabeth, and Thomas H. Norrell. 1996. "Faculty and Family Policies in Higher Education." *Journal of Family Issues* 17:204–26.

O'Laughlin, Elizabeth M., and Lisa G. Bischoff. 2005. "Balancing Parenthood and Academia: Work/Family Stress as Influenced by Gender and Tenure Status." *Journal of Family Issues* 26:79–106.

Schutt, Russell K. 2001. *Investigating the Social World: The Process and Practice of Research.* Thousand Oaks, CA: Pine Forge Press.

Solomon, Catherine Richards. 2008. "Personal Responsibility in Professional Work: The Academic 'Star' as Ideological Code." Pp. 180–202 in *People at Work: Life, Power, and Social Inclusion in the New Economy,* edited by M. L. DeVault. New York, NY: New York University Press.

———. 2011. "'Sacrificing at the Altar of Tenure': Assistant Professors' Work/Life Management." *The Social Science Journal* 48:335–44.

———. 2010. "The Very Highest Thing Is Family": Male Assistant Professors' Work/Family Management. Pp. 233–255 in *Interactions and Intersections of Gendered Bodies at Work, at Home, and at Play,* edited by M. T. Segal. Bingley, UK: Emerald Group Publishing Limited.

Thompson, Linda. 1991. "Family Work: Women's Sense of Fairness." *Journal of Marriage and the Family* 12:181–96.

UC Faculty Family Friendly Edge. 2003. "The UC Faculty Family Friendly Edge: Turning a Problem into UC's Competitive Advantage." Retrieved August 1, 2012 (http://ucfamilyedge.berkeley.edu/index.html).

Ward, Kelly, and Lisa Wolf-Wendel. 2004. "Academic Motherhood: Managing Complex Roles in Research Universities." *The Review of Higher Education* 27:233–57.

Weiss, Robert S. 1994. *Learning from Strangers: The Art and Method of Qualitative Interview Studies.* New York: The Free Press.

West, Martha S., and John W. Curtis. 2006. "AAUP Faculty Gender Equity Indicators 2006." Retrieved August 1, 2012 (http://www.aaup.org/NR/rdonlyres/63396944-44BE-4ABA-9815-5792D93856F1/0/AAUPGenderEquityIndicators2006.pdf)

Williams, Joan. 2000. *Unbending Gender: Why Work and Family Conflict and What to do About it.* Oxford: Oxford University Press.

Williams, Joan, Tamina Alon, and Stephanie Bornstein. 2006. "Beyond the 'Chilly Climate': Eliminating Bias Against Women and Fathers in Academe." *Thought and Action* Fall:79–96.

Wilson, Robin. 1999. "Timing is Everything: Academe's Annual Baby Boom." *The Chronicle of Higher Education,* June 25.

Wolfinger, Nicholas H., Mary Ann Mason, and Marc Goulden. 2009. "Stay in the Game: Gender, Family Formation, and Alternative Trajectories in the Academic Life Course." *Social Forces* 87:1591–621.

WorkLifeLaw. 2009. "Take Action: Model Policies and Practices." Retrieved August 1, 2012 (http://www.worklifelaw.org/GenderBias_takeAction.html).

Young, Diane S., and Ednita M. Wright. 2001. "Mothers Making Tenure." *Journal of Social Work Education* 37:555–68.

Chapter Three

Do Work/Life Policies Matter?

*The Importance of Work/Life Policies for
Reducing Faculty Intention to Quit*

Catherine White Berheide and Rena Linden

Work/family conflict arises when roles and responsibilities at home and at work are incompatible, forcing workers to make hard choices about how to divide their fixed pool of resources, especially time and energy, between the two spheres (Berheide and Anderson-Hanley 2012; Gerson 1986; Greenhaus and Beutell 1985; Jacobs and Winslow 2004). Despite having more autonomy and more flexible schedules than many employees, college and university faculty report high levels of work/family conflict as well as dissatisfaction with their demanding workweek (Amelink and Creamer 2007; Elliott 2003; Fox, Fonseca, and Bao 2011; Gatta and Roos 2004; Misra, Lundquist, and Templer 2012; O'Laughlin and Bischoff 2005; Ward and Wolf-Wendel 2012; Watanabe and Falci 2014; Wonch Hill, Holmes, and McQuillan 2014). Some faculty leave positions at elite colleges and universities for institutions they believe will allow them to integrate their work and family lives, particularly ones that do not require as much scholarly productivity, such as community colleges (Anderson et al. 2014; Ollilainen and Solomon 2014; Ward and Wolf-Wendel 2012). Others leave higher education for jobs in the corporate, not-for-profit, or public sectors that demand fewer hours, especially during the evening and the weekend. Others may opt out of the labor force or move to a part-time position at least temporarily because of caregiving demands (Pavalko and Henderson 2006; Perry-Smith and Blum 2000; Richman et al. 2008).

To decrease work/life conflict and improve the well-being of their employees, therefore, increasing numbers of employers, including colleges and universities, have introduced work/life policies (Drago et al. 2006; Hollenshead et al. 2005; Lundquist, Misra, and O'Meara 2012; Mason and Goulden 2004; Moen and Sweet 2004). Employees may not feel able to take advantage of formal work/life policies, however (Blair-Loy and Wharton 2002; Eaton 2003; Fried 1998; Lundquist, Misra, and O'Meara 2012; Wharton and Estevez 2014). Nonetheless, employers increasingly believe that finding effective ways to reduce work/life conflict may be an important part of creating a positive work environment with higher productivity and job satisfaction as well as lower absenteeism and intentions to quit (Brandon and Temple 2007; Butts, Casper, and Yang 2013; Eaton 2003; Grover and Crooker 1995; Kelly, Moen, and Tranby 2011).

This chapter examines the importance of work/life policies for faculty at two highly selective liberal arts colleges. We explore whether faculty members' perceptions of the importance of five work/life policies affected how seriously they had considered the possibility of leaving their current job. We hypothesize that the more important a faculty member considered each of the five work/life policies, the less likely a faculty member agreed he or she had considered quitting 1) his or her job; 2) to obtain better work/life balance; and 3) for his or her spouse's career. If the data support these hypotheses, then colleges and universities will have evidence that adopting work/life policies is one way to lower faculty intentions to quit. Reducing the number of faculty who leave benefits not only the individual but also the employing institution by eliminating the considerable costs of hiring replacements.

NEW INSTITUTIONALISM AND WORK/LIFE POLICIES

According to new institutionalism theory, institutions establish rules and enforcement mechanisms that are designed to meet the goals of both the actors and the institution (Ingram and Clay 2000). The economic approach to new institutionalism theory argues that individuals behave according to their self-interests based on limited information. It examines choice-within-constraints or bounded rationality. Rational choice new institutionalism, heavily influenced by economics, identifies the institution's rules and policies as central to individual decision-making. Critiquing the notion of a rational actor, Granovetter (1985) argued that individuals are "embedded" in so many social, economic, and political relationships that it is impossible to define rational decision making uniformly, as rationality depends on the social context of the actor.

Sociological new institutionalism argues instead that the interplay between the broader social environment and the institution determines individuals' decisions. This approach emphasizes the effect of organizational culture on actors. The development of sociological new institutionalism theory focused organizational analysis on how the routines, scripts, and schemas as well as the values, norms, and beliefs within the larger environment in which an organization is embedded shape its policies, practices, and structures (Powell and DiMaggio 1991). Actors are bound together by common organizational and/or professional values, such as devotion to work and to the separation of work and family life, which may affect their willingness to accept new organizational policies and practices, such as work/life policies. This sociological approach to new institutionalism provides a theoretical framework for studying the interactions among employees, workplace policies, and the employing organization's culture.

According to Powell and DiMaggio (1991), workers do not choose which rules or policies to enact; instead they rely on the norms of the institutional context to guide their behavior. Ellickson (1991) posited that members of groups, such as work groups, establish norms to increase the welfare of their members. Organizational norms are a form of social capital that produces greater group outcomes than when employees base their decision-making on obtaining personal advantages (Nee 1998). As a result, workers often conform to group norms even when rational choice theory would suggest that they would not.

In contrast to the rational choice institutionalism approach, the sociological approach to new institutionalism highlights the gap between the formal policies and the informal norms of the workplace. Co-workers are embedded within social relationships. They establish their own workplace culture and implicit set of norms that are not necessarily congruent with the formal rules. According to Mennino, Rubin, and Brayfield (2005), everyday interactions as well as organizational culture shape the behavior of organizational actors in conjunction with formal rules and procedures. The sociological approach to new institutionalism suggests that merely adopting work/life policies may not be sufficient to reduce intentions to quit if the workplace culture is not supportive of employees who want to take advantage of these policies.

LITERATURE REVIEW

Previous research has described the effects of work/life policies on organizations, the role of workplace culture as the gateway to accessing these policies, and the role of gender in work/life management. Some research has examined these same topics in specific industries and occupations. We end our review of the literature by focusing on previous research specifically about work/life policies at colleges and universities.

The Effects of Work/Life Policies

Research (e.g., Brandon and Temple 2007; Kelly, Moen, and Tranby 2011; Richman et al. 2008) has demonstrated that work/life policies benefit organizations. Previous research has found that work/family policies can reduce absenteeism (Brandon and Temple 2007) and increase productivity (Brandon and Temple 2007; Eaton 2003). While many studies focus on the effects of specific work/life policies, such as on-site childcare or dual career hiring, Perry-Smith and Blum (2000) studied work/life bundles, that is, combinations of several complementary family-friendly policies, finding that they were positively associated with a firm's sales growth and market performance. A meta-analysis conducted by Butts, Casper, and Yang (2013) revealed that work/family policies had positive effects on job satisfaction, commitment, and intentions to stay. Grover and Crooker (1995) found that employees with access to work/life policies were less likely to quit their jobs, even if they did not use the policies themselves. Despite this body of research that connected work/life policies to positive organizational outcomes, some scholars (Eaton 2003; Kossek, Lewis, and Hammer 2010) questioned whether work/family policies actually improve work/life management or simply serve as public relations tools. In her study of a Fortune 500 company, Hochschild (1997) found that work/life policies increased the number of hours employees spent at work, resulting in decreased family time. Similarly Lapierre and Allen (2006) found that telework increased work/family conflict. In short, there is some disagreement in the previous research on whether work/life policies actually reduce work/family conflict.

The Role of Workplace Climate and "Embedded" Social Relationships

According to previous research (Eaton 2003; Fried 1998), employees must perceive that work/life policies are accessible for such policies to reduce work/family conflict. As Lewis (1997, 18) noted, work/life policies are incongruent with conventional organizational values of long hours and the separation between family responsibilities and work ones. A workplace climate that discourages employees from taking advantage of policies because doing so might damage career prospects diminishes the positive effects of work/life policies (Kossek et al. 2010; Fried 1998). Blair-Loy and Wharton (2002, 839) found that "while many employees desire to use work/family policies, only some will have access to the kinds of positions that are compatible with policy use with minimal career costs." Specifically, Blair-Loy and Wharton (2002) concluded that employees were more likely to use work/life policies if powerful supervisors and colleagues could protect them from the negative effects on their careers. Hochschild (1997, 80) found similar results in her study, noting the division between

> the powerful men at the top of the company hierarchy, who had the authority and skill to engineer a new family-friendly work culture but lacked any deep interest in doing so [. . . and . . .] advocates of family-friendly policies lower down the corporate ladder, who had a strong interest in such changes but little authority to implement them.

In addition, Callan (2007) found that employees were ambivalent about using work/life policies, fearing that taking parental leave might increase the workload for their coworkers or suggest that they felt entitled to what other workers, and especially managers, might perceive as generous amounts of time off. In short, work/life policies will not reduce work/family conflict if employees feel unable to use the policies.

Indeed, after conducting a meta-analysis, Butts, Casper, and Yang (2013) concluded that organizational support for family may be more important in improving employee attitudes about work/family management than formal work/life policies. For example, Mennino, Rubin, and Brayfield (2005) found that the availability of work/life policies, such as dependent care benefits and flextime, did not reduce negative work-to-family and family-to-work conflict, whereas family-supportive workplace cultures did. They concluded that the workplace culture is more important than the availability of work/life policies in enabling employees to manage their work and family lives. In sum, many researchers have concluded that a positive workplace culture that supports family obligations must accompany work/life policies for them to be effective in reducing work/life conflict (Pavalko and Henderson 2006; Fried 1998). Thus, adopting new policies is not sufficient to reduce work/life conflict if the workplace culture has not also changed to support use of those policies.

The Role of Gender

Previous research offers contradictory findings about whether gender affects work/life conflict. According to Hochschild and Machung (1989), work/life conflict disproportionately affected women as a result of their traditional responsibilities in the home. In contrast, Bagger, Li, and Gutek (2008) concluded that men were more affected by work/life conflict because of the incongruence between their traditional identities as devoted workers and their newer identities as involved fathers. Women were more likely than men to allow family responsibilities to spill into the workplace and as a result experienced *less* work/family conflict. Using spillover theory, which conceptualizes work/life conflict as bidirectional, Mennino, Rubin, and Brayfield (2005) found that both men and women experienced higher levels of work-to-family spillover than family-to-work spillover, while women reported significantly higher levels of work-to-family spillover than did men. In short, previous research has found that there is potential for all employees to experience negative spillover, regardless of gender.

Faculty Work/Life Management at Colleges and Universities

Similar to other workers, college and university professors struggle to manage their work and family lives (Berheide and Anderson-Hanley 2012; Jacobs and Winslow 2004; O'Laughlin and Bischoff 2005). Indeed, Anderson, Morgan, and Wilson (2002) found that university employees, particularly faculty, have more negative attitudes toward the work/family climate at their workplaces than do corporate employees. Amelink and Creamer (2007) found that when faculty are more satisfied with their own work/life balance, they are more satisfied with their jobs.

Even as women have entered faculty positions in greater numbers, gendered expectations that women will be responsible for a large share of household labor continue to place a greater burden on women faculty than on men (Misra, Lundquist, and Templer 2012; O'Laughlin and Bischoff 2005). Competing responsibilities for paid and care work create work/family conflict for women faculty at research universities (Amelink and Creamer 2007; Fox, Fonseca, and Bao 2011; Gatta and Roos 2004) as well as liberal arts colleges (Berheide and Anderson-Hanley 2012; Ward and Wolf-Wendel 2012). Drago et al. (2006) found that women faculty at teaching institutions were more likely than women faculty at research institutions to report missing important events in their children's lives in order to appear committed to work. In contrast, Ward and Wolf-Wendel (2012) found that women at both types of institutions reported similar amounts of work/life conflict. The difference they found between types of institutions was in the source of the conflict. For women faculty at research universities it was their research that interfered with family life whereas for the women faculty at liberal arts colleges it was their teaching and service that interfered with family life.

Fox, Fonseca, and Bao (2011) found that both work-to-family and family-to-work conflict is higher for women faculty at research universities than for men and that women experience greater family-to-work conflict than work-to-family. Similarly, O'Laughlin and Bischoff (2005) found that women faculty reported greater work/family conflict and also perceived less institutional support for balancing work and family than men. One reason may be that men are more likely to have spouses who did all or most of the childcare (Jacobs and Winslow 2004; Solomon 2010). Solomon (2011) reported that in an effort to spend more time with their families, men with children or spouses were almost as likely as their female colleagues and more likely than their single colleagues to respond to work/family conflict by resisting the "ideal worker" norm that prioritizes work over family.

While colleges and universities have begun to offer formal policies to address work/life conflict, a nationwide survey of 255 colleges and universities revealed that they offered, on the average, only two of eight possible policies (Hollenshead et al. 2005). The most common policy was "stop the tenure clock," which was available at 43 percent of the institutions surveyed, while the least common was employment assistance for spouses/partners, which was only provided by 9 percent of the institutions. Research universities offered the highest average number of family-friendly policies (three), which was twice as many as other types of institutions, with the exception of elite liberal arts colleges. Hollenshead et al. (2005, 47) found that the top one hundred liberal arts colleges in *U.S. News and World Report*, a group that includes the two colleges we studied, have nearly as many formal work/family policies as research universities, specifically they "had 2.53 policies on average, while other baccalaureates had 0.69 policies." Hollenshead et al. (2005, 47) surmised that elite liberal arts colleges compete with research universities for the best faculty and therefore they "have developed a greater number of family-friendly policies as a recruitment strategy."

Mason and Goulden (2004, 15) found that university faculty did not use the formal work/family policies either because they did not know about the policies, they did not know whether they were eligible to use the policies, or they were afraid of the consequences of taking advantage of the policies. Lundquist, Misra, and O'Meara (2012) found considerable faculty concern at one public research university about the consequences of taking family leave and that very few men faculty, in particular, take paid leave. Similarly, only 4 out of a sample of 257 tenure-track faculty members at another public research university took any formal family leave, a reaction to what Drago et al. (2006) identified as informal bias against faculty who are caregivers. Hollenshead et al. (2005) too concluded that a "chilly climate" reduces the likelihood that faculty will use work/family policies.

According to Amelink and Creamer (2007), informal cultural norms and the symbolic message that university faculty could balance their personal and professional lives, communicated by the existence of work/life policies, influence faculty attitudes about work/life management more than the formal policies actually did. Watanabe and Falci (2014) found that a supportive work/family department culture reduced the likelihood that faculty at a public research university were considering leaving their jobs to reduce work/family conflict. Based on the previous research on work/life policies, faculty work life, and employee retention, we expect that the importance of work/life policies for intentions to quit would not differ by the faculty members' family and job characteristics but that family-friendly department climates would reduce intentions to quit at the two elite liberal arts colleges being examined.

METHODS

Research Design

This research is part of a larger project comparing faculty experiences at two comparably ranked highly selective small private liberal arts colleges in the same Northeastern metropolitan area, one formerly all female and the other formerly all male. The most prominent differences between the two colleges reflect their gendered pasts. Although virtually identical in the number of tenure-line faculty and the size of the student body, the former men's college has more students and faculty in the natural sciences and engineering while the former women's college has more students and faculty in the arts and humanities. While both colleges had been coeducational for almost forty years at the time the survey was conducted, the former women's college still has more women students (approximately 60 percent) while women constitute only half the students at the former men's college. The larger research project examined whether faculty experiences at these two colleges differed, specifically whether women faculty had more positive experiences at the former women's college than at the former men's college. For this part of the project, we asked whether it is easier for faculty, especially women faculty, to integrate their work and their lives at the former women's college than at the former men's college.

Data Collection

This analysis used data from a survey administered online to the population of 341 tenured and tenure-track faculty members at two comparably ranked, highly selective, small private liberal arts colleges located in the Northeastern United States during the spring 2009. The 70 percent response rate yielded a total of 237 respondents.

We constructed a survey instrument by drawing questions that were applicable to liberal arts colleges from faculty work/life surveys previously administered at research universities (i.e., Callister 2006; Khare and Owens 2006; Settles et al. 2006). We revised some items to fit the specific circumstances of the two colleges, particularly those that referred to the formal work/life policies and programs available at one or both of the colleges. The final instrument included fifty-three questions covering tenure and promotion, department climate, resources, job satisfaction, time use, personal well-being, and demographic characteristics (see Berheide and Anderson-Hanley 2012, Berheide et al. 2013, and Fox et al. 2010 for more information about the survey design and the sample).

Family and Job Characteristics

Drawing on the results of previous analyses of the faculty survey data from these two colleges (Berheide and Anderson-Hanley 2012; Berheide et al. 2013; Berheide and Walzer 2014; Berheide et al. 2014; Fox et al. 2010) as well as from other work/life research (Blair-Loy and Wharton 2002; Elliott 2003; Perry-Smith and Blum 2000), we used six control variables to account for family and job characteristics that might affect faculty perceptions of the importance of work/life policies. We created dummy variables to control for gender, parental status, marital status, college of employment, discipline, and professorial rank. For gender, women were coded as 1 and men as 0. Respondents who have cared for or currently care for children were coded as 1, while faculty who were not parents were coded as 0. Three-quarters of the faculty were married and living with a spouse while another 5 percent were married but not living with their spouse and another 6 percent were not married but living with a domestic partner. Marital status of the respondents was therefore coded as 1 = married and living with spouse and 0 = not married, married but not living with spouse, and not married but living with a domestic partner. This variable was not included in regression analysis of the factors predicting how strongly respondents agreed to having considered quitting for their spouse or partner's career, because the question was only asked of married faculty.

To test whether the two colleges differed, we controlled for college of employment (0 = former women's college and 1 = former men's college). To test for disciplinary differences, we used the National Science Foundation's definition of the sciences, which encompasses the social, behavioral, and economic sciences in addition to the natural and mathematical sciences, to determine which departments to include in the variable measuring STEM (natural and social sciences, computer science, engineering, and mathematics). The STEM dummy variable separates faculty in the mathematical, natural, and social sciences as well as engineering (coded as 1) from those in the arts, humanities, and other professions (coded as 0). (We did conduct the analysis substituting a dummy variable that omitted the social sciences, which is not shown here. It replicated the findings reported here.)

Because previous research (Blair-Loy and Wharton 2002; Hochschild 1997) showed that power within organizations affected several facets of job experience, we controlled for rank, coding full professors as 1 and associate and assistant professors as 0. We had previously found that full professors reported less work/life conflict even when controlling for the presence of children at home than do the other ranks (Berheide and Anderson-Hanley 2012; Berheide et al. 2014). In fact, we found that rank was a more powerful predictor of work/family integration than gender. (We performed an analysis substituting a dummy variable for being tenured for the full professor dummy variable, which is not shown here, and found that the rank variable was a more powerful predictor than the tenured variable.) Full professors, at least at these two colleges, simply have more power to control their teaching, research, and service workloads, among other things, than either tenured associate professors or untenured assistant professors.

Department Support for Family Obligations

To measure the family-friendliness of the work unit, we used Khare and Owens' (2006) departmental support for family obligations index. It consisted of five statements respondents rated on a six-point Likert scale: "most faculty in my department are supportive of colleagues who want to balance their family and career lives," "department meetings frequently occur at times which conflict with family obligations," "the department is supportive of family leave," "it is difficult for faculty in my department to adjust their work schedules to care for children or other family members," and "faculty who have children are considered to be less committed to their careers." To measure family-friendliness, the latter two items were reverse coded so that 1 = strongly disagree and 6 = strongly agree, while the first three items retained the original coding of 1 = strongly agree and 6 = strongly disagree, yielding an acceptable Cronbach's alpha of .74. Scores ranged from 5 to 30. The higher the score on the index, the more family-friendly the respondent reported the department to be. In twenty-two cases, we replaced missing data with the mean for the individual item.

Importance of Work/Life Policies

The respondents were asked to "think about what you need to help you do your job as a faculty member more successfully, especially to help you attain tenure or promotion to full professor if you have not already. Please rate the importance of the following programs or policies" on a scale that ranged from very important (6) to very unimportant (1). The five work/life policies were on-campus childcare, on-campus summer and afterschool childcare, dual-career hiring, split or shared appointment, and the suspension of the tenure clock for parental responsibilities. When combined to form the importance of work/life policies index, responses ranged from a low of 5 to a high of 30 with the higher scores indicating greater importance. The work/life policies index had an excellent reliability with a Cronbach's alpha of .90. Although faculty at both colleges were asked to rate the importance of on-campus childcare and of on-campus childcare during the summer, the former women's college offered both programs, while the former men's college did not. The other three policies were available at both colleges.

The five work/life policy variables had more missing data than other questions. Because the policies aimed to ameliorate specific work/life conflicts most often faced by faculty with children and/or spouses, we divided respondents into one of the four family types: married with children, married without children, not married with children, or not married without children. Respondents who were married with children were more likely to answer these policy questions than faculty who were married without children, not married with children, or not married without children (see Table 3.1).

Analysis of variance revealed that the means for each family type were significantly different for four of the five work/life policies (analysis not shown). Therefore, we replaced the missing data for each of the five work/life policies with the mean for the respondent's respective family type rather than the policy's overall mean. We then combined the five work/life policy items into a work/life policy index that had a Cronbach's alpha of .88 indicating good reliability. Seven respondents were excluded from the analyses because they did not answer questions about their marital or parental status or both, reducing the sample size to 230.

Table 3.1. Response rate for five work/life policies questions by family fype (in percentages)

Work/life policies	Married with children (N = 129)	Married without children (N = 44)	Not married with children (N = 12)	Not married without children (N = 45)	Total (N = 230)
On-campus childcare	82 (106)	59 (26)	67 (8)	58 (26)	70 (166)
Childcare on-campus after school or during the summer	81 (104)	57 (25)	67 (8)	56 (25)	68 (162)
Suspension of tenure clock for parental responsibilities	81 (105)	57 (25)	67 (8)	64 (29)	70 (167)
Split or shared appointments	74 (96)	55 (24)	50 (6)	64 (29)	65 (155)
Dual career hiring	68 (88)	57 (25)	58 (7)	62 (28)	62 (148)

Intention to Quit

We used three dependent variables to measure faculty retention. The first was a general measure, based on the intention to quit index developed by Callister (2006). The intention to quit index included two statements: "I will probably look for a new job soon" and "I often think about leaving my job." Faculty responded to these statements using a six-point scale that was coded so that 1 = strongly disagree and 6 = strongly agree. Responses ranged from a low of 2 to a high of 12 with the higher score measuring a greater likelihood of quitting. The intention to quit index had good reliability with a Cronbach's alpha of .82.

The second and third measures of intention to quit used the same scale. The second asked respondents to rate how strongly they agreed with the statement, "I have seriously considered leaving [the college] in order to achieve better balance between work and professional life." The third asked respondents how strongly they agreed with "I have seriously considered leaving [the college] in order to enhance my spouse/partner's career opportunities." Scores ranged from 1 to 6 for both items.

FINDINGS

Family and Job Characteristics

Table 3.2 displays the means, medians, and standard deviations of the three measures of intention to quit, the importance of work/life policies index, the department support for family obligations index, and the family and job characteristics. The sample was divided evenly between men and women. Including the social sciences, 58 percent of respondents worked in STEM departments. Almost 40 percent of respondents were full professors. Three-quarters of faculty members were married and living with their spouse. Over 60 percent of them have cared for or are caring for children. Finally, slightly fewer of the respondents worked at the former men's college (48 percent) than at the former women's college (52 percent).

Importance of Work/Life Policies

Table 3.3 reveals that over half of all faculty deemed all five work/life policies as important or very important to their job success and two-thirds deemed them as at least somewhat important. The two policies faculty considered most important for their job success were on-campus childcare (48 percent rated it very important) and suspension of the tenure clock (42 percent rated it very important). Given that on-campus childcare was only available at the former women's college, while other policies were available at

**Table 3.2.   Means, medians, and standard deviations of intentions to quit, work/
life policies, department support for family obligations, and family and job characteristics**

Variable	Mean	Median	SD	N
Importance of work/life policies	21.5	22.1	6.11	(230)
Intention to quit	4.3	3.0	2.64	(223)
Intention to quit for better work/ life balance	2.7	2.0	1.88	(225)
Intention to quit for spouse/ partner's career	2.4	2.0	1.64	(186)
Departmental support for family obligations	24.0	25.0	4.37	(230)
Women	0.5	1.0	0.50	(230)
STEM	0.6	1.0	0.50	(230)
Full professor	0.4	0.0	0.49	(230)
Living with spouse	0.8	1.0	0.43	(230)
Have children	0.6	1.0	0.49	(230)
Former men's college	0.5	0.0	0.50	(230)

both colleges, it is somewhat surprising to see that this item has the highest
percentage of faculty rating it as very important. The only statistically significant differences between the faculty at the two colleges in their ratings of the
importance of the five work/life policies for successful job performance was
for these two programs (analysis not shown). Not surprisingly, 83 percent of
the faculty at the former women's college rated on-site childcare and 80
percent rated on-site summer day camp as at least somewhat important
whereas only 64 percent and 65 percent of the faculty at the former men's
colleges rated these two programs that were not available on their campus as
at least somewhat important.

Department Support for Family Obligations

According to Table 3.4, 90 percent of faculty somewhat agreed, agreed, or
strongly agreed that their department is supportive of family leave. Almost as
many (88 percent) somewhat agreed, agreed, or strongly agreed that their
department supports work/family balance. Slightly fewer (85 percent) somewhat disagreed, disagreed, or strongly disagreed that faculty with children
are considered to be less committed to their careers. Similarly, 73 percent
somewhat disagreed, disagreed, or strongly disagreed that it is difficult for
faculty to adjust their work schedules to care for children or other family

Table 3.3. Importance of work/life policies for success as a faculty member index (in percentages)

	Very unimportant	Unimportant	Somewhat unimportant	Somewhat important	Important	Very important
On-campus childcare (N = 166)	16.3	6.0	3.6	9.6	16.3	48.2
Childcare on-campus after school or during the summer (N = 162)	14.2	5.6	7.4	18.5	22.2	32.1
Suspension of tenure clock for parental responsibilities (N = 167)	9.0	2.4	5.4	18.0	22.8	42.5
Split or shared appointments (N = 155)	17.4	7.1	5.2	14.8	25.8	29.7
Dual career hiring (N = 148)	16.2	6.1	6.8	18.9	22.3	29.7
						$\alpha = .90$

Note: Some percentages may not total 100% due to rounding.

members, but 83 percent agreed that department meetings occur at times that conflict with family responsibilities.

Intention to Quit

A mean of 4 out of a possible score of 12 on the intention to quit index indicates that on average, faculty members disagreed with the two intention to quit items. They also disagreed with the two specific reasons for thinking about quitting, though quitting for better work/life balance did have a slightly higher mean (2.7) than quitting for spouse/partner's career (2.4).

Table 3.5 indicates that the three intention to quit variables were positively correlated with each other. The importance of work/life policies was not related to intention to quit, but it was moderately positively related to intention to quit for better work/life balance ($r = .20; p < .01$) and for spouse's career ($r = .20; p < .01$). It was also not related to college of employment despite the fact that there were differences in the availability of the five

Table 3.4. Departmental support for family obligations index (in percentages)

	Dis- agree strongly	Dis- agree	Some- what disagree	Some- what agree	Agree	Agree strongly
Faculty are supportive of work/family balance (N = 223)	1.8	4.9	5.4	13.0	40.4	34.5
Department is supportive of family leave (N = 213)	2.8	1.4	5.6	15.0	35.7	39.4
Faculty with children are considered to be less committed to their careers (r) (N = 219)	53.0	23.3	9.1	8.7	3.7	2.3
Department meetings occur at times which conflict with family obligations (r) (N = 221)	38.5	34.8	10.0	7.7	6.3	2.7
Difficult for faculty to adjust work schedules to care for children or other family (r) (N = 220)	20.5	31.8	20.5	15.0	5.9	6.4
						$\alpha = .74$

Note: Some percentages may not total 100% due to rounding.

work/life policies and programs at the two colleges with the former women's college but not the former men's college offering both on-site childcare and an on-site summer day camp. In contrast, there was a strong negative relationship between the department supports family obligations index and the intention to quit index ($r = -.41$; $p < .01$), intention to quit for better work/life balance ($r = -.39$; $p < .01$), and intention to quit for spouse's career($r = -.30$; $p < .01$).

Table 3.5. Correlations of intentions to quit, work/life policies, department support for family, and family and characteristics

	Considered quitting for better balance	Considered quitting for spouse's career	Impor- tance of work/life policies	Dept. supports family	Women	STEM	Full prof.	Living with spouse	Have children
Intention to quit (N = 223)	.68**	.43**	.13	-.41**	.03	-.13	-.16*	-.00	-.05
Considered quitting for better balance (N = 221)		.47**	.20**	-.39**	.07	-.12	-.18**	-.03	-.06
Considered quitting for spouse/partner's career (N = 184)			.20**	-.30**	-.07	-.09	-.11	.04	-.08
Importance of work/ life policies (N = 223)				-.15*	.10	-.09	-.06	.07	.28**
Department supports family (N = 223)					-.06	.27**	.22**	.10	-.01
Women (N = 223)						-.11	-.13*	-.15*	.02
STEM (N = 223)							.09	.20**	.17**
Full professor (N = 223)								.08	.04
Living w. spouse (N = 223)									.47**
Have children (N = 223)									

$p < .05; **p < .01$

Hypothesis 1: Intention to Quit

Table 3.6 reports OLS regressions of the general index of intention to quit, intention to quit for better work/life balance, and intention to quit for a spouse or partner's career on importance of work/life policies, departmental support for family obligations, and family and job characteristics. These variables explained 17 percent of the variance in the intention to quit index ($R^2 = .17$). The regression equation was significant at the $p < .001$ level ($F = 6.67$). The department support for family obligations index was the only statistically significant variable ($\beta = -.40$; $p < .001$). Controlling for the importance of work/life policies, gender, discipline, rank, marital status, parental status, and college of employment, the higher a faculty member's score on departmental support for family obligations index, the lower his or her intention to quit. Contrary to the first hypothesis, the importance of work/life policies has no effect on intention to quit.

Hypothesis 2: Intention to Quit for Better Work/Life Balance

The importance of work/life policies, departmental support for family obligations, and family and job characteristics explained 17 percent of the variance

Table 3.6. Regression of intentions to quit on importance of work/life policies, department support for family obligations, and family and job characteristics

	Intention to quit	Intention to quit for work/life balance	Intention to quit for spouse/ partner's career
	β	β	β
Importance of work/life policies	.10	.17**	.22**
Department support for family	-.40***	-.35***	-.26***
Women	.01	.03	-.11
STEM	-.02	.02	.00
Full professor	-.07	-.09	-.05
Living with spouse	.10	.08	—
Have children	-.12	-.15*	-.15*
Former men's college	.10	-.03	.07
R^2	.17***	.17***	.12***
F	6.67	6.54	4.44
N	223	225	186

$*p < .05$; $**p < .01$; $***p < .001$

(R^2 = .17) in faculty members' intentions to quit for better work/life balance. This regression equation was also significant at the $p < .001$ level ($F = 6.54$). Controlling for gender, discipline, rank, marital status, and college of employment, the importance of work/life policies, departmental support for family obligations, and having children were statistically significant predictors of intention to quit for better work/life balance. The standardized betas showed that departmental support for family obligations ($\beta = -.35$; $p < .001$) had the largest statistically significant effect while the importance of work/life policies ($\beta = .17$; $p < .01$) had the second largest effect, and having children ($\beta = -.15$; $p < .05$) had the smallest effect on intention to quit for better work/life balance. Contrary to the second hypothesis, the *more* important faculty members rated the work/life policies, the greater their intentions to quit for better work/life balance. In contrast, departmental support for family obligations had a negative relationship with the dependent variable, suggesting that the more the department supported family obligations, the lower the faculty member's intention to quit for better work/life balance. Finally, having children also lowered a faculty member's intention to quit for better work/life balance.

Hypothesis 3: Intention to Quit for Spouse/Partner's Career Opportunities

Importance of work/life policies, departmental support for family obligations, gender, discipline, rank, marital status, parental status, and college of employment explained only 12 percent of the variance (R^2 = .12; $F = 4.44$; $p < .001$) in respondents' intentions to quit for a spouse's career. The importance of work/life policies, departmental support for family obligations, and parental status had statistically significant effects on intention to quit for a spouse's career. Controlling for importance of the work/life policies, gender, discipline, rank, marital status, parental status, college of employment, and departmental support for family obligations ($\beta = -.26$; $p < .001$) had the strongest statistically significant effect on intention to quit for a spouse's career. The more a department supports family obligations, the less strongly faculty members agreed that they considered quitting for a spouse's or partner's career. The importance of work/life policies ($\beta = .22$; $p < .01$) had the second largest effect on intention to quit for a spouse or partner's career, controlling for all other variables. Contrary to the third hypothesis, the *more* important a faculty member rated work/life policies, the higher his or her intention to quit for a spouse's career. Finally, having children ($\beta = -.15$; $p < .05$) had the smallest effect on intention to quit for a spouse's career of the three statistically significant variables. The negative relationship demonstrated that respondents with children were also less likely to have considered quitting for a spouse's career.

DISCUSSION

The importance of the five work/life policies had no effect on one of the measures of intention to quit, and in the two regression models where it was a significant predictor, it operates in the opposite direction from the one hypothesized. It positively affected respondents' intentions to quit for the two specific measures of intention to quit (for better work/life balance and for a spouse's career) and had no effect on the general measure. Although most faculty valued the work/life policies provided by the college that employed them, those who regarded these policies as important did not have lower intentions to quit than those who regarded them as unimportant. In fact, those who placed the greatest importance on these five work/life policies were most likely to have considered quitting for better work/life balance and for spouses' career opportunities. It may be that the reasons that led a faculty member to value these work/life policies most highly are the same reasons that led them to consider quitting for better work/life balance and for spouses' career opportunities.

The results are consistent with previous research that found that workplace culture was more important than work/life policies (Butts et al. 2013; Mennino, Rubin, and Brayfield 2005), including at a research university (Amelink and Creamer 2007). Studying a public research university, Watanabe and Falci (2014) also found that a department culture that supports work/family management reduced the likelihood that faculty were considering leaving their jobs to reduce work/family conflict. While policies for addressing work/family conflict were important, this research supports the conclusion of other studies that the policies do not work as intended unless the workplace culture supports their use (Blair-Loy and Wharton 2002; Eaton 2003; Fried 1998; Kossek et al. 2010; Pavalko and Henderson 2006), including at colleges and universities (Hollingshead et al. 2005; Lundquist et al. 2012).

The finding that a family-friendly workplace culture was a better indicator of intention to quit than the importance of work/life policies supports the sociological new institutionalism theory's emphasis on workplace culture, rather than policies, for fostering organizational change. These results underscore the shortcomings of the rational choice institutionalism argument that if a policy exists, individuals will use it when it helps them achieve their goals. The power of department climate as a predictor suggests that formal policies are simply less important than the informal workplace culture.

Only one formal work/family policy was specifically covered in the items measuring department climate. The department support for family obligations index included a question that asked respondents whether departments were supportive of faculty who used family leave. Only 39 percent of faculty strongly agreed that their department is supportive of faculty who take family leave, providing evidence of the incongruence between the policy's formal availability and the informal climate supporting its use. The climate index also included an item measuring what Drago and his colleagues (2006) labelled caregiver bias. Only 53 percent of the respondents strongly disagreed that faculty with children are considered to be less committed to their careers, revealing that a substantial portion of the faculty see some signs of bias against colleagues who engage in caregiving. Not surprisingly, then, only a third (34 percent) strongly agreed that the department faculty are supportive of work/family balance. These percentages suggest that departments at these two colleges have a long way to go before their cultures can be described as strongly supportive of work/life management.

The department support for family obligations index also included two measures of the day-to-day ways that a department can accommodate family needs when setting faculty schedules or times for department meetings. These items suggest that family-friendly workplaces require more than formal policies that handle major events such as the birth of a child or spousal accommodation at the point of hire. They also need to address day-to-day problems, including the provision of childcare and adjusting work schedules to accommodate family needs. Formal policies and programs, such as on-site day care and flextime, can and do help with these needs, but so too do coworkers who support caregiving, leave-taking, and work-life integration and are willing to make informal adjustments as needed.

Finally, family and job characteristics did not predict faculty members' intentions to quit, except when faculty members reported having cared for children. Faculty members with children were less likely to have considered quitting for better work/life balance or for a spouse's career. In contrast to the body of literature that demonstrated that caring for children significantly increased work/life conflict (Elliott 2003; Frone and Yardley 1996; Pavalko and Henderson 2006), this analysis suggests that children can tie employees to their current job and to their community, including the schools their children attend and a support network of friends and caregivers, thereby reducing intentions to quit for either balance or for spouse's career. Overall, these results confirmed the importance of embeddedness, as the sociological approach to new institutionalism argued, by demonstrating that an informal family-friendly department culture and having children deterred faculty members from considering quitting their jobs.

In conclusion, then, the existence of work/life policies does not guarantee that employees will feel able to use them. Colleges must promote supportive department climates that take family needs into account when setting work schedules and that encourage faculty to take advantage of the work/life policies they offer. Colleges need to go further than providing work/life policies by fostering family-friendly departments. To solve the faculty time bind, Jacobs (2004) suggested that departments implement policies, such as limiting the number of department meetings and travel on weekends, to establish an institution-wide norm that decreases work/life conflict. Other possible methods of achieving supportive department climates include stressing excellence in teaching and research rather than time spent in the office, scheduling meetings when they do not conflict with family obligations, and encouraging department chairs, especially, to promote work/life policies. Supportive coworkers are integral to accessing work/life policies, which not only benefit faculty members but also transform the college from a place of employment to a community that recognizes that its employees hold a variety of professional and personal roles. Birnbaum (1988) has called liberal arts colleges examples of "total communities" where faculty and staff are dedicated to supporting the growth and development of their almost exclusively full-time residential student body. Faculty and staff would benefit from that same degree of support for managing their work and family lives.

ACKNOWLEDGMENTS

An earlier version of this paper was presented at the Eastern Sociological Society meeting, held February 2012, in New York. This research is based upon work supported by the National Science Foundation (NSF) under Grant Numbers 0820080 and 0820032. We want to acknowledge the work on the larger research project of a co-Principal Investigator, Cay Anderson-Hanley, as well as the undergraduate research assistants, Tara Kelley, Emily Cooper, Joelle Sklaar, Ilona Abramova, and Christina Gomes, and two invaluable administrative assistants, Anita Miczek and Linda Santagato. We would also like to thank Alice Dean, Kimberley Frederick, Holley Hodgins, Muriel Poston, Monica Raveret Richter, Barbara Danowski, Kristin Fox, Suthathip Yaisawarng, and especially Brenda Johnson for their contributions to the larger NSF project. Any opinions, findings, and conclusions or recommendations expressed in this material are those of the authors and do not necessarily reflect the view of NSF or Skidmore College.

REFERENCES

Amelink, Catherine T., and Elizabeth G. Creamer. 2007. "Work-Life Spillover and Job Satisfaction of Married/Partnered Faculty Members." *Journal of Women and Minorities in Science and Engineering* 13:317–32.

Anderson, Cynthia D., Christine Mattley, Valerie Martin Conley, and David A. Koonce. 2014. "Community Colleges and the Reproduction of Gender in the Academy: Experiences of Women Stem Faculty." Pp. 41–62 in *Gender Transformation of the Academy*, Vol. 19, *Advances in Gender Research*, edited by V. Demos, C. W. Berheide, and M. T. Segal. Bingley, UK: Emerald Group Publishing Limited.

Anderson, Donna M., Betsy L. Morgan, and Jennifer B. Wilson. 2002. "Perceptions of Family-Friendly Policies: University versus Corporate Employees." *Journal of Family and Economic Issues* 23:73–92.

Bagger, Jessica, Andrew Li, and Barbara A. Gutek. 2008. "How Much Do You Value Your Family and Does It Matter? The Joint Effects of Family Identity Salience, Family-Interference-with-Work, and Gender." *Human Relations* 61:187–211.

Berheide, Catherine White, and Cay Anderson-Hanley. 2012. "Doing It All: The Effects of Gender, Rank, and Department Climate on Work-Family Conflict for Faculty at Liberal Arts Colleges." Pp. 165–88 in *Social Production and Reproduction at the Interface of Public and Private Spheres*, Vol. 16, *Advances in Gender Research*, edited by M. T. Segal, E. Ngan-Ling Chow, and V. Demos. Bingley, UK: Emerald Group Publishing Limited.

Berheide, Catherine White, Lisa Christenson, Rena Linden, and Una Bray. 2013. "Gender Differences in Promotion Experiences at Two Elite Private Liberal Arts Colleges in the United States." *Forum on Public Policy* 2013:1–19.

Berheide, Catherine White, and Susan Walzer. 2014. "Processes and Pathways: Exploring Promotion to Full Professor at Two Liberal Arts Colleges in the United States." Pp. 177–98 in *Gender Transformation of the Academy*, Vol. 19, *Advances in Gender Research*, edited by V. Demos, C. W. Berheide, and M. T. Segal. Bingley, UK: Emerald Group Publishing Limited.

Berheide, Catherine White, Megumi Watanabe, Christina Falci, Diane C. Bates, Elizabeth Borland, and Cay Anderson-Hanley. 2014. "Still Gendered after All These Years: A Comparison of Faculty Work-Life Integration across Institutional Type." Paper presented at the American Sociological Association meetings, San Francisco, CA, August.

Birnbaum, Robert. 1988. *How Colleges Work: The Cybernetics of Academic Organization and Leadership*. San Francisco: Jossey-Bass Publishers.

Blair-Loy, Mary, and Amy S. Wharton. 2002. "Employees' Use of Family-Responsive Policies and the Workplace Social Context." *Social Forces* 80:813–45.

Brandon, Peter D., and Jeromey B. Temple. 2007. "Family Provisions at the Workplace and Their Relationship to Absenteeism, Retention, and Productivity of Workers: Timely Evidence from Prior Data." *Australian Journal of Social Issues* 42:447–59.

Butts, Marcus M., Wendy J. Casper, and Tae Seok Yang. 2013. "How Important Are Work–Family Support Policies? A Meta-Analytic Investigation of Their Effects on Employee Outcomes." *Journal of Applied Psychology* 98:1–25.

Callan, Samantha. 2007. "Implications of Family-Friendly Policies for Organizational Culture: Findings from Two Case Studies." *Work, Employment and Society* 21:673–91.

Callister, Ronda Roberts. 2006. "The Impact of Gender and Department Climate on Job Satisfaction and Intentions to Quit for Faculty in Science and Engineering Fields." *Journal of Technology Transfer* 31:367–75.

Drago, Robert W., Carol Colbeck, Kai D. Stauffer, Amy Pirretti, Kurt Burkum, Jennifer Fazioli, Gabriela Lazarro, and Tara Habasevich. 2006. "The Avoidance of Bias against Caregiving: The Case of Academic Faculty." *American Behavioral Scientist* 49:1222–47.

Eaton, Susan C. 2003. "If You Can Use Them: Flexibility Policies, Organizational Commitment, and Perceived Performance." *Industrial Relations* 42:145–67.

Ellickson, Robert. 1991. *Order without Law*. Cambridge, MA: Harvard University Press.

Elliott, Marta. 2003. "Work and Family Role Strain among University Employees." *Journal of Family and Economic Issues* 24:157–81.

Fox, Kristen, Catherine White Berheide, Kimberly Frederick, and Brenda Johnson. 2010. "Adapting Mentoring Programs to the Liberal Arts College Environment." Pp. 27–41 in *Mentoring Strategies to Facilitate the Advancement of Women Faculty*, edited by K. Karukstis, B. Gourley, M. Rossi, and L. Wright. Washington, DC: American Chemical Society.

Fox, Mary Frank, Carolyn Fonseca, and Jinghui Bao. 2011. "Work and Family Conflict in Academic Science: Patterns and Predictors among Women and Men in Research Universities." *Social Studies of Science* 41:715–35.

Fried, Mindy. 1998. *Taking Time: Parental Leave Policy and Corporate Culture*. Philadelphia, PA: Temple University Press.

Frone, Michael R., and John K. Yardley. 1996. "Workplace Family Supportive Programmes: Predictors of Employed Parents' Importance Ratings." *Journal of Occupational and Organizational Psychology* 69:351–66.

Gatta, May L., and Patricia A. Roos. 2004. "Balancing without a Net in Academia: Integrating Family and Work Lives." *Equal Opportunities International* 23:124–42.

Gerson, Kathleen. 1986. *Hard Choices: How Women Decide About Work, Career and Motherhood.* Berkeley: University of California Press.

Granovetter, Mark. 1985. "Economic Action and Social Structure: The Problem of Embeddedness." *American Journal of Sociology* 91:481–93.

Greenhaus, Jeffrey H., and Nicholas J. Beutell. 1985. "Sources of Conflict Between Work and Family Roles." *The Academy of Management Review* 10:76–88.

Grover, Steven L., and Karen J. Crooker. 1995. "Who Appreciates Family-Responsive Human Resources Policies: The Impact of Family-Friendly Policies on the Organizational Attachment of Parents and Non-Parents." *Personnel Psychology* 48:271–88.

Hochschild, Arlie. 1997. *The Time Bind: When Work Becomes Home and Home Becomes Work.* New York: Henry Holt and Company.

Hochschild, Arlie, and Anne Machung. 1989. *The Second Shift: Working Parents and the Revolution at Home.* New York: Viking.

Hollenshead, Carol S, Beth Sullivan, Gilia C. Smith, Louise August, and Susan Hamilton. 2005. "Work/Family Policies in Higher Education: Survey Data and Case Studies of Policy Implementation." *New Directions for Higher Education* 130:41–65.

Ingram, Paul, and Karen Clay. 2000. "The Choice-within-Constraints New Institutionalism and Implications for Sociology." *Annual Review of Sociology* 26:525–46.

Jacobs, Jerry A. 2004. "The Faculty Time Divide." *Sociological Forum* 19:3–27.

Jacobs, Jerry A., and Sarah E. Winslow. 2004. "Overworked Faculty: Job Stresses and Family Demands." *Annals of the American Academy of Political and Social Science* 596:104–29.

Kelly, Erin L., Phyllis Moen, and Eric Tranby. 2011. "Changing Workplaces to Reduce Work-Family Conflict: Schedule Control in a White-Collar Organization." *American Sociological Review* 76:265–90.

Khare, Manorama M., and Linda Owens. 2006. "Faculty Work Climate Survey: Final Report." University of Illinois at Chicago. Retrieved September 25, 2011 (http://www.uic.edu/depts/oaa/faculty/climatesurvey.html).

Kossek, Ellen E., Suzan Lewis, and Leslie B. Hammer. 2010. "Work-Life Initiatives and Organizational Change: Overcoming Mixed Messages to Move from the Margin to the Mainstream." *Human Relations* 63:3–19.

Lapierre, Laurent M., and Tammy D. Allen. 2006. "Work-Supportive Family, Family-Supportive Supervision, Use of Organizational Benefits, and Problem-Focused Coping: Implications for Work-Family Conflict and Employee Well-Being." *Journal of Occupational Health Psychology* 11:169–81.

Lewis, Suzan. 1997. "'Family Friendly' Employment Policies: A Route to Changing Organizational Culture or Playing about at the Margins?" *Gender, Work, and Organization* 4:13–23.

Lundquist, Jennifer H., Joya Misra, and KerryAnn O'Meara. 2012. "Parental Leave Usage by Fathers and Mothers at an American University." *Fathering* 10:337–63.

Mason, Mary Ann, and Marc Goulden. 2004. "Do Babies Matter (Part II)? Closing the Baby Gap." *Academe* 90:10–15.

Mennino, Sue F., Beth A. Rubin, and April Brayfield. 2005. "Home-to-Job and Job-to-Home Spillover: The Impact of Company Policies and Workplace Culture." *Sociological Quarterly* 46:107–35.

Misra, Joya, Jennifer H. Lundquist, and Abby Templer. 2012. "Gender, Work Time, and Care Responsibilities among Faculty." *Sociological Forum* 27:300–23.

Moen, Phyllis, and Stephen Sweet. 2004. "From 'Work-Family' to 'Flexible Careers.'" *Community, Work and Family* 7:209–26.

Nee, Victor. 1998. "Sources of New Institutionalism." Pp. 1–16 in *The New Institutionalism in Sociology*, edited by M. C. Brinton and V. Nee. Stanford, CA: Stanford University Press.

O'Laughlin, Elizabeth M., and Lisa G. Bischoff. 2005. "Balancing Parenthood and Academia: Work/Family Stress as Influenced by Gender and Tenure Status." *Journal of Family Issues* 26:79–106.

Ollilainen, Marjukka, and Catherine Richards Solomon. 2014. "Carving a 'Third Path': Faculty Parents' Resistance to the Ideal Academic Worker Norm." Pp. 21–40 in *Gender Transformation of the Academy, Vol. 19, *Advances in Gender Research*, edited by V. Demos, C. W. Berheide, and M. T. Segal. Bingley, UK: Emerald Group Publishing Limited.

Pavalko, Eliza K., and Kathryn A. Henderson. 2006. "Combining Care Work and Paid Work: Do Workplace Policies Make a Difference?" *Research on Aging* 28:359–74.

Perry-Smith, Jill E., and Terry C. Blum. 2000. "Work-Family Human Resource Bundles and Perceived Organizational Performance." *Academy of Management Journal* 43:1107–17.

Powell, Walter W., and Paul J. DiMaggio, eds. 1991. *The New Institutionalism in Organizational Analysis*. Chicago, IL: University of Chicago Press.

Richman, Amy L., Janet T. Civian, Laurie L. Shannon, E. Jeffrey Hill, and Robert T. Brennan. 2008. "The Relationship of Perceived Flexibility, Supportive Work-Life Policies, and Use of Formal Flexible Arrangements and Occasional Flexibility to Employee Engagement and Expected Retention." *Community, Work, and Family* 11:183–97.

Settles, Isis H., Lilia M. Cortina, Janet Malley, and Abigail J. Stewart. 2006. "The Climate for Women in Academic Science: The Good, the Bad, and the Changeable." *Psychology of Women Quarterly* 30:47–58.

Solomon, Catherine Richards. 2011. "'Sacrificing at the Altar of Tenure': Assistant Professors' Work/Life Management." *The Social Science Journal* 48:335–44.

———. 2010. "The Very Highest Thing Is Family": Male Assistant Professors' Work/Family Management. Pp. 233–55 in *Interactions and Intersections of Gendered Bodies at Work, at Home, and at Play*, Vol. 14, *Advances in Gender Research*, edited by V. Demos and M. T. Segal. Bingley, UK: Emerald Group Publishing Limited.

Ward, Kelly, and Lisa Wolf-Wendel. 2012. *Academic Motherhood: How Faculty Manage Work and Family*. New Brunswick, NJ: Rutgers University Press.

Watanabe, Megumi, and Christina Falci. 2014. "A Demands and Resources Approach to Understanding Faculty Turnover Intentions due to Work-Family Balance." *Journal of Family Issues*, 0192513X14530972, first published on May 1, 2014 as doi:10.1177.

Wharton, Amy S., and Mychel Estevez. 2014. "Department Chairs' Perspectives on Work, Family, and Gender: Pathways for Transformation." Pp. 131–50 in *Gender Transformation of the Academy*, Vol. 19, *Advances in Gender Research*, edited by V. Demos, C. W. Berheide, and M. T. Segal. Bingley, UK: Emerald Group Publishing Limited.

Wonch Hill, Patricia, Mary Anne Holmes, and Julia McQuillan. 2014. "The New Stem Faculty Profile: Balancing Family and Dual Careers." Pp. 3–20 in *Gender Transformation of the Academy*, Vol. 19, *Advances in Gender Research*, edited by V. Demos, C. W. Berheide, and M. T. Segal. Bingley, UK: Emerald Group Publishing Limited.

Chapter Four

"Could I be THAT Guy?"

*The Influence of Policy and Climate on
Men's Paternity Leave Use*

Erin K. Anderson

Stimulated by the passage of the 1993 Family and Medical Leave Act (FMLA) and pressured by competition with industry and a variety of activists in academia, institutions of higher education have developed a number of policies to assist employees in managing the competing demands of family and work. Several such policies focus on the time period surrounding the birth or adoption of a new child, including stoppage of the tenure clock, modified workplace duties, part-time teaching, and at some schools, paid parental leave (Spalter-Roth and Erskine 2006; Sullivan et al. 2004).

The FMLA, which provides up to twelve weeks of leave, is a policy that a significant proportion of eligible employees feel they are unable to use, largely because the leave is unpaid. Many families cannot forgo the income in order to utilize this parental leave and they may have access to only a short absence from work supported by paid sick days, vacation time, or personal leave days (Albelda and Mandell 2010). This is especially true for fathers, who are far less likely to have access to paid parental leave than are mothers (Matos and Galinsky 2012). Yet, as men's roles in marriage and the family change, there is growing interest among men to be able to utilize parental leave when a new child comes into the family (Harrington et al. 2014). A recent survey of American fathers found an overwhelming majority, 89 percent, rated paid parental leave provided by an employer as an important workplace benefit (Harrington et al. 2014). It is clear that men now report that they, like women, experience pressures in managing work and family roles (Bellavia and Frone 2005; Roehling, Moen, and Batt 2003).

In response, a small but growing number of U.S. employers are offering parental leave policies that provide for at least some period of paid leave (Hollenshead, Sullivan, Smith, August, and Hamilton 2005; Sullivan et al. 2004; Van Giezen 2013). This is true not only in industry, but in the academy as well. Institutions of higher education are required to comply with FMLA requirements, therefore, some form of leave is available to most faculty and staff. But when it comes to parental leave, little of this is paid. Excluding the availability of paid sick, vacation, or personal leaves, only about one third of U.S. colleges and universities have a paid parental leave policy (Center for the Education of Women 2007; Yoest 2004). Where they do exist, paid leave policies are most commonly maternity leave policies and therefore available only to women. Large research universities have traditionally offered more in the way of work/life policies, including maternity leave (Hollenshead et al. 2005). However, private elite institutions are more likely than public colleges and universities to offer gender neutral parental leave policies; approximately one quarter of private institutions have a paid parental leave policy available to both women and men while only 10 percent of public institutions do (Yoest 2004).

The notion of men taking any significant amount of time away from work for the birth or adoption of a child has been somewhat unusual given gendered family roles throughout American history. Men's family contributions have customarily been centered on their economic support of wives and children (Coltrane and Adams 2001; Lamb 1986; LaRossa 1998; Pleck 1987). Such roles have been promoted by the ideals of hegemonic masculinity, characterized by breadwinning, competition, and dominance (Connell 1999). However, many American fathers today report an interest in a more active and involved parenthood (Coltrane 1996; Coltrane and Adams 2001; Lamb 1986; Pleck 1987). It is well documented that contemporary fathers are more likely to be present at the birth of their children, involved in their care as infants, participate in daily childcare activities, and maintain an intimate and expressive relationship with sons and daughters (Coltrane 1996; Griswold 1993; Pleck 1987; Rotundo 1993). Given this growing desire on the part of men in the United States to be more involved in the care of their children, a greater expressed interest in paid paternity leave, and the implementation of family-friendly policies in academia, one might expect more men in higher education to take advantage of paid leave. This, however, is not the case. In fact, it seems that few men who are eligible for such leave actually utilize it (Armenia and Gerstel 2006; Drago et al. 2006; Hollenshead et al. 2005; Kaufman et al. 2010; Lundquist, Misra, and O'Meara 2012). This might lead one to question whether men are merely offering an endorsement of the expansion of family roles and workplace support for them, or if they truly would like to be able to contribute more in the caretaking of their children. The factors that might influence men's use of paid parental leave,

particularly at academic institutions, are of interest if we are to better understand both why men want access to this family-friendly policy and why they
might also be hesitant to use leave when it is available.

METHODS

This case study examines the situations of thirteen men employed at River
Bend College (pseudonyms are used for all institutions and individuals refer-
enced here) and their decisions to use or not use parental leave. River Bend
College, a private liberal arts college, has slightly more than 1,400 students
and employs over 700 people in full-time positions; about 100 of these are
tenure-line faculty. Implemented in 2004, River Bend College has a policy of
paid parental leave available to employees who meet the eligibly requirements for the FMLA. The college's leave policy extends beyond the twelve
weeks required by the FMLA; fifteen weeks of paid leave are available to
qualifying faculty and staff for the birth or adoption of a child. River Bend's
domestic partner policy allows employees who have a domestic partner (of
the same or opposite sex) to take advantage of this policy as well. There is,
however, one restriction on the use of parental leave for couples in which
both partners work for the college: fifteen weeks of paid leave is available to
the couple, who may split it however they wish (i.e., each partner may take a
portion of the leave or one partner can take all fifteen weeks).

The paid parental leave policy was first available to faculty and staff in
2004. Although no official data is available from the institution, it is commonly believed among employees that the policy was not used by a man at
the institution until 2009. In contrast, all women who have been eligible for
paid leave are believed to have taken all or nearly all leave available to them.
The thirteen men interviewed for this study comprise nearly the entire population of men currently employed at River Bend College who have been
eligible to take the full fifteen weeks of paid parental leave at some point
during their employment. It should be noted that men whose partners were
also employed at the college and would have been eligible for a shared leave
of fifteen weeks were excluded from this study. Because this study seeks to
understand the influences and factors men take into consideration when deciding if and how they will use the paid leave policy, men who would have to
negotiate a shared leave with a spouse or partner (and therefore might opt to
take little or no leave so their wives/partners might have the maximum recovery time after childbirth) are not included in this population.

Both faculty and staff at River Bend College have the same fifteen weeks
of paid leave available to them. Although in general few men have utilized
the full leave period, staff fathers are far less likely to take advantage of this
policy than are faculty fathers. To understand the factors at play for staff and

faculty men in their decisions to use or not use the paid leave available to them faculty and staff men were interviewed to find out what they thought about the policy and its usage.

Each participant completed a pre-interview survey to collect demographic and leave-use information, followed by a semi-structured interview, lasting between thirty and sixty minutes. This data was analyzed using a grounded theory approach. Grounded theory, one of the most widely employed methods of qualitative analysis in the social sciences, is preferred for this research because it allows one to focus on patterns of action and interaction as well as the processes experienced by men in this decision-making position. Grounded theory analysis generates a systematic examination of the conditions, contexts, actions, strategies, and consequences of the phenomenon being studied (Corbin and Strauss 2014). The factors most influential to men as they consider parental leave and the contrast between faculty and staff ranks are explored here.

FINDINGS

Of these thirteen men, only five had taken the full fifteen weeks of paid leave available to them; four of these were faculty and one was a staff member (see Table 4.1). Of the eight men who were eligible but chose a shortened leave or negotiated other arrangements, four were faculty and four were members of the college staff. All the staff men in this study occupied positions based on the specialized technical, athletic, or administrative skills they possessed; they were not general laborers.

As with most colleges or universities, the classification of positions of faculty and staff at River Bend College has some important distinctions. The two groups are guided by separate employee handbooks that outline policies and procedures relevant to their positions. Staff positions accrue sick leave and vacation days; faculty positions do not. Most staff have twelve-month appointments while faculty largely have responsibilities on campus only nine months of the year. The academic calendar (based on a two-semester system) generally governs faculty teaching activities. This semester schedule is significant for staff as well, but the workload of many of these positions is governed by a different schedule (such as the "busy seasons" for admissions or athletics) or is influenced by year-round responsibilities (such as information technology or facilities management). However, these two groups of employees are also subject to many of the same workplace policies at River Bend College, including the FMLA and paid parental leave policies. For these fathers, the awareness of the parental leave policy, the logistics of taking leave, relationships with coworkers, and consequences for one's career were all identified as factors that influenced a man's consideration and

Table 4.1.   Staff and faculty fathers

	Staff fathers	
Anthony	15 weeks leave	
Edward	2 weeks leave, 8 weeks part-time work	
Jared	2 weeks leave, 2 weeks part-time work	
Keith	2 weeks leave	
Marcus	No leave, 1 week part-time work	
	Faculty fathers	
Douglas	15 weeks leave	Tenured
Greg	15 weeks leave	Untenured
Nathan	15 weeks leave	Untenured
Russell	15 weeks leave	Untenured
Brent	1 week leave	Untenured
Carson	3 days leave	Untenured
Francis	No time off	Untenured
Joel	1 week leave, two-thirds teaching load for 2 semesters	Untenured

subsequent decision to take any time away from work for a new child in the family.

Policy Awareness

The fact that River Bend College offers both mothers and fathers leave that is 1) paid and 2) exceeds the twelve weeks of FMLA leave makes the institution somewhat rare among academic institutions (Center for the Education of Women 2007; Hollenshead et al. 2005; Yoest 2004). Two men stated they were specifically attracted to the institution because of such policies and what their existence might mean for work/family balance. For instance, during his job interview, faculty member Nathan was impressed with the "kind of a progressive policy for an institution of this size and this location, that there was both maternal and paternal leave paid . . . I was delighted that there was a family leave policy."

Most men, however, had little knowledge of the policy until they were expecting a child and sought information about time off that might be available to them. Very few men knew much about the policy or anyone who had utilized it. Whereas women might seek a fuller understanding of such policies as they are considering a career, negotiating employment, or undergoing a new employee orientation process, making time to meet the (non-economic) needs of a new child in the family was not at the forefront of most men's minds. This difference may be a function of men's and women's different biological experiences of pregnancy, childbirth, and recovery, the assumption that parental leave policies only exist for women, or the cultural differences in the roles of mothers and fathers in the lives of young children. While women often anticipate the need to arrange for an absence from their workplace for the birth or adoption of a child, men are more likely to see value in their economic contributions for a new child and less likely to consider taking time from work (Townsend 2002).

Keith, a father in a staff position, said "I didn't even think about the leave . . . I didn't do a good job of investigating the policy and there wasn't like anybody [who] sat down with me like, 'your wife's pregnant. These are the things you could do.'" Keith acknowledged, however, his own lack of effort to investigate his options and continued, "it would be very easy for somebody to sit here and be like 'well, nobody came and told me that.' Well, I have a [staff] handbook. I mean, it's right there in front of me. I could have looked it up myself. I could have gone to [the human resources representatives] and been like . . . 'what exactly do I have here?'" Anthony, also a staff member, explained, "actually, I didn't know that it existed until my colleague, Carla Morris, went on leave. And when we found out that we were pregnant I said, 'oh, okay, so I wonder if I can take a similar leave' and she said 'yes, it's open to men as well' . . . and that's when I read the policy."

In general, faculty men seemed to have a greater awareness of the policy. Whether it was due to advertising and recruitment efforts in the hiring of new faculty, a more thorough faculty orientation process, or the regular meetings of the entire faculty where such policies might be mentioned or discussed, these college employees were more likely to indicate they knew the leave policy was available even if they didn't take advantage of it. Brent, a faculty father who took only one-week leave when his child was born, explained, "I knew that they [maternity/paternity leave policies] existed . . . I mean it came up in faculty meetings and stuff . . . [my child] was born in, I guess 2009 and it [the leave policy] started in 2004. I probably didn't know about it in 2004. I probably didn't know about it until like three or four years later." Faculty member Greg, who did take a full semester's leave, said, "Initially I knew very little except that we had one [a leave policy] and I assumed that it was simply an excused, but unpaid leave of absence and so I sought clarity on that from Russell, a colleague, because I knew that he had taken it and he clarified to me that it was fully paid, before I talked to the dean about it." Very often it was an immediate supervisor or other colleague, as in the cases of Anthony and Greg, who volunteered or provided information about the workplace policy and actually encouraged a man to look into it.

The awareness of such policies has clear implications for who might utilize work/family policies. At River Bend College, faculty men were better informed about the existence of paid parental leave, were more willing to investigate their options and discuss them with colleagues, and were ultimately more likely to utilize the policy. The lack of awareness of the policy and questions about one's eligibility at this institution highlight an area of concern discussed by Spalter-Roth and Erskine (2006) who identify a lack of research on how information about policies is distributed at academic institutions. Most employees in academia are likely to have some knowledge of FMLA because it is a federally mandated policy, but knowledge of other work/family policies is skewed by gender. Faculty mothers are far more likely to know about these policies in their workplaces than are faculty fathers (Spalter-Roth and Erskine 2006). Although mothers are not examined in the current study, it is obvious that fathers at River Bend College generally have little knowledge of the parental leave policy. Many of these men were aware that women had paid leave available, often because they saw coworkers and colleagues use it, but they had little initial awareness that they too were eligible for parental leave that would not reduce their income. Spalter-Roth and Erskine (2006) find that in the academy, parents are often not encouraged to investigate or use work/family policies. Further, these are often seen as "a reward not a resource" (Spalter-Roth and Erskine 2006, 9).

Logistics

The arrangements that must be made when a River Bend College employee takes leave differ based on one's workplace position. Given that teaching responsibilities are heaviest during two predictable fifteen-week periods (semesters) per year, and childbearing or adoption tend to be events one has a lengthy period to plan for (as opposed to leave for an illness), faculty are able to plan for leave with few concerns. Replacing a faculty member for a semester of leave, whether it is for parental leave, a research sabbatical, or an administrative reason, is a fairly routine process. The human resources office posts a job opening and solicits applicants and the department chair and search committee interview candidates for a replacement position; a visiting professor is hired. Once a faculty member's parental leave commences, they are excused from teaching, advising, and committee service work during their fifteen weeks of leave. They do, however, continue to have access to all income and regular benefits, including insurance, retirement contributions, and pre-tax set asides, associated with their position.

The work life of a staff member, however, may be governed less by the academic calendar, and more by other needs of the institution. For this reason, the timing of one's leave might be less routine and more of a challenge for the employee and their coworkers. Edward, a member of the college's fund raising department and father who took "a couple of weeks off" and then returned to work part-time for two months after the birth of his child, explained, "my sense is that [faculty] live in a different world. . . . There's probably both, depending on the time of year, more or less flexibility, you know . . . it's not apples to apples because, you know, I manage relationships with various people." Edward feared the consequences for the institution and for his position if he were to try to put those relationships on hold or pass them on to a colleague for fifteen weeks, so he negotiated a different work/ family arrangement.

Many men acknowledged that the process of making sure their duties were fulfilled during a leave was very different for staff than it was for faculty and this presented a substantial hurdle to using or even considering the full parental leave. The institution was unable or unwilling to hire outside replacements for many of the staff positions for a fifteen-week leave period, therefore making sure work continued without interruption was a challenge. Another significant difference between faculty and staff where leave was concerned was the responsibility for covering one's work during a leave period. Whereas for faculty this burden was taken on by a department chair or a committee who hired a visiting professor, for staff this was largely left up to the employee seeking leave. Jared, a staff member, rationalized his two weeks of leave and two weeks of part-time work before returning full-time to his technology support position in this way,

> Basically, I think it's the case in a lot of people's positions in a smaller group, it's difficult to find one person who could fill a spot as a temporary person to get people to cover you. You could get people who have sort of shared, you know, abilities to cover and then just put off some things, but to be able to do it for an extended period of time, I think it would have been more difficult to do.

Marcus, a staff member working in athletics who did not take leave, also expressed concern for the institution and the ability to replace the work he did with a temporary position, "there's three [people with my qualifications in the county] and they all work here. So, it's not realistic to try to bring somebody in as a flex or temp job, so it makes it difficult."

These comments highlight an important distinction between faculty and staff at River Bend College and perhaps most schools. Although employed at the same institution, these two classes of workers are guided by different time tables, different demands, and different organizational approaches to dealing with life events that might interrupt one's work. The college offers a very predictable, very uniform, and largely impersonal way for faculty to excuse themselves from workplace commitments in order to attend to the needs of a new child in the family. The dean, department chair, and a search committee seek a qualified replacement and a visiting faculty member is assigned a complement of courses to teach. Staff, however, are tasked with negotiating with their colleagues and supervisors to create a plan and assign workplace responsibilities while they are away. The fact that they must be more involved in the logistics of this means they are less likely to request leave. Whether they are uncertain about how things might be handled in their absence or uncomfortable with burdening coworkers, these men take this personal responsibility seriously. Staff fathers, like many American fathers (Kaufman et al. 2010), are more likely to use vacation or sick leave for a short-term absence from work after the birth of a baby. These men are also more likely to work out informal arrangements that are not part of the official parental leave policy, such as flextime or part-time work. They see these short-term absences and arrangements as more acceptable for their work group, colleagues, and their own needs and interests. Such patterns echo the findings of Callan (2007) who found employees were less likely to utilize leave if they feared their coworkers would be negatively impacted by their absence.

In this way, the same policy for both classes of employees does not seem to be effective. Faculty calendars and personnel procedures are structured in a way that offers faculty fathers a more clearly institutionalized method for utilizing paternity leave. Many staff men don't really feel they can or should take fifteen weeks of parental leave. Although it will not cost them financial support in lost wages, it may cost them social capital in the relationships they have with others in their workplace.

Relationships

Related to these logistics are the relationships affected by men taking parental leave. While some faculty men cited concern for their students, colleagues, or the department in general as a reason not to take parental leave, this unease was usually articulated as a worry about what might not get done in their absence, such as courses taught, student theses advised, and curriculum advanced. Staff, on the other hand, were often reluctant to utilize parental leave because their coworkers would have to take on more work while they were away and staff were hesitant to burden their workplace peers who had their own job responsibilities. Jared feared that if his small work group lost him for parental leave it would put additional stress on his colleagues who continued working and had to pick up the slack if he were to take more than a couple of weeks of leave. He said,

> We didn't have any provisioning for a temporary [worker] or anything like that . . . It's not really the kind of job that would be easy to get just a temporary person to fill in, so basically whenever anybody is taking, whether it is leave time or vacation time or whatever, we just basically have to cover. So in that

case it was, I didn't feel that it was fair to take fifteen weeks, you know, for everybody else.

Keith also feared that his colleagues in athletics would suffer if he were away from the workplace too long, but he also recognized that he might be subject to some criticism from his male colleagues,

> Well, obviously I can speak for athletics more than I can anything else . . . within the guys there is a little bit of, like, fraternity-like atmosphere amongst the guys . . . [the guy] in the office right next to me, I know he would give me a lot of crap if I took a month off because, you know, I'm home with my kid . . . the ones that would grumble wouldn't do it behind my back either, they would do it to my face.

Anthony, the only staff father who did take the full leave available said, "It's not a vacation and a lot of staff here questioned that with me . . . it's not a vacation taking care of a newborn. It's a lot of work . . . It took a lot of my coworkers here some time to understand why I was taking it." He further explained, "I just got the feeling that many people really weren't respectful of the fact that I did take the time off."

Given that a typical faculty career incorporates periodic leaves, generally for research sabbaticals, men faculty were much more likely to expect their colleagues would accept their absence for a semester. They also felt they had less to worry about in terms of being away from their offices or classrooms for fifteen weeks. Staff, on the other hand, keenly understood the consequences of their absence and potential reactions from coworkers. The distinctions in the frequency of leaves of absence from the workplace and how colleagues and the overall institution might be impacted where faculty and staff are concerned is noteworthy. While the same fifteen weeks of paid leave is available to both categories of employees, the workplace climate and the procedures for ensuring the continuity of work impact faculty and staff very differently, thus influencing the likelihood one will utilize parental leave.

Staff men seemed to prioritize the needs of their coworkers and justify them as a reason not to take more than a few days to a few weeks of leave. Faculty men, on the other hand, were more likely to see the needs of their partners and children as acceptable reasons to take time away from the workplace to devote their energies to needs at home. The difference in these views might be attributed to educational and social class differences between the staff and faculty. The more highly educated a man is, the more likely he is to utilize parental leave (Plantin 2007). Although, it is worth noting that most of the staff men in this study possessed educational credentials and specialized skills that would locate them in a white collar social class category. And half of the faculty men here did not use leave. In general, however, a significant influence for all of these men when they were considering leave seemed to be how the institution facilitated, or didn't, an employee's time away from the workplace. Faculty were able to make the decision to utilize the leave and not have to worry about covering their teaching, advising, and service work while they were away from campus. Staff positions were not offered this same support; a man who wanted to take leave was largely responsible for arranging for the completion of his own workplace duties in his absence. The effort and social capital required to so do might have been a great enough hurdle for these men to dissuade them from putting their family needs first.

Career Consequences

Many of these men were ambivalent about the parental leave policy. While they all expressed support for the policy and praised the institution for having such a policy on the books, most also communicated some concern for the actual consequences of using it. This was true of both faculty and staff men.

Tenure-line faculty are obviously influenced by the evaluative process that leads to tenure and the job security that comes with it. How children might impact the tenure process is reported to be a concern for fathers as well as mothers (Solomon 2010). Most faculty men who became fathers before they were tenured acknowledged the tenure decision was taken into consideration when they were deciding how to approach the issue of parental leave. The decision to grant tenure at River Bend College is made based on, among other things (e.g., publication record, course evaluations, student recommendations), an evaluation of a faculty member by his or her departmental colleagues, faculty from other departments, and the college's dean. For this reason, the opinions of campus colleagues can be quite significant in one's decision-making process. Brent, who didn't know of any other men who had used the parental leave policy at the time his child was born, said, "I didn't want to be THAT guy, the first guy." With no frame of reference for how leave utilization might actually be interpreted, many men were reluctant to be the guinea pig for men managing work and family with the policy. A faculty member on parental leave has the option to put their tenure clock on hold until they return, however few men were aware this was an option. Those who did know were reluctant to stop the tenure clock because they were not aware of any of their male colleagues who had done so and therefore didn't know what the professional consequences might be. Joel rationalized, "the biggest concern about being away was that I have one semester less visibility on campus, so I wanted to be here in the year leading up to tenure . . . I wanted to be here, being visible, creating observables for evaluation for tenure." Carson's tenure decision was expected in the same semester his child was born, but he would have had to apply for leave in the months before the semester or the decision on his tenure application. In negotiating these demands he felt he had to weigh the immediate and long-term needs of his family before ultimately deciding not to request leave, "of course tenure for us meant stability for the entire family, for the child. And that's part of the reason that it's such a scary situation to try and take paternity leave when you're up for tenure, because this is the bread and butter for that child as well." It is interesting to note that many of these men's women colleagues had taken parental leave and had taken advantage of stopping the tenure clock, and had subsequently been tenured. There was no precedence for denying a faculty member tenure after taking parental leave or stopping the tenure clock at this college.

Staff do not have the same type of job protection that faculty are able to come to expect through tenure. There are no employee unions at River Bend College and staff can lose their jobs due to workplace reorganization, a shift in the goals of the college's leadership, or poor job performance. Therefore, maintaining the appearance of adding value to the college is at the forefront of many of their daily experiences. Edward witnessed a number of changes in the college's organization and wanted to ensure his contributions to the college were appreciated. He explained that amid these changes, taking a significant amount of time off for parental leave could cause him to miss some opportunities,

> It was at a point where I was getting an opportunity to work with President Smith on some things . . . so there were just a lot of opportunities there for me to kind of step up and, you know, it was sort of professional opportunities to help me advance my career more quickly and, you know, any time, organizationally, any time that there is upheaval or change, there's invariably opportunities that go along with that, an opportunity to advance, to take on more responsibility, and to grow professionally.

Some staff men even thought ahead to their next career move and sought to ensure that the reputation they had in their current position would help them get ahead in a future workplace. Marcus, for instance, was very conscious of the ways success for the college athletes he worked with would influence future career opportunities, "I came here with some very specific goals about success for the team and we were hitting the marks. We were right there. We had a really good year . . . these jobs are fickle and if I wanted to move on, having this success would have been a great thing on the resume." Thus, Marcus limited his time away from work to attend to the needs of his wife and new child in order to avoid compromising a career advancement opportunity that might not even come for several years.

For many of these men, like American fathers in general, success in their current positions is an important priority and parental leave may be passed over in order to ensure future opportunities or accomplishments (Blair-Loy and Wharton 2002). Poising oneself for success in a future position or workplace is also central to their decision-making process. Their achievements in their current or potential workplace role are seen as an important part of meeting the needs of their families. Anything that might inhibit their workplace rewards or opportunities could also negatively impact their role as a father or husband. Being a good provider is part of being a good father and good husband, part of the "package deal" in men's lives that Townsend (2002) identified.

Hindsight

Many of the men who used little or none of the leave available to them, both faculty and staff, stated that in hindsight they may have made a different decision about managing their work and family responsibilities. Faculty men who opted not to take leave out of concern for their careers were likely to look back and feel they had missed an opportunity in their families while focusing on the career impact of parental leave. Some men, like Brent, second-guessed their fears about not attaining tenure, "In retrospect, I think it would have been fine. I think I would have gotten tenure." These men began to think differently about the existence of the policy and the consequences for using it. Other men, generally first-time fathers, re-evaluated the experience of trying to balance the needs of a new infant, a working spouse, and their own career after they lived through the early months of parenthood. Carson identified with this experience in reflecting on his choices, "You wonder like, should I have . . . should I have taken paternity leave right after the child was born . . . I should have asked for a reduced load. That would have made me feel better. It would have given me more time to be with my family . . . even right after the decision was made, I said to myself 'ahhh, I should have gone ahead and taken paternity leave.'"

Some staff fathers who had not utilized the leave available to them also reconsidered their actions. Even after his wife suffered complications in childbirth and his son spent several days in the NICU after birth, Keith returned to work almost immediately. Although he was "officially" taking two weeks off, he appeared on campus frequently during those two weeks. However, what seemed like pressing issues at work then, seemed less important in hindsight, "Looking back now, I probably would have done it [taken the leave] knowing what I know now about that. It's like maybe I didn't have to be that hands-on [at work] and I could have just let it go. . . . To take paternity leave seemed like a luxury that I couldn't afford at the time. Looking back now, with a more wise view of things . . . I probably could have." Likewise, Edward, who had negotiated a lengthy period of part-time work after the birth of his child, reflected, "I'm glad that I took the time I did and in some ways feel like I may have missed out on some things for not taking the rest of the time."

None of the five fathers who did take the full fifteen weeks of leave regretted doing so. None of them felt that their careers, their colleagues, students, or departments in the college had suffered. In fact, they communicated a clear intention to challenge the "ideal worker" norm that prioritizes work over family (Solomon 2011) and believed they had a responsibility to educate their colleagues on the feasibility of using the policy without negative workplace consequences.

Douglas, for instance, explained

> I was gonna take it just to make sure that folks knew that it wasn't something that was just on the books and that men not only had it available, but that they should feel free to take it . . . I had a colleague who had a child here. He was eligible to take it. He wasn't tenured and didn't take it because he thought it would reflect poorly on him. I was quite upset with that. Not with him, but for him feeling as though he had to make that decision. . . . So as I said, [it was important I took leave] in terms of symbolic notion of taking it, to make sure that people knew that men were taking this and that they should feel free to take it.

Greg had benefited from talking with a colleague who had utilized paternity leave and was subsequently willing to be a resource for other men on campus who wanted to know more about how to make the policy work for them. He described "a sort of wall of silence around the whole thing" that needed to be addressed, "if anyone were to come to me and ask me about it, I would be happy to share with them and I would encourage them. I just don't think that, I don't think there's a lot to fear with regard to assistant professors, in particular, that it's gonna impact the tenure decision."

Staff serving as such a resource for one another seems less likely for several reasons. First, the lack of examples of successful staff paternity leaves is a limitation; only one eligible staff member has taken the leave to date. Second, the variety of staff positions across the college is much more significant than the variety among faculty. There are more similarities between faculty positions in different departments than there are between staff positions in different departments as well as a wide range of skill levels, credentials, and work schedules. Staff may be less likely to identify with one another and recognize their shared interests. Third, staff are less likely to interact with one another for the purposes of challenging policies or practices on campus. While all faculty attend a monthly meeting where such issues are raised and discussed or sit on committees where policies are developed, this cooperation among staff is not encouraged, fostered, or facilitated. They are less likely to see opportunities to work together and advocate for their shared interests and may actually fear negative repercussions for attempting to do so.

CONCLUSION

There are important lessons to be learned by looking at the availability of a family-friendly policy, the actual use of such policy, and the perception employees have of the policy and its impact on their careers. River Bend College offers the same fifteen-week paid parental leave to all employees who meet the eligibility requirements of the FMLA, but the employees themselves see their situations and desires quite differently.

The majority of the men are hesitant to utilize the full period of paid leave available to them. A primary reason for this, concerns about how colleagues and supervisors might judge their commitment to their jobs and workplace, echoes the findings of much previous research (Blair-Loy and Wharton 2002; Butts, Casper, and Yang 2013; Eaton 2003; Fried 1998; Hollenshead et al. 2005; Lundquist, Misra, and O'Meara 2012; Pavalko and Henderson 2006). A "chilly climate" (Hollenshead et al. 2005) toward parental leave, real or perceived, reduces the likelihood a new father would utilize this parental leave policy. Many of these men were concerned about their reputations if they were to take time off work and continue to collect a paycheck while burdening their colleagues by their absence. The fact that this leave would be to provide care for a new baby was not enough to overcome the potential stigma for most (Lester 2013).

The consequences for one's career were also at the forefront of most men's decision to forgo parental leave. Whether it was the immediate outcome or the long-term impact an absence might have on a resume, vita, or reference, they were hesitant to take a leave which might limit their career advancement. Consistent with other findings (Hollenshead et al. 2005; Jacobs and Gerson 2004; Solomon 2008; Wolf-Wendel, Twombly, and Rice 2003), both faculty and staff in this study were concerned that their commitment to their careers might be questioned if they used the full leave available to them. Clear support offered by colleagues and supervisors was a meaningful influence in faculty and staff decisions to prioritize family needs over work roles that could be performed by others or suspended during a leave period. The recognition of family needs and overt support offered by supervisors is especially important for employees to feel they have the freedom to utilize work/life policies when they are needed without negative repercussions (Blair-Loy and Wharton 2002).

Gender also plays a persistent role in the use of work/life policies. The fact that women are more likely than men to use such policies contributes to the perpetuation of a gendered division of labor in the private sphere (Hochschild 1989; Misra, Lundquist, and Templer 2012; Nyberg 2012, Rhoads and Rhoads 2012). Men's ability to "opt out" of caretaking needs for a new child might serve to disadvantage the careers not only of their partners, but also of their female colleagues. If women faculty or staff take the fifteen weeks of leave available to them and men do not, women's commitment to their careers may be questioned, their ability to manage work and family responsibilities might be scrutinized, and their professional accomplishments could be stalled. Men's resistance to using parent leave has negative consequences for women both in the family and in the workplace. A workplace that offers men the opportunity to take parental leave and provides economic support to do so has the power to increase men's caretaking contributions in the family as well as normalize leave taking from the workplace, thus positively impacting women's experiences in the workplace and the family.

Lessons to be learned from this, and previous research, are that work/life policies are only beneficial if employees feel they are able to use them. There must be an institutional structure and workplace culture that encourage their use. The provision of a policy, such as the parental leave policy at River Bend College, may be ineffective if the process of utilizing it is significantly different for staff than it is for faculty. One class of employees, faculty, may feel more able to manage work and family responsibilities because the practice of leave taking is institutionalized. Staff, on the other hand, work within a structure that places additional burdens on them if they want to utilize the paid leave to which they are entitled; these burdens may make the policy ultimately seem unattractive or inaccessible. The lack of awareness of the policy, whether it is a federal policy such as FMLA or an employer specific one, also makes it challenging for an employee to understand what options they have available. Greater publicity of such work/life policies might further normalize their use. Finally, challenging the norms of hegemonic masculinity is essential for de-stigmatizing caretaking behaviors and the use of parental leave by men. While perhaps the hardest of these things to change, this not only offers something for men to gain in their relationships with children and partners, it has great potential to expand the opportunities and rewards for women in the workplace.

ACKNOWLEDGEMENTS

An earlier version of this paper was presented at the Eastern Sociological Society meeting, held March 2013, in Boston. Support for this research was provided by the Washington College Faculty Enhancement Fund.

REFERENCES

Albelda, Randy, and Betty Mandell. 2010. "Paid Family and Medical Leave." Pp. 47–62 in *The Crisis of Caregiving: Social Welfare Policy in the United States*, edited by B. R. Mandell. New York: Palgrave MacMillan.
Armenia, Amy, and Naomi Gerstel. 2006. "Family Leaves, the FMLA and Gender Neutrality: The Intersection of Race and Gender." *Social Science Research* 35:871–91.

Bellavia, Gina, and Michael Frone. 2005. "Work-Family Conflict." Pp. 113–47 in *Handbook of Work Stress*, edited by J. Barling, E. K. Kelloway, and Michael Frone. Thousand Oaks, CA: Sage Publications.

Blair-Loy, Mary and Amy S. Wharton. 2002. "Employees' Use of Family-Responsive Policies and the Workplace Social Context." *Social Forces* 80:813–45.

Butts, Marcus M., Wendy J. Casper, and Tae Seok Yang. 2013. "How Important Are Work–Family Support Policies? A Meta-Analytic Investigation of Their Effects on Employee Outcomes." *Journal of Applied Psychology* 98:1–25.

Callan, Samantha. 2007. "Implications of Family-Friendly Policies for Organizational Culture: Findings from Two Case Studies." *Work, Employment and Society* 21:673–91.

Center for the Education of Women. 2007. "Family-friendly Policies in Higher Education: A Five-year Report." University of Michigan Research Brief.

Connell, Robert W. 1999. "Understanding Masculinities and Change." *Diskurs* 9: 6–69.

Coltrane, Scott. 1996. *Family Man: Fatherhood, Housework, and Gender Equity.* New York: Oxford University Press.

Coltrane, Scott, and Michele Adams. 2001. "Men's Family Work: Child-Centered Fathering and the Sharing of Domestic Labor." Pp. 72–99 in *Working Families: The Transformation of the American Home*, edited by R. Hertz and N. L. Marshall. Berkeley: University of California Press.

Corbin, J., and Strauss, A. 2014. *Basics of Qualitative Research: Techniques and Procedures for Developing Grounded Theory*, 4th edition. Thousand Oaks, CA: Sage Publications.

Drago, Robert, Carol L. Colbeck, Kai D. Stauffer, Amy Pirretti, Kurt Burkum, Jennifer Fazioli, Gabriela Lazzaro, and Tara Habasevich. 2006. "The Avoidance of Bias Against Caregiving: The Case of Academic Faculty." *American Behavioral Scientist* 49:1222–47.

Eaton, Susan C. 2003. "If You Can Use Them: Flexibility Policies, Organizational Commitment, and Perceived Performance." *Industrial Relations* 42:145–67.

Fried, Mindy. 1998. *Taking Time: Parental Leave Policy and Corporate Culture.* Philadelphia, PA: Temple University Press.

Griswold, Robert L. 1993. *Fatherhood in America: A History.* New York: Basic Books.

Harrington, Brad, Fred Van Deusen, Jennifer Sabatini Fraone, Samantha Eddy, and Linda Haas. 2014. "The New Dad: Take Your Leave—Perspectives on paternity leave from fathers, leading organizations, and global policies." Boston College Center for Work and Family. Retrieved August 19, 2014 (http://www.bc.edu/content/dam/files/centers/cwf/news/pdf/BCCWF percent20The percent20New percent20Dad percent202014 percent20FINAL.pdf).

Hochschild, Arlie R. 1989. *The Second Shift: Working Parents and the Revolution at Home.* New York: Viking.

Hollenshead, Carol S., Beth Sullivan, Gilia C. Smith, Louise August, and Susan Hamilton. 2005. "Work/family Policies in Higher Education: Survey Data and Case Studies of Policy Implementation." *New Directions for Higher Education* 130:41–65.

Jacobs, Jerry A., and Kathleen Gerson. 2004. *The Time Divide: Work, Family, and Gender Inequality.* Cambridge, MA: Harvard University Press.

Kaufman, Gayle, Clare Lyonette, and Rosemary Crompton. 2010. "Post-Birth Employment Leave Among Fathers in Britain and the United States." *Fathering: A Journal of Theory, Research, and Practice about Men as Fathers* 8:321–40.

Lamb, Michael E. 1986. "The Changing Role of Fathers." Pp. 3–27 in *The Father's Role: Applied Perspectives*, edited by M. E. Lamb. New York: John Wiley and Sons.

LaRossa, Ralph. 1988. "Fatherhood and Social Change." *Family Relations* 37:451–58.

Lester, Jaime. 2013. "Work-life Balance and Cultural Change: A Narrative of Eligibility." *The Review of Higher Education* 36:463–88.

Lundquist, Jennifer, Joya Misra, and KerryAnn O'Meara. 2012. "Parental Leave Usage by Fathers and Mothers at an American University." *Fathering* 10:337–63.

Matos, Kenneth, and Ellen Galinsky. 2012. *2012 National Study of Employers.* New York: Families and Work Institute. Retrieved July 25, 2014 (http://familiesandwork.org/site/research/reports/NSE_2012.pdf).

Misra, Joya, Jennifer H. Lundquist, and Abby Templer. 2012. "Gender, Work Time, and Care Responsibilities among Faculty." *Sociological Forum* 27:300–23.

Nyberg, Anita. 2012. "Gender Equality Policy in Sweden: 1970s–2010s." *Nordic Journal of Working Life Studies* 2:67–84

Pavalko, Eliza K., and Kathryn A. Henderson. 2006. "Combining Care Work and Paid Work: Do Workplace Policies Make a Difference?" *Research on Aging* 28:359–74.

Plantin, Lars. 2007. "Different Classes, Different Fathers? On Fatherhood, Economic Conditions and Class in Sweden." *Community Work and Family* 10: 93–110.

Pleck, Joseph H. 1987. "American Fathering in Historical Perspective." Pp. 83–97 in *Changing Men: New Directions in Research on Men and Masculinity*, edited by M. S. Kimmel. Newbury Park, CA: Sage Publication.

Rhoads, Steven E., and Christopher H. Rhoads. 2012. "Gender Roles and Infant/Toddler Care: Male and Female Professors on the Tenure Track." *Journal of Social, Evolutionary, and Cultural Psychology* 6:13–31.

Roehling, Patricia, Phyllis Moen, and Rosemary Batt. 2003. "Spillover." Pp. 101–21 in *It's About Time: Couples and Careers*, edited by P. Moen. Ithica, NY: Cornell University Press.

Rotundo, E. Anthony. 1993. *American Manhood: Transformations in Masculinity from the Revolution to the Modern Era.* New York: Basic Books.

Solomon, Catherine Richards. 2008. "Personal Responsibility in Professional Work: The Academic 'Star' as Ideological Code." Pp. 180–202 in *People at Work: Life, Power, and Social Inclusion in the New Economy*, edited by M. L. DeVault. New York: New York University Press.

———. 2011. "'Sacrificing at the Altar of Tenure': Assistant Professors' Work/Life Management." *The Social Science Journal* 48:335–44.

———. 2010. "'The Very Highest Thing is Family': Male Untenured Assistant Professors' Construction of Work and Family." Pp. 233–55 in *Interactions and Intersections of Gendered Bodies at Work, at Home, and at Play*, Vol. 14, *Advances in Gender Research*, edited by V. P. Demos and M. T. Segal. Bingley, UK: Emerald Group Publishing Limited.

Spalter-Roth, Roberta, and William Erskine. 2006. "Resources or Rewards? The Distribution of Work-Family Policies." ASA Research Brief, American Sociological Association.

Sullivan, Beth, Carol Hollenshead, and Gilia Smith. 2004. "Developing and Implementing Work-Family Policies for Faculty." *Academe* 90:24–27.

Townsend, Nicholas W. 2002. *The Package Deal: Marriage, Work and Fatherhood in Men's Lives.* Philadelphia, PA: Temple University Press.

Van Giezen, Robert. 2013. "Paid leave in private industry over the past 20 years." *Beyond the Numbers: Pay and Benefits.* Vol. 2, no. 18 Bureau of Labor Statistics. Retrieved July 25, 2014 (http://www.bls.gov/opub/btn/volume-2/paid-leave-in-private-industry-over-the-past-20-years.htm).

Wolf-Wendel, Lisa, Susan B. Twombly, and Suzanne Rice. 2003. *The Two-body Problem: Dual-career-couple Hiring Practices in Higher Education.* Baltimore: Johns Hopkins University.

Yoest, Charmaine. 2004. "Parental Leave in Academia." Report to the Alfred P. Sloan Foundation and the Bankard Fund at the University of Virginia. Retrieved June 15, 2014 (http://www.faculty.virginia.edu/familyandtenure/institutional percent20report.pdf).

Chapter Five

Caring for Aging Parents

Managing the Personal and Professional in Academia

Rona J. Karasik, Debra L. Berke, and Scott D. Scheer

Work and family represent central life roles and are gaining increasing attention from both employers and researchers (Bianchi and Milkie 2010). While many work/life issues are common to employees across the employment spectrum (e.g., finding and affording suitable childcare), each profession and work venue also give rise to their own unique challenges. The academic profession is no exception. Often stereotyped as an elite, extremely flexible workplace, academia nonetheless poses some very specific work/life challenges (e.g., cost and time required for education; limited employment opportunities, leading many to relocate away from family and other support systems; and ever-increasing expectations for tenure and promotion) (Baker 2010; Damiano-Teixeira 2006; Jacobs and Winslow 2004; Philipsen 2008; Philipsen and Bostic 2010; Solomon 2011).

Much of the current research on managing the personal with the professional in academia centers on the early stages of both family and academic career (e.g., childbearing and rearing of children while on the tenure track) (Bassett 2005; Connelly and Ghodsee 2011; Williams 2005), although several studies (Berke, Karasik, and Scheer 2007, 2009; Solomon 2011) do intentionally address these issues for single faculty and married faculty without children. Research addressing the interaction of later stages of family and career for academics (e.g., elder care for parents while post tenure) has received much less attention, most often in the form of a casual reference or tangential note regarding how academics can become sandwiched between child and parent care (Hagedorn and Sax 2004; Philipsen 2008). As the population continues to age, however, parent care has become a growing concern for employees in other types of work (Cullen et al. 2009; Gautun and

Hagen 2010; Katz et al. 2011), and promises to be a growing concern for academics as well. Using a life course perspective lens, this study examines two data sets reflecting the professional and personal trajectories of academics in the United States as they relate to concerns regarding aging parents (e.g., elder care).

THE ACADEMIC WORKPLACE

Despite public perceptions of the academic workplace as an intellectual "ivory tower" where overpaid faculty work flexible twelve-hour workweeks, numerous studies have emerged to contradict these myths about the academic work experience. With regard to flexibility, Philipsen and Bostic (2010) note that the absence of a time clock to punch does not eliminate the need to meet the ever-increasing expectations of academic productivity, especially for junior faculty seeking tenure. Rather, flexibility may simply mean that faculty work (with the exception of class schedules) does not have set starting and ending times, allowing it to spill over into nights, weekends, and other traditionally "family-designated" segments of time. Furthermore, Basset (2005) identifies academic work as having "an emphasis on competition and individual achievement" (1), and Fischer, Ritchie, and Hanspach (2012) argue that academia has moved to a model of productivity that values quantity over quality.

For women, the challenges of negotiating work and family may be further complicated by the reality that "(a)cademic workplaces largely remain structured around a traditionally hierarchical, male workplace model and culture, which can inhibit women's career advancement" (Schlehofer 2012, 112). While both men and women are challenged by the increasing demands of their work (e.g., serving as educators, researchers, advisors, supervisors, committee members), several authors suggest that the impact may be greater on women (Baker 2010; Bonawitz and Andel 2009; Cummins 2005; Philipsen 2008; Townsley and Broadfoot 2008), particularly those who bear children at a culturally expected but academically inconvenient (e.g., pre-tenure) life stage (Bassett 2005; Kemkes-Grottenthaler 2003). For example, studies show that women who have children early in their careers are less likely to achieve tenure than women who have children later or not at all. Conversely, for faculty who are men, early parenting has been shown to have a more positive effect on their chances of promotion (Mason and Goulden 2002), although both men and women may delay having children until they reach tenure (Solomon 2011). Jacobs and Winslow (2004) suggest "that the demanding nature of academic jobs combines with the gender segregation of academic fields to contribute to reduce the representation of women as tenured faculty" (144). Despite the increase in women entering the academy, many find that the gender imbalance regarding tenure and promotion still weighs heavily against women faculty (Baker 2010; Conley 2005; O'Laughlin and Bischoff 2005; Williams 2005).

"Family-friendly" policies within academic institutions emerged with the goal of counterbalancing these trends. Findings from studies of the so-called "mommy-track," where women are given the opportunity to "stop the tenure clock" for family-related needs (e.g., childbearing) have been mixed with regard to their impact on outcomes such as salary and promotion (Connelly and Ghodsee 2011; Manchester, Leslie, and Kramer 2010). Cummins (2005) also cautions that some institutions may attempt to "mommy-track" women faculty regardless of their maternal status. Furthermore, O'Meara and Campbell (2011) found that both men and women may be reluctant to take advantage of "family-friendly" policies for fear of their potential for a negative career impact while Munn and Hornsby (2008) discuss how lesbian and gay families are often disadvantaged by how family is defined. Similarly, Lester (2013) suggests that an institution's culture plays a role in the stigma associated with such policies. On the other hand, Spalter-Roth and Erskine (2005) contend that while family-friendly policies may be beneficial for some academic mothers, it is the "best and the brightest" who are most able to access them successfully. Thus, Gerten (2011) distinguishes between "family-friendly" and "career-friendly" policies, with the former leaving mothers at a potential disadvantage career-wise and the latter a goal still to be achieved.

WORK AND CARING FOR AGING PARENTS

It is no secret that the population of older adults in the United States is expanding as more people are living longer (Vincent and Velkoff 2010). The vast majority of these older adults are relatively healthy and able to take care of themselves. The overall increase in the number of older persons, however, also increases the number of working adult children who will eventually face work/life issues associated with caring for the needs of an older parent. While few studies focus exclusively on work and elder care issues in academia, several at least mention it as one work/family issue among many (Hagedorn and Sax 2004; Philipsen 2008; Philipsen and Bostic 2010). Outside of academia, however, elder care has become a growing concern both for employers and employees. One thread in the current work/elder care literature examines concerns from the employee's perspective, exploring issues such as filial responsibility, role strain (Gordon et al. 2012; Silverstein and Giarrusso 2010; Silverstein, Gans, and Yang 2006) and workers becoming "sandwiched" between their careers, their children, and their aging parents (Pines et al. 2011). The physical and emotional impact of caregiving on employed caregivers and caregiver burden are also of concern (Duxbury, Higgins, and Smart 2011; Trukeschitz et al. 2013), as are gender issues of work and elder care for dual-earner families (Baker 2010; Chesley and Poppie 2009; Pope, Kolomer, and Glass 2012).

A second theme in the literature focuses on employers' perspectives and policies that govern employees and elder care. Some of these studies examine the impact of elder care on worker productivity (Gordon and Rouse 2013; Katz et al. 2011; Trukeschitz et al. 2013). Katz et al. (2011), for example, found that employers noticed that employees' elder caregiving disrupted workers' productivity, particularly with regard to work time lost due to employee tardiness, absence, and leaves. Katz et al. (2011) also found that employers' attitudes toward family leave policies were mixed, with some in favor of such policies in order to bring attention to the issues, and many others feeling the policies were unnecessary either because formal policies might limit what could be done informally or because elder care was the employee's problem rather than their own. Ryan and Kossek (2008) indicate that how work/life policies are implemented influences their overall impact on work and employee outcomes. Thus, it is not just the policy but how it is viewed within the institutional culture that leads to its eventual acceptance and subsequent use or not.

A LIFE COURSE PERSPECTIVE

The current study examines faculty parent care work/life experiences following the life course perspective. This perspective focuses on age norms and the timing of life transitions (Elder, Johnson, and Crosnoe 2003; Roehling, Roehling, and Moen 2001). From this perspective, family life transitions (e.g., marriage, career, childbearing, aging parents) may be placed into social and historical context (e.g., as "on-time" or "off-time"). Individual life experiences and their outcomes (e.g., bearing children, gaining tenure, caring for aging parents) may then be interpreted with regard to the impact of such timing (e.g., at what point during one's academic career do the issues of elder care arise and how do they affect outcomes such as tenure and promotion). Similarly, this perspective takes into account the reality that not all faculty enter academia and/or the tenure track at the same time. Some faculty, especially women, may begin their academic career later in their life course (e.g., "off-time") (Townsley and Broadfoot 2008). Given the continuing gender differences associated with the academic experience (Baker 2010; Connelly and Ghodsee 2011; Philipsen 2008), the current study pays particular attention to gender as an important intervening variable with regard to the role that parent care plays in the work and family lives of academics in the United States.

METHODS

Procedure

The current study represents one aspect of two phases of data collection. In the first phase, in-depth semi-structured interviews were conducted with a small number of academics (N = 15) from four different educational institutions in the East Coast and Midwest. The goal was to identify key themes in the work and family lives of faculty in higher education. Questions were developed based on previous research (e.g., Becker and Moen 1999) and addressed areas such as detailed descriptions of respondents' work, family and educational timelines, work load, locations where work was performed, definitions of managing work and family demands, institutional policies, and how "family-friendly" their institutions were. None of the interview questions specifically asked about aging or parent care. The average length of the interviews was one hour with a range of one to two and a half hours. Each respondent was asked the same open-ended questions so that comparable data would be available across cases. Data from this first phase were analyzed using qualitative open-coding techniques (Strauss and Corbin 1990). While this phase of the study covered a broad range of work/life issues, reported here are only responses that emerged as pertaining to issues of aging parents and/or elder care.

In the second phase of this study, a written survey of work and family life was developed based on findings from the initial interviews. An electronic survey using SurveyMonkey (https://www.surveymonkey.com) was disseminated to various professional listservs that reach university faculty, including campus-wide lists at several colleges and universities. Data from this second phase were analyzed using descriptive and inferential statistics, as well as the qualitative methods described above for open-ended responses. Analysis of the data did not include significance testing to establish causality, rather the findings describe participants' perceptions of their experiences. In this second phase, a broad range of family/work issues were addressed by the survey. Again, reported here are only responses pertaining to issues of aging parents and/or elder care.

Sample

Phase I

Participants for phase I (N = 15) were purposefully selected based on being either a tenured or tenure-track faculty member. While efforts were made to create as diverse a sample as possible, the majority of this group were married (N = 10, 66.7 percent); white (N = 11, 73.3 percent), associate professors

(N = 8, 53.3 percent) with at least one child (N = 12, 80 percent). Nine participants (60 percent) were women, six (40 percent) were men and their ages ranged from 32 to 61 years, with a mean age of 45.5 years. Participants represented different academic disciplines and institutional classifications, including four-year bachelor's level college (N = 5, 33.3 percent); master's level institution (N = 5, 33.3 percent); and research/doctoral level institution (N = 5, 33.3 percent). See Table 5.1 for additional demographic details.

Phase II

In the second phase, survey responses (N = 775) were received from college and university faculty across the United States. Respondents ranged in age from 22 to 72 years, with a mean age of 43.9 years. A large portion of respondents were white/Caucasian (N = 665, 87.7 percent), women (N = 612, 81.2 percent), and married (N = 487, 65.6 percent). Two hundred (26.2 percent) had a master's degree while a majority of the respondents (N = 476, 62.4 percent) held doctoral degrees. With regard to tenure status, 206 (38.6 percent) were tenured; 140 (26.2 percent) were on the tenure track but not yet tenured; 188 (35.2 percent) were not on a tenure track; and the remaining participants did not respond to this question. Note: In phase II, not all participants chose to respond to all of the questions. Percentages were calculated based on the number of responses for each question. See Table 5.1 for additional demographic details.

FINDINGS

Phase I

Although not specifically asked about aging or elder care, eleven of the fifteen interviewees (73.3 percent) reflected on issues concerning their aging parents. The responses of these eleven are reported here. Overriding themes within these parental issues included: caregiving, filial-separation, and bereavement. Within each theme, several subthemes were also identified.

Caregiving

Of the eleven respondents raising the topic of their aging parents, only four (36.4 percent) indicated that they were currently providing or had recently provided direct care to one or more of their older parents or parents-in-law. For those who did, however, the impact was significant in terms of time, economics (cost of care), and the need to manage care with their academic and additional family duties. One tenure-track, married, forty-five-year-old woman with two children brought her ailing mother from overseas to provide care for four months before her mother's death. During that time, she " . . .

Table 5.1. Demographics

Respondent Group	Phase 1 (N = 15)	Phase 2[a] (N = 775)	Phase 2[a] Elder Subsample (N = 45)
Gender			
Men	6 (40.0%)	142 (18.8%)	3 (7.0%)
Women	9 (60.0%)	612 (80.1%)	40 (93.3%)
Race			
African American/black	3 (20.0%)	23 (3.0%)	4 (9.1%)
Asian/Pacific Islander	1 (0.7%)	16 (2.1%)	1 (2.3%)
Caucasian/white	11 (73.3%)	665 (87.7%)	32 (72.7%)
Hispanic/Latino/a	0 (0.0%)	18 (2.4%)	3 (6.8%)
Mixed	0 (0.0%)	19 (2.5%)	1 (2.3%)
Other	0 (0.0%)	17 (2.2%)	3 (6.8%)
Marital status			
Single	2 (13.3%)	125 (16.8%)	8 (18.6%)
Married	10 (66.7)	487 (65.5%)	23 (53.5%)
Domestic partnership	2 (13.3%)	76 (10.2%)	8 (16.3%)
Divorced	1 (0.7%)	46 (6.2%)	4 (9.3%)
Separated	0 (0.0%)	6 (0.8%)	0 (0.0%)
Widowed	0 (0.0%)	3 (0.4%)	1 (2.3%)
Academic rank			
Assistant professor	4 (26.7%)	159 (27.1%)	4 (12.1%)
Associate professor	8 (53.3%)	128 (21.8%)	10 (30.3%)
Full professor	2 (13.3%)	76 (12.9%)	5 (15.2%)
Instructor/adjunct	0 (0.0%)	57 (9.7%)	4 (12.1%)
Other	1 (0.7%)	167 (28.4%)	10 (30.3%)
Tenure status			
Tenured	9 (60.0%)	206 (38.6%)	15 (51.7%)
On tenure track	6 (40.0%)	140 (26.2%)	2 (6.9%)
Not on tenure track	0 (0.0%)	188 (35.2%)	12 (41.4%)
Children			
No	3 (20.0%)	305 (40.3%)	14 (31.1%)
Yes	12 (80.0%)	452 (59.7%)	31 (68.9%)

[a]In phase II, not all participants chose to respond to all of the questions. Percentages were calculated based on the number of responses for each question.

did everything. From dressing her, to bathing her, to taking her to . . . the bathroom, changing her, feeding her, taking her to the doctor . . . at the point where she was out of the hospital; I was the single provider of that."

Another tenure-track woman, single with no children, age fifty, contemplated whether the direct care for her parent fell to her because of her birth order, her gender, or her family status:

> I think there is probably certain things that are expected . . . I am the oldest . . . I'm not married and don't have other responsibilities with my own immediate family. . . . So, who does that fall to? It's falling to me. Would it fall to the oldest sibling if the oldest sibling was male? I don't know. Or would it just fall to the oldest female? So, it could be simply because of birth order. It could be because of a couple of other combination of things but I think it's probably related to gender . . . assuming that caretaker role.

On the other hand, another woman, age forty-six, who married after she had tenure and did not have children, reflected that despite the challenges of providing parent care, her academic job gave her more flexibility than some others she knew: "I have a girlfriend . . . she works for [a mobile network operator], she's at her job every night until 11:30 . . . It's a very high pressure job. So . . . I feel no right to complain at all in any way. But I think having some flexibility . . . [helps]."

While not all of the women in this sample reported providing parent care, all those in the sample who did indicate they provided parent care were women. As described above, these care-providing respondents noted that although the benefits of academia such as flexibility assisted them in managing work and caregiving, the costs of caregiving were also significant in terms of time and energy (e.g., physical, emotional).

Filial-Separation

Geographic distance was a concern for each of the eleven interviewees who talked about parental issues. Cultural issues relating to parent care and filial expectations were also an important theme among the respondents. International respondents seemed particularly aware of the challenges of long-distance parent care, although several were only in the "anticipation" stage of care. For example, one man, a forty-three-year-old tenure-track faculty member from an African nation noted "I also try to help my father out but he primarily supports himself. But being the first child and the type of culture I come from, that is an expectation that I will also take care of him. You know that we do not have nursing homes and a place like that so I have to worry about his upkeep."

While none of the interviewees lived close to their parents, at least initially, several indicated they had to take time off to care for their parent. For example, another man, a thirty-seven-year-old on the tenure track, described getting permission from his Provost to help his mother: "[she said] 'it's okay, you can leave now and I'll make sure that you get people to teach your courses.' And this not only happened one time . . . when people were teaching the classes and I was able to go home again." This same faculty member also faced similar caregiving challenges with his mother-in-law:

> For the first two years we went back to [our home country] four times . . . and doctors told us, you know, she was going to die one time in November, when I was able to get others to teach the classes and we flew back and she was fine. We went back the following summer just to visit and also to do some research . . . we got a call again close to Christmas. "You got to be home" so we flew back. She was fine. So we went back and forth.

Several other respondents similarly reported the need to coordinate care long-distance. Some indicated that other family members who were geographically closer (e.g., their siblings) might provide some help to their parents; however, these respondents still felt responsibility and some remorse in regard to their parent's care. As one tenured thirty-nine-year-old woman faculty member noted: "my brother and sister are over there so . . . they're on the front line and I have the guilt of not being on the front line." When asked to reflect on whether long-distance or front-line care was more challenging, this respondent noted: "They are equally hard. They are different. I would think the front line is harder. They have the day-to-day stuff." As an important reminder that support and caregiving among adult children and their aging parents is rarely one-sided, this same respondent also spoke to the limits geographic distance placed on her ability to receive reciprocal support: "I live here, my family's over there . . . so we have a lot of issues just around having a child . . . we have to deal with having a child, but we don't have my parents [help]."

As reflected by the stories above, geographic distance posed a variety of challenges for these respondents, ranging from what to do when hands-on direct care is required, to mixed feelings about needing to rely on others (e.g., siblings) for any care their parent(s) might need currently or in the future. Greater geographical separation (e.g., internationally) appeared to exacerbate such challenges. Coping mechanisms used or anticipated for this group included respondents moving their parents/in-laws closer and/or using resources such as time and money to arrange care assistance—either by traveling to the family member in need or by accessing caregiving assistance proximate to those requiring care.

Bereavement

In addition to parent care, death of a parent also emerged as a common theme for several interviewees. In these instances, not only was distance a challenge for respondents, but so was finding the time to grieve. As the tenure-track, married, forty-five-year-old woman described earlier as bringing her mother from overseas to live with her notes:

> [With] the death of my dad [abroad], I found myself having to make arrange-
> ments. Up to this point, I hadn't really had to do that as an adult . . . then . . .
> the death of my mom's sister who was living with my mom after my dad died.
> That was also in [my home country]. Then my trip to . . . bring my mom here
> and then my mom's death in summer . . . I fell apart when my mom died . . . I
> would go to the cemetery every day and I would think of her and cry.

Here again, geographic distance plays a role in the way faculty may manage competing work/family concerns related to older parents. As demonstrated above in the cases both of parent care and bereavement, additional challenges arise from the reality that neither challenge follows a finite, proscribed timeframe that easily meshes with the expectations and timing within academia.

Phase II

Caregiving

In this larger, Phase II survey-based study, many respondents indicated that their work life had been impacted at some point by various caregiving responsibilities (e.g., childcare, N = 305, 56.1 percent; parent care, N = 131, 24.2 percent). Only a small portion (N = 45, 5.8 percent), however, responded in the affirmative to the question "Are you responsible for the care of an elder or person with a disability for at least three hours a week?" Of this group of respondents currently caring for an elder, the vast majority (N = 40, 88.9 percent) were women, married (N = 23, 52.3 percent), tenured (N = 15, 51.7 percent), and held a doctoral degree (N = 31, 68.9 percent). Ages for this subsample ranged from 34 to 66 years of age, with an average age of 50.8 years. See Table 5.1 for additional demographic details of this subsample.

Among this currently caregiving subsample, twenty-one (61.8 percent) were providing care for their mother, six (17.6 percent) were caring for their father, five (14.7 percent) were caring for their mother-in-law, and three (8.8 percent) were caring for their father-in-law. Six respondents (17.7 percent) were caring for a child with a disability. Two respondents (4.4 percent) reported caring for both of their parents, while one other (2.2 percent) reported caring for both parents plus a mother-in-law. Several of these caregivers (N = 15, 39.5 percent) provided care in their own home year-round, while others (N = 8, 21.1 percent) provided care in the care recipient's home year-round. Three quarters of the caregivers (N = 34, 75.6) reported providing assistance with instrumental activities of daily living (IADL) tasks, including: transportation, shopping, cooking, help with doctor's appointments, finances, yard and housework. Some respondents (N = 10, 22.2 percent) indicated that they provided companionship and emotional support. Some (N = 10, 22.2 percent) also indicated that they were involved with the more time-consuming provision of direct care to a parent, helping with their activities of daily living (ADL) tasks (e.g., medication assistance, bathing, feeding, toileting, dressing, and mobility).

Managing Work and Family

In both the elder caregiving subsample (N = 32, 100 percent) and those not currently providing elder care (N = 449, 87.7 percent), respondents overwhelmingly agreed with the statement "I have had to make sacrifices to balance work and family." Similarly, a larger percentage of the caregiving subsample (N = 17, 53.2 percent) agreed that they "had difficulty achieving a promotion," contrasted with only 30 percent (N = 146) of those not currently providing elder care. A large proportion of both groups (N = 27, 84.4 percent) and (N = 382, 75.2 percent), respectively, felt "pulled between work and family."

Parent care did impact many of the caregivers' work, with several indicating that it had a negative impact on their research productivity (N = 19, 63.3 percent); ability to attend professional events/conferences (N = 15, 50 percent); and professional mobility (N = 15, 53.6 percent), although few felt that it affected their academic rank (N = 7, 23.3 percent) or their employment status (N = 1, 3.3 percent). Only one of the caregiving subsample (3.8 percent), however, reported having taken family and medical leave to care for her parents. A similarly small proportion of the non-elder-care sample (N = 14, 2.9 percent) also reported using family and medical leave for parent care.

Institutional Impact on Elder Care

A majority of both the elder-caregiving subsample (N = 19, 61.3 percent) and the non-caregiving group (N = 335, 67 percent) agreed with the statement "The work culture at my institution allows for flexibility." On the other hand, a majority of both the elder-caring subsample (N =20, 66.7 percent) and the non-caregiving group (N = 259, 52.2 percent) also agreed with the statement "I would change the family polices at my work if I could."

In regard to questions specifically on elder care, those currently providing elder care were less likely than the other respondents to agree with the statement "My institution does what it can to make doing eldercare and the tenure-track compatible." Rather, over half of the elder-caregiving subsample ($N = 15$, 51.7 percent) disagreed with the above statement, as compared to those not currently providing elder care ($N = 132$, 28.1 percent). On the other hand, a much larger percent of elder-caregivers ($N = 13$, 43.3 percent) agreed with the statement "My department does what it can to make doing eldercare and the tenure-track compatible" than did those not currently providing elder care ($N = 70$, 14.9 percent).

In addition to the fixed-response survey questions, respondents were asked in open-ended questions to give family policy suggestions. Respondents suggested that changes could occur on the individual institution level but that the academy as well as society itself needs to change. "I could write a book on this, but will leave it at 'allow more flexibility in scheduling to allow balancing work/family demands and don't penalize people who take advantage of flexibility'" wrote one respondent. Other macro-level changes included suggestions such as "acceptance of pathways that impact women in different stages in their careers and open full possibilities for tenure-track academic advancement to women completing PhDs at older ages" and "I would somehow promote an awareness that family is always more important than work—this should be true not just for faculty members with children, but for faculty who want to spend more time with their spouses, parents, etc." Still other respondents noted we need a change at the societal level, "As a country we do not support family life. We could have nationalized childcare, medical care, elder care, family support, etc."

As described above, when the need for elder care intersected with employment transitions, individuals were forced to make choices. Individuals in our sample noted that caring for parents or someone with a disability had an impact on their life course both professionally and personally. While all remained employed, many had not advanced in their careers as quickly as they could have because of their commitment to family, staying on-time with family transitions but off-time with work ones. Individuals also recognized that they often had few resources available to aid with caregiving and were forced to rely on themselves, their families, and/or their individual institutions to provide assistance.

DISCUSSION

Overall, these findings confirm that elder care is a concern for a portion of the academic faculty population. While many of the respondents in the current two-phased study had not yet reached a life stage with aging parents in need of care, for those who had, the impact was extremely powerful with regard to issues of caregiving, filial responsibility, bereavement, work/life management, and institutional work/family polices.

Caregiving

The majority of the respondents who provided care for an older parent were women, supporting previous research (e.g., Baker 2010; Chesley and Poppie 2009; Pope et al. 2012) that showed responsibility of caregiving typically and substantially falls to women. While this is not out of line with current social and cultural caregiving expectations, these findings may be particularly salient for women as they continue to fight for equality in academia. In spite of the gains women have made in recent years, women represent only 23 percent of those in tenure track and 44 percent of those in tenured positions (Thornton and Curtis 2012), and numerous studies report an ongoing imbalance against women faculty with regard to tenure and promotion (Baker 2010; Conley 2005; O'Laughlin and Bischoff 2005; Williams 2005). Additionally, while Sax et al. (2002) did not find that caregiving responsibilities directly affected scholarly productivity for either men or women, our research indicates that activities necessary for advancement in academia (research productivity, attendance at professional events/conferences, and professional mobility) were impacted greatly. Sax et al. (2002) did find that many academics, particularly women, are overextended as they manage work and family responsibilities. As the population of women faculty ages, more are likely to find themselves overextended as they become "sandwiched" between work and both child and elder care (Hagedorn and Sax 2004; Philipsen 2008). For those faculty who are pre-tenure or up for promotion at the time their parents need care, this very likely may push their tenure or promotion track "off-time."

Radical changes are needed to address this issue. One option is to redesign the tenure process, for example, creating different timelines and requirements for promotion to assistant, associate, and full professor and for gaining tenure. The processes presently in place put work and family life course careers at opposition. Another possibility is to create different tracks with different tenure and promotion requirements (e.g., a teaching track versus a research track). Currently, the promotion and tenure requirements are not the same across all academic institutions and women may be self-selecting out of higher paying and more prestigious employment at Research 1 institutions because of the different demands for promotion and tenure. Some women may think the demands of a teaching institution are more amenable to managing work/family. Each type of institution, however, comes with its own costs and rewards.

The current findings also suggest that while many of the faculty respondents were not presently providing care for an older parent, some had done so in the past and many anticipated the need to do so in the future. As the older population continues to grow, this is not an unreasonable expectation. Moreover, while women faculty respondents were more likely to be currently providing care, studies suggest that both men and women are likely to provide some form of care for older relatives if the need arises (Bookman and Kimbrel 2011). Thus, elder care is likely to be a growing issue for all faculty, regardless of gender.

One preventative measure is to revise current elder care policies to take into account the wide range of care types that are possible and provide opportunities for individuals to "bank" time or money (e.g., elder care flex plan dollars) to use for care. For example, studies have found that women are more likely to provide direct, hands-on forms of care, while men are more likely to provide assistance with instrumental activities of daily living and/or to finance the purchase of services from a professional caregiver (e.g., Bookman and Kimbrel 2011; Silverstein et al. 2006; Silverstein and Giarrusso 2010). Thus, the course for faculty who provide direct care may be different from those whose care duties are more of a financial or service-coordination nature. Similarly, there likely will be differences for faculty members based on their age and life stage when an older parent requires care. For "on-time" faculty, parent care is likely to fall later in their academic career than childcare might. For faculty entering their academic career later (e.g., "off-time"), this might not be the case, with greater potential for tenure, promotion, and parent care responsibilities to coincide and conflict.

Filial-Separation

Long-distance caregiving was a concern for many respondents in both data sets. This concern is expected given that long-distance elder care provision is a trend that will increase in the next decade (Koerin and Harrigan 2002). In addition to issues such as added cost and travel, long-distance care providers may experience different types of caregiver burden than those who are more geographically proximate. For example, while physical and work-related stress seem to be higher for caregivers who live closer to care recipients, long-distance caregivers may experience higher levels of emotional and psychological stress from trying to provide care from a distance (Cagle and Munn 2012; Koerin and Harrigan 2002). Caregiving from an extremely long distance, as illustrated by the experiences of a number of international respondents in the current study, may add an additional dimension to long-distance caregiving. Several respondents expressed concerns or described the challenges they faced in providing care to parents in another country. These challenges ranged from the expense and timing of travel at inopportune periods during the academic year, to trying to manage the varying cultural expectations about elder care provision (Zechner 2008).

The increasing availability of distance-learning technology in academia may be able to provide some relief for faculty whose positions are at a distance from parents in need of care. For example, institutions could embrace the use of technology for supplementing face-to-face classes, holding meetings as well as having virtual office hours so that faculty (and students) could participate from any location. Institutions could also schedule classes either online and/or on nights and weekends so caregivers could teach during times when other family members might be available for caregiving.

Bereavement

While information on bereavement issues in the current study is somewhat limited, what was found is consistent with Fitzpatrick's (2007) findings that some faculty struggle with managing their grief needs with the demands of academia, while others may find the environment more supportive than other types of work settings. In part, this may be tied to the varying levels of support that faculty experience within their departments and across their campuses. The current findings suggest that faculty perceptions of support from their colleagues and administrators vary widely. No direct information on the impact of the timing of bereavement was collected but one might anticipate that life course placement would play an important role. For example, having colleagues who are at similar stages in the life course and who are experiencing parental loss may lead to a more sympathetic environment. While more research into the factors that mediate these experiences of support is warranted, educating management and colleagues about bereavement issues and providing on-site and/or online family life education programming and support groups can help facilitate the process. Bereavement leave is also provided by many institutions, yet faculty may not know that it is available or may be unable to afford taking it for any length of time if the leave is unpaid.

Managing Work and Family

The overwhelming number of faculty respondents who reported making sacrifices to manage work and family and who often feel pulled between work and family is consistent with findings of academics experiencing role overload (e.g., Damiano-Teixeira 2006; Elliott 2003). While only a small portion of respondents reported serious challenges managing elder care with their academic work, those who did found the impact to be substantial. As the population continues to age, it can be expected that more and more faculty will experience such challenges. This may be particularly salient to women faculty who were more likely than their counterparts who are men to report conflict between caregiving and employment responsibilities (Fox, Fonseca, and Bao 2011).

As these trends continue to evolve, additional questions regarding the impact of life stage and career tracks will need to be examined. For example, as academic trajectories and family trajectories both move in the same direction, is there more flexibility and understanding for a full professor dealing with parent care issues than for an assistant professor in the same situation? How has an increased awareness and value of parenting, particularly fathering, impacted attitudes toward caregiving of children versus caregiving of elderly parents? Conversely, as suggested by the current findings, how will "off-time" faculty negotiate elder care needs with their later entrance onto the academic tenure and promotion track?

Having resources (financial, physical, social/emotional) available to faculty is important. Some of the resources are similar regardless of timing of transition (e.g., care centers either for children or older parents who need assistance, located on-campus or nearby campus). Providing options for faculty to set aside pre-tax dollars for elder care and providing faculty with technology will enable them to be successful regardless of location. Facilitating family life education programming and support groups for on-time and off-time transitions, (e.g., becoming a parent, death of a parent) on campus or online for all faculty can benefit individuals experiencing the same events by providing numerous kinds of support (e.g., information, social/emotional).

Institutional Impact on Elder Care

The Family and Medical Leave Act (FMLA) of 1993 allows for unpaid leave for care of a family member which could include an aging parent (Yang and Gimm 2013), yet only a handful of the respondents in this study reported having taken advantage of the FMLA for elder care. Although more institutions now have formal policies including FMLA, research has shown that many faculty are hesitant to utilize these options for fear of becoming stigmatized as being less committed to their careers (Jacobs and Gerson 2004; Wolf-Wendel, Twombly, and Rice 2003). For women whose commitment to academia may already be suspect, this may pose yet another barrier. Creating paid leave and a culture which embraces the care of family as well as the recognition that faculty productivity is not limited to an on-campus presence will be important at the departmental, college, and institutional level in addition to the societal level.

Another consideration specific to elder care is the uncertainty regarding the timing, location, and overall duration of parent caregiving. As documented in the literature (Vincent and Velkoff 2010) and illustrated by the experiences of our interview respondents, health in later life varies widely from person to person and can fluctuate for quite some time. Unlike other life stage events (e.g., marriage, pregnancy), one cannot plan or control if or when elder care will be needed. Additionally, the length of time necessary for elder care may be more unpredictable than other types of caregiving and perhaps not fit within the FMLA guidelines. Similarly, the end result of elder care may be the death of the care recipient—necessitating a subsequent need for bereavement leave. Also, unlike childcare, where typically the child resides with the parents or caregivers, the older individual needing care is likely at a distance and often a significant distance. Additionally, with elder care, caregiving responsibilities may include not only caring for an aging parent, but the elder person's residence as well. It would be useful to explore further what, if any, other formal or informal policies and resources are made available to faculty in these circumstances.

CONCLUSION

This study is one of the few to examine how elder care impacts work and family for faculty in academia. Through a life course perspective lens, the findings suggest that while parent care currently impacts a relatively small segment of faculty, the impact on work and family life for those who experience it is significant. As the population in the United States continues to age, and as more faculty follow divergent paths to enter the academic work world, the impact of parent care is likely to grow considerably. While both men and women are affected, the impact is more profound for women and faculty who are geographically distant from their aging parents. It may also be more challenging for "off-time" faculty who are managing the demands of tenure and promotion with parent care responsibilities.

Changes at a variety of levels are needed to address the current and anticipated challenges of managing work/family life in academia. Institutions should examine strategies to address work/life issues beyond benefits of parental leave or childcare. Such strategies could include redesigning both the tenure process and current family care policies to accommodate the wide range of work/life challenges faculty encounter. Additionally, institutions can take a more proactive stance by not only offering additional management resources to faculty, but also widely promoting their availability and actively supporting their use. In doing so, academic institutions may create a work culture that enables faculty to better manage work and family life without fear of damaging one's career. Of course, change is needed on a broader level as well. As a society we need to reexamine our attitudes and values toward family care, not just in terms of elder care, but toward practices such as paid leave for family care overall. Thus, change occurring both within and outside the academy is essential to enabling faculty to manage the personal and professional.

REFERENCES

Baker, Maureen. 2010. "Choices or Constraints? Family Responsibilities, Gender and Academic Career." *Journal of Comparative Family Studies* 41:1–18.

Bassett, Rachel Hile. 2005. "Introduction." Pp. 1–16 in *Parenting and Professing: Balancing Family Work with an Academic Career,* edited by R. Bassett. Nashville, TN: Vanderbilt University Press.

Becker, Penny Edgell, and Phyllis Moen. 1999. "Scaling back: Dual-Earner Couples' Work-Family Strategies." *Journal of Marriage and the Family* 61:994–1007.

Berke, Debra L., Rona J. Karasik, and Scott D. Scheer. 2009. "Why Don't I Give Myself and My Family a Break? Negotiating the Demands of Academic Life." Paper copresented at the National Council on Family Relations Conference, San Francisco, California.

———. 2007. "Work-Family Intersections over the Life Course: How Family Friendly are Academic Institutions?" Paper copresented at the National Council on Family Relations Conference, Pittsburgh, Pennsylvania.

Bianchi, Suzanne M., and Melissa A. Milkie. 2010. "Work and Family Research in the First Decade of the 21st Century." *Journal of Marriage and Family* 72:705–25.

Bookman, Ann, and Delia Kimbrel. 2011. "Families and Elder Care in the Twenty-first Century." *The Future of Children* 21:117–40.

Bonawitz, Mary, and Nicole Andel. 2009. "The Glass Ceiling is Made of Concrete: The Barriers to Promotion and Tenure of Women in American Academia." *Forum on Public Policy: A Journal of the Oxford Round Table* 5:1–16.

Cagle, John G., and Jean C. Munn. 2012. "Long-distance Caregiving: A Systematic Review of the Literature." *Journal of Gerontological Social Work* 55:682–707.

Chesley, Noelle, and Kyle Poppie. 2009. "Assisting Parents and In-laws: Gender, Type of Assistance, and Couples' Employment." *Journal of Marriage and Family* 71:247–62.

Conley, Valerie Martin. 2005. "Career Paths for Women Faculty: Evidence from NSOPF: 99." *New Directions for Higher Education* 2005:25–39.

Connelly, Rachel, and Kristen Ghodsee. 2011. *Professor Mommy. Finding Work-family Balance in Academia.* Lanhan, MD: Rowman and Littlefield.

Cullen, Jennifer C., Leslie B. Hammer, Margaret B. Neal, and Robert R. Sinclair. 2009. "Development of a Typology of Dual-Earner Couples Caring for Children and Aging Parents." *Journal of Family Issues* 30:458–83.

Cummins, Helene A. 2005. "Mommy Tracking Single Women in Academia When They Are Not Mommies." *Women's Studies International Forum* 28:222–31.

Damiano-Teixeira, Karla M. (2006). "Managing Conflicting Roles: A Qualitative Study with Female Faculty Members." *Journal of Family and Economic Issues* 27:310–34.

Duxbury, Linda, Christopher Higgins, and Rob Smart. 2011. "Elder Care and the Impact of Caregiver Strain on the Health of Employed Caregivers." *Work* 40:29–40.

Elder, Glen H., Jr., Monica Kirkpatrick Johnson, and Robert Crosnoe. 2003. "The Emergence and Development of Life Course Theory." Pp. 3–19 in *Handbook of the Life Course,* edited by J. T. Mortimer and M. J. Shanahan. NY: Springer.

Elliott, Marta. 2003. "Work and Family Role Strain Among University Employees." *Journal of Family and Economic Issues* 24:157–81.

Fischer, Joern, Euan G. Ritchie, and Jan Hanspach. 2012. "Academia's Obsession with Quantity." *Trends in Ecology and Evolution* 27:473–74.

Fitzpatrick, Tanya R. 2007. "Bereavement Among Faculty Members in a University Setting." *Social Work in Health Care* 45:83–107.

Fox, Mary Frank, Carolyn Fonseca, and Jinghui Bao. 2011. "Work and Family Conflict in Academic Science: Patterns and Predictors Among Women and Men in Research Universities." *Social Studies Science* 41:715–35.

Gautun, Heidi, and Kare Hagen. 2010. "How Do Middle-Aged Employees Combine Work with Caring for Elderly Parents?" *Community, Work, and Family* 13:393–409.

Gerten, Annette M. 2011. "Moving Beyond Family-friendly Policies for Faculty Mothers." *Affilia: Journal of Women and Social Work* 26:47–58.

Gordon, Judith R., Rachel A. Pruchno, Maureen Wilson-Genderson, Wendy Marcinkus Murphy, and Miriam Rose. 2012. "Balancing Caregiving and Work: Role Conflict and Role Strain Dynamics." *Journal of Family Issues* 33:662–89.

Gordon, Judith R., and Elizabeth D. Rouse. 2013. "The Relationship of Job and Elder Caregiving Involvement to Work-caregiving Conflict and Work Costs." *Research on Aging* 35:96–117.

Hagedorn, Linda Serra, and Linda J. Sax. 2004. "Marriage, Children, and Aging Parents: The Role of Family-related Factors in Faculty Job Satisfaction." *Journal of Faculty Development* 19:65–76.

Jacobs, Jerry A., and Kathleen Gerson. 2004. *The Time Divide: Work Family, and Gender Inequality.* Cambridge: Harvard University Press.

Jacobs, Jerry A., and Sarah E. Winslow. 2004. "The Academic Life Course, Time Pressures and Gender Inequality." *Community, Work, and Family* 7:143–61.

Katz, Ruth, Ariela Lowenstein, Dana Prilutzky, and Dafna Halperin. 2011. "Employers' Knowledge and Attitudes Regarding Organizational Policy Toward Workers Caring for Aging Family Members." *Journal of Aging and Social Policy* 23:159–81.

Kemkes-Grottenthaler, Ariane. 2003. "Postponing or Rejecting Parenthood? Results of a Survey Among Female Academic Professionals." *Journal of Biosocial Science* 35:213–26.

Koerin, Beverly B., and Marcia P. Harrigan. 2002. "P.S. I Love You: Long-Distance Caregiving." *Journal of Gerontological Social Work* 40:63–81.

Lester, Jaime. 2013. "Work-life Balance and Cultural Change: A Narrative of Eligibility." *The Review of Higher Education* 36:463–88.

Manchester, Colleen Flaherty, Lisa M. Leslie, and Amit Kramer. 2010. "Stop the Clock Policies and Career Success in Academia." *The American Economic Review* 100:219–23.

Mason, Mary Ann, and Marc Goulden. 2002. "Do Babies Matter? The Effect of Family Formation on the Lifelong Careers of Academic Men and Women." *Academe* 88:21–27.

Munn, Sunny L., and Eunice Ellen Hornsby. 2008. "Work-Life: Policy and Practice Impacting LG Faculty and Staff in Higher Education." *Online Submission ERIC*, EBSCOhost. Retrieved May 12, 2014.

O'Laughlin, Elizabeth M., and Lisa G. Bischoff. 2005. "Balancing Parenthood and Academia: Work/Family Stress as Influences by Gender and Tenure Status." *Journal of Family Issues* 26:79–106.

O'Meara, KerryAnn, and Corbin M. Campbell. 2011. "Faculty Sense of Agency in Decisions about Work and Family." *The Review of Higher Education* 34:447–76.

Pines, Ayala Malach, Margaret B. Neal, Leslie B. Hammer, and Tamar Icekson. 2011. "Job Burnout and Couple Burnout in Dual-earner Couples in the Sandwiched Generation." *Social Psychology Quarterly* 74:361–86.

Philipsen, Maike Ingrid. 2008. *Challenges of the Faculty Career for Women: Success and Sacrifice.* San Francisco: Jossey-Bass.

Philipsen, Maike Ingrid, and Timothy B. Bostic. 2010. *Helping Faculty Find Work-life Balance: The Path Toward Family-friendly Institutions.* San Francisco: Jossey-Bass.

Pope, Natalie D., Stacey Kolomer, and Anne P. Glass. 2012. "How Women in Late Midlife Become Caregivers for Their Aging Parents." *Journal of Women and Aging* 24:242–61.

Roehling, Patricia V., Mark V. Roehling, and Phyllis Moen. 2001. "The Relationship Between Work-life Policies and Practices and Employee Loyalty: A Life Course Perspective." *Journal of Family and Economic Issues* 22:141–70.

Ryan, Ann Marie, and Ellen Ernst Kossek. 2008. "Work-life policy implementation: Breaking Down or Creating Barriers to Inclusiveness?" *Human Resource Management* 47:295–310.

Sax, Linda J., Linda Serra Hagedorn, Marisol Arredondo, and Frank A. Dicrisi, III. 2002. "Faculty Research Productivity: Exploring the Role of Gender and Family-related Factors." *Research in Higher Education* 43:423–46.

Schlehofer, Michele. 2012. "Practicing What We Teach? An Autobiographical Reflection on Navigating Academia as a Single Mother." *Journal of Community Psychology* 40:112–28.

Silverstein, Merrill, Daphna Gans, and Frances M. Yang. 2006. "Intergenerational Support to Aging Parents: The Roles of Norms and Needs." *Journal of Family Issues* 27:1068–84.

Silverstein, Merril, and Roseann Giarrusso. 2010. "Aging and Family Life: A Decade Review." *Journal of Marriage and Family* 72:1039–58.

Solomon, Catherine. 2011. "'Sacrificing at the Altar of Tenure': Assistant Professors' Work/Life Management." *The Social Science Journal* 48:335–44.

Spalter-Roth, Roberta, and William Erksine. 2005. "Beyond the Fear Factor: Work/Family Polices in Academia: Resource or Rewards?" *Change* 37:18–25.

Strauss, Anselm, and Juliet Corbin. 1990. *Basics of Qualitative Research: Grounded Theory Procedures and Techniques.* Newbury Park, CA: Sage.

Thornton, Saranna, and John W. Curtis. 2012. "A Very Slow Recovery." *The Annual Report on the Economic Status of the Profession 2011–12.* Washington, DC: American Association of University Professors.

Townsley, Nikki C., and Kirsten J. Broadfoot. 2008. "Care, Career, and Academe: Heeding the Calls of a New Professoriate." *Women's Studies in Communication* 31:133–42.

Trukeschitz, Birgit, Ulrike Schneider, Richard Muhlmann, and Ivo Ponocny. 2013. "Informal Eldercare and Work-related Strain." *Journals of Gerontology, Series B: Psychological Sciences and Social Sciences* 68:257–67.

Vincent, Grayson K., and Victoria A. Velkoff. 2010. *The Next Four Decades: The Older Population in the United States: 2010 to 2050.* Washington, DC: U.S. Department of Commerce, Economics and Statistics Administration, U.S. Census Bureau.

Williams, Joan C. 2005. "The Glass Ceiling and the Maternal Wall in Academia." *New Directions for Higher Education, 2005* 130:91–105.

Wolf-Wendel, Lisa, Susan B. Twombly, and Suzanne Rice. 2003. *The Two-body Problem: Dual-career-couple Hiring Practices in Higher Education.* Baltimore: Johns Hopkins University.

Yang, Y. Tony, and Gilbert Gimm. 2013. "Caring for Elder Parents: A Comparative Evaluation of Family Leave Laws." *Journal of Law, Medicine and Ethics* 4:501–13.

Zechner, Minna. 2008. "Care of Older Persons in Transnational Settings." *Journal of Aging Studies* 22:32–44.

Part II

Tales from the Trenches: The Goals, Challenges, and Realities of Policy Implementation

Chapter Six

Introduction to Case Studies

Erin K. Anderson and Catherine Richards Solomon

In response to work/family conflict of faculty, some universities offer family-friendly policies and programs to help faculty manage their work and family responsibilities (Hollenshead, Sullivan, Smith, August, and Hamilton 2005; Lundquist, Misra, and O'Meara 2012; Mason and Goulden 2004). In this chapter, we provide a brief overview of the types and prevalence of family-friendly policies at a variety of universities.

FAMILY-FRIENDLY POLICIES AT UNIVERSITIES

Family-friendly policies fall into two basic categories: government policies and university-specific policies. The most prevalent government policy is the federal Family and Medical Leave Act (FMLA). This policy allows employees who work more than twenty-five hours a week to take up to twelve weeks of job-protected leave for a variety of circumstances. These include: the birth of a child; the placement of a foster or adopted child; a serious health condition of a child, spouse, or parent; the employee's own serious health condition; the provision of care to an injured family member who is part of the military. However, a number of restrictions exist that limit employee eligibility. For instance, employees must have worked for their employer for at least twelve months and a minimum of 1,250 hours in the previous year, and employees are only covered by this policy if there are fifty or more employees at their worksite. Due to these and other policy restrictions, only about 60 percent of Americans have FMLA leave available to them (Albelda and Mandell 2010). Other government policies exist at the state level and usually extend the FMLA unpaid leave by two to four weeks. For instance, Connecticut's unpaid FMLA is sixteen weeks; four weeks may be added to the FMLA twelve-week leave. Hawaii offers an additional four weeks of unpaid leave; Washington provides an additional twelve weeks of unpaid leave for a total of twenty-four weeks. California, in contrast, improves upon the twelve weeks of unpaid leave by providing paid leave for up to six weeks for employees for the same circumstances as the FMLA.

University-specific policies vary between institutions (AAUP 2001; CEW 2007). According to a study of over two-hundred universities and colleges (Hollenshead, Sullivan, Smith, August, and Hamilton 2005), the most progressive and generous policies are offered by top-tier research universities. One such example is the University of California's Faculty Family Friendly Edge initiative (UC Faculty Family Friendly Edge 2013). Under this initiative, universities in the UC system offer: up to two quarters or semesters of reduced duties for new caregivers, a tenure extension policy, a part-time option for tenure-track faculty, a one-year unpaid parental leave, and a one-year unpaid leave to care for oneself or a family member with a serious health issue (twelve weeks of which may be paid with approval from the UC Chancellor) (UC Faculty Family Friendly Edge 2013). According to the Center for the Education of Women (CEW), most other universities offer much less generous leave policies (2007). The most commonly offered policies are six weeks of paid maternity leave and tenure clock extension (CEW 2007). Paid maternity leave is generally offered through accrued sick leave or disability leave (Hollenshead et al. 2005). In contrast, paid parental leave for fathers is relatively rare. A 2004 study of parental leave policies in academia found that only 18 percent of schools extended parental leave to men (Yoest 2004). Such policies are most commonly found at elite, private institutions.

The Center for the Education of Women reports that less than a third of universities and colleges offer a paid parental leave for new parents. Less than a quarter of universities offer "modified duties," which can include offering reduced teaching duties following the birth or adoption of a child for professors who provide at least half of the caregiving duties (CEW 2007; Hollenshead et al. 2005; UC Faculty Family Friendly Edge 2003; WorkLife-Law 2009). A tenure extension policy generally adds a full year to the tenure clock (CEW 2007; Hollenshead et al. 2005). This policy is sometimes automatically applied to a faculty member's tenure clock and can be used separately or in conjunction with parental leave (CEW 2007; WorkLifeLaw 2009).

CONTRIBUTIONS IN THIS BOOK

Section two includes case studies of the process of formulating family-friendly policies and their adoption at a variety of universities as well as the evaluation of some long-standing policies. The focus of these chapters includes use of the Family and Medical Leave Act, the enactment of a parental leave policy, the development of a unique "life cycle professorship program," and strategies used to implement new policies. These case studies provide descriptions of how faculty and staff needs were identified and the processes of policy development as well as advice to faculty and administrators who seek to develop similar policies at their institutions.

In chapter seven, "A Tale of Two Policies: Lessons Learned in Writing and Adopting Parental Leave Policies at a University," Brandy A. Randall and Virginia Clark Johnson discuss the need they saw at their university for a policy that would provide paid leave for women faculty who give birth as well as a modified-duties policy to accommodate various life events. Because these needs were not covered by FMLA and could have significant impacts on the careers of faculty, they initiated the efforts to create policies that would allow for better work/life balance. The initial obstacles they encountered, claims that such a policy violated state and federal law, the belief that informal arrangements were sufficient, and a general resistance to the potential cost of new university policies, did not dissuade them from seeking a solution to this problem. Randall and Johnson outline the steps they took as a faculty member and an administrator, personnel they worked with, and hurdles they encountered in the four years it took them to accomplish the task of instituting childbearing leave and modified-duties policies. They advise others to "think creatively" and "don't reinvent the wheel" when it comes to designing family-friendly policies. It is in this spirit they detail their own experience, to assist in policy creation at other colleges and universities.

The process of effecting change and the creation of work/life policies is also addressed by Leslie E. Tower in chapter eight, "Changing Work/Life Policies in Institutions of Higher Education: A Case Study." As a faculty member at an institution that did not initially offer much official support for parental leave, she details how she was able to make the case for work/life policies, identify and work with stakeholders, and achieve success. Through this case study, a series of steps, informed by organizational change theory, are outlined. Tower describes how her strategy and steps were carried out, where she met with resistance, and how she overcame this, ultimately succeeding in establishing a paid parental leave work policy. This process relies on seeking information from peer institutions and outside entities, surveying the needs of university employees, and finding and working with allies to develop realistic and sustainable policies.

In chapter nine, "Understanding Family and Medical Leave at a Large Public University," Stacy Oliker and Amanda Seligman detail the findings from a task force charged with studying leave policy and practices at the University of Wisconsin–Milwaukee. A survey of faculty and staff found that the process for using FMLA was not well understood by many employees. Furthermore, the options and outcomes for leave taking seemed to vary significantly among faculty and staff and women and men. Oliker and Seligman argue that a decentralized system of decision making related to leave allows for beneficial flexibility but also has the effect of institutionalizing problematic variability in policy use. The application of policies, leave options, and workplace roles of faculty and staff introduces challenges to the fair implementation of work/family policies. Out of this research, Oliker and Seligman offer suggestions for the study, creation, and implementation of leave policies on other campuses.

In chapter 10, "Life Happens: The Vilas Life Cycle Professorship Program at the University of Wisconsin-Madison," Jennifer Sheridan, Christine Maidl Pribbenow, Molly Carnes, Jo Handelsman, and Amy Wendt review a unique program to address work/life management. Initiated through an NSF ADVANCE grant, the University of Wisconsin-Madison has perpetuated this program that offers financial assistance to faculty who have suffered some "life event" which has compromised their ability to conduct research, and thus progress in their academic careers. This program has proved valuable as a safety net for professionals committed to their research work, but also trying to manage critical life events that might be sudden, unexpected, or traumatic and thus interfere with productivity. Evaluations of the first decade of this grant program have revealed the funding for research-related activities has improved faculty retention, especially for women and minorities, and led to positive outcomes for faculty and the university in terms of further grant funding, prestige, and loyalty. Such a program illustrates another way higher education can create an environment that allows personnel to manage their professional and personal lives for the benefit of the individual and the institution.

REFERENCES

Albelda, Randy, and Betty Mandell. 2010. "Paid Family and Medical Leave." Pp. 47–62 in *The Crisis of Caregiving: Social Welfare Policy in the United States*, edited by B. R. Mandell. New York, NY: Palgrave MacMillan

American Association of University Professors (AAUP). 2001. "Statement on Principles of Family Responsibilities and Academic Work." *Academe* 87:55–61.

Center for the Education of Women. 2007. "Family-friendly Policies in Higher Education: A Five-year Report." University of Michigan Research Brief.

Hollenshead, Carol S., Beth Sullivan, Gilia C. Smith, Louise August, and Susan Hamilton. 2005. "Work/Family Policies in Higher Education: Survey Data and Case Studies of Policy Implementation." *New Directions for Higher Education* 130:41–65.

Lundquist, Jennifer H., Joya Misra, and KerryAnn O'Meara. 2012. "Parental Leave Usage by Fathers and Mothers at an American University." *Fathering* 10:337–63.

Mason, Mary Ann, and Marc Goulden. 2004. "Marriage and Baby Blues: Redefining Gender Equity in the Academy." *Annals of the American Academy of Social and Political Science* 596:86–103.

UC Faculty Family Friendly Edge. 2003. "The UC Faculty Family Friendly Edge: Turning a Problem into UC's Competitive Advantage." Retrieved August 1, 2012 (http://ucfamilyedge.berkeley.edu/index.html).

WorkLifeLaw. 2009. "Take action: Model policies and practices." Retrieved August 1, 2012 (http://www.worklifelaw.org/GenderBias_takeAction.html).

Yoest, Charmaine. 2004. "Parental Leave in Academia." Report to the Alfred P. Sloan Foundation and the Bankard Fund at the University of Virginia. Retrieved June 15, 2014 (http://www.faculty.virginia.edu/familyandtenure).

Chapter Seven

A Tale of Two Policies

Lessons Learned in Writing and Adopting
Parental Leave Policies at a University

Brandy A. Randall and Virginia Clark Johnson

Parental leave policies at academic institutions vary substantially, and in some cases may be absent altogether. A lack of policy supporting faculty parents in managing the sometimes competing demands of work/family can be particularly challenging for untenured faculty, who tend to be at an age when family formation coincides with the demands associated with earning tenure. Having models of successful policy change can be helpful to those wishing to pursue developing or changing parental leave policies at their institution. Federal policy provides the overarching context for such policies.

Federal policy in the United States does not require paid leave for childbearing. The Family and Medical Leave Act (FMLA) does guarantee up to twelve weeks unpaid leave for individuals employed by companies with fifty or more employees, but only for employees who have been at the company for 1,250 hours over the previous twelve months (U.S. Department of Labor: Wage and Hour Division). Additionally, the Pregnancy Discrimination Act of 1978 specifies that institutions with fifteen or more employees cannot treat pregnancy differently than any other medical condition, which includes access to sick leave benefits for pregnancy and childbirth-related conditions (U.S. Equal Employment Opportunity Commission). The absence of a federal pregnancy and childbirth policy that supports the needs of families gives employers a great deal of latitude in the accommodations they are required to make for parenthood. This latitude has resulted in substantial inconsistency in terms of how academic institutions approach faculty members' advent into and responsibilities during parenthood. This chapter begins by reviewing the literature on the rationale for, and impact of, family-friendly policies on academic faculty. Following this we share our experiences with developing and institutionalizing policies for childbearing leave and modified duties at our institution. We highlight the obstacles we encountered and the lessons we learned that may be informative for others. We hope that our experience provides encouragement and a starting place for anyone seeking to help their institution adopt family-friendly policies.

WHY WE NEED WORK/FAMILY POLICIES IN THE ACADEMY

American society is changing, yet many academic institutions have been slow to respond to these shifts, leaving university employees less satisfied than corporate employees on multiple dimensions of the work/life climate at their place of employment (Anderson, Morgan, and Wilson 2002). Women earn approximately half of doctoral degrees awarded today (Mason, Wolfinger, and Goulden 2013). Parity for women in doctoral degree attainment has not led to similar parity in academic employment; women are still less likely than men to obtain a tenure-line faculty position (Mason et al. 2013). Mason et al. (2013) suggest that this is, in part, due to the impact of having children on women's academic careers, as women continue to shoulder the majority of childcare responsibilities (Kotila, Schoppe-Sullivant, and Dush 2013). Their data suggests that parenthood has a detrimental effect on women's academic careers, with academic mothers far less likely than academic fathers to obtain a tenure-line position. Mason et al. (2013) further suggest that an overall lack of institutional friendliness in accommodating the needs of faculty's families might play an important role in explaining the gap between the number of women earning PhDs and the number of women in tenure-line positions. Policies supporting parents in their dual responsibilities to their institutions and their families are a necessary element for movement toward attaining gender parity in academia.

An additional change that has affected colleges and universities is the configuration of the American family. Fewer families conform to the traditional norm of male wage earner with a stay-at-home wife (Cancian and Reed 2009). Female faculty members are more likely than male faculty members to have a spouse who is employed full-time (Mason et al. 2013). Thus, the policies and benefits offered by institutions of higher education that were organized around a traditional family model where faculty members were men with stay-at home wives are no longer functional for many who are pursuing or might wish to pursue a tenure-line position.

It is critical that university family policies are inclusive of both women and men, but that the actual role in caregiving is also considered. Research on the impact of Sweden's government-mandated paid parental leave suggested that fathers who took more leave were significantly more involved in childcare and more satisfied with the amount of contact they had with their children (Haas and Hwang 2008). Rhoads and Rhoads (2012) found that academic men who took more parental leave did more childcare, although there were still substantial gender differences in the amount of childcare performed. In fact, men who took leave did significantly less of the childcare than women who did not take leave. Only three of the 108 men in their sample did at least half of the childcare. Unfortunately, they also heard stories of men who misused institutional parental leave policies in order to have more time for research. Such behaviors have led some institutions to require that parental leave applicants certify that they will be fulfilling at least 50 percent of the childcare responsibilities. Clearly these sorts of behaviors stand to disadvantage those faculty who are utilizing the policies in the intended manner if it creates an appearance of reduced productivity by these faculty relative to their supposedly caregiving peers. However, other analyses suggest that institutional policies are an essential element in changing the cultural norms that assume fathers are not caregiving parents (e.g., Leonard 2013; Reddick et al. 2012; Sallee 2013; Smithson and Stokoe 2005). This appears to be rather a catch-22 for institutions, as they seek to provide equitable working conditions for men and women, as well as for parents and nonparents. Continued examination of the effects of these policies is needed.

Although institutions may not feel that the societal benefits of providing family-friendly policies are enough reason to develop such policies, they may be more swayed by the fiscal arguments for doing so, particularly in terms of successful completion of doctoral programs by enrolled graduate students and in the recruitment and retention of faculty and staff. Doctoral degree attainment requires a substantial investment of money and time at many levels—by the individual, the faculty mentors, the degree-granting institution, grant and fellowship sources, etc.—with a typical program costing between $242,000 to $300,000 (Education Portal N.d.). Furthermore, institutions invest a great deal in hiring new faculty members, and in replacing them if they do not stay or do not attain tenure. Harvard University's Collaborative on Academic Careers in Higher Education estimates that the cost for the hiring process for each new faculty member is approximately $96,000 (The Higher Education Recruitment Consortium N.d.). Hollenshead et al. (2005, p. 61) reported that universities feel that work/family policies "inspired loyalty and a sense of community among faculty," making it more likely that they would stay. Further, these policies are seen as an important tool in faculty recruitment (Hollenshead et al. 2005). Thus, creating and supporting policies for families may save institutions money in the long-term (American Council on Education N.d.).

WORK/FAMILY POLICY VARIATIONS

Substantial variability exists among institutions with respect to the number and nature of formal work/family policies available. The Faculty Work/Family Policy Study examined the work/family policies from a representative sample of U.S. institutions (Hollenshead et al. 2005). They found that 32 percent of Research I and II class institutions had a formal policy permitting modified duties, which is a provision that allows faculty to temporarily shift job duties from one category to another (e.g., reducing teaching obligations for a semester) without a reduction in pay. Interestingly, the study indicated that although the legal requirement of the Pregnancy Discrimination Act (1978) is to provide commensurate paid time off for pregnancy and childbirth if paid time off is provided for other health conditions, faculty women experience challenges with the provisions offered by their institutions (Hollenshead et al. 2005). One major issue for the faculty sampled is that at many institutions, only twelve-month employees can access traditional sick leave, yet faculty typically have appointments that are less than twelve months. Although 69 percent of the institutions indicated that women could access sick leave following childbirth, this conflicted with the women's own reports of what was available to people in their job category. Thus, although institutions may be complying with the federal law, their offerings do not provide supportive conditions for women faculty who experience childbirth. Findings such as this highlight the marked discrepancies between what institutional representatives may believe is available to their employees, and the actual options as experienced by the employees themselves.

The absence of formal policies can leave faculty members who are becoming parents to essentially fend for themselves. Wolf-Wendel and Ward (2006) interviewed women assistant professors with young children about how they managed their dual roles and then developed vignette profiles using content from the interviews. The vignette based on interviews from women at research universities poignantly captures the sentiments of these women regarding childbearing leave at their institutions. For example, one woman said, "I didn't take any leave. The campus maternity leave is pretty much non-existent and when I asked about it I was told to work it out with my chair. I told my chair I had everything worked out. My chair seems supportive but somehow it felt safer to stay away from talk about a leave" (Wolf-Wendel and Ward 2006, 499). As this vignette demonstrates, women whose campuses lack a formal leave policy feel that it is somehow risky to ask for leave. Unfortunately, this is the situation in which many faculty members find themselves.

There is evidence that some faculty members strategically avoid bias by not becoming parents, delaying parenthood, not using available family policies, and by hiding family-related obligations (Drago et al., 2005). Weigt and

Solomon (2008), in their interviews with female assistant professors, found that many women reported hiding their use of workplace flexibility to attend to family-related needs, and that there was a stigma attached to wanting to take maternity leave. However, Drago and colleagues (2005) showed that faculty are more likely to use formal policies when their institution has more formal family policies on the books. Additionally, Spalter-Roth and Erskine (2006) found that mothers who used at least one work/family policy produced a higher number of publications than mothers who had not used any policies and childless women, though this appeared to be explained in part by their publication productivity in graduate school. Finally, Solomon's (2011) interviews with pre-tenured faculty members suggests that a sizeable number of faculty members, particularly those with children, value having a full personal life and are not willing to sacrifice that to work. Additionally, her research on pre-tenure male faculty members confirmed that for some men, the flexibility of a faculty position facilitated their sharing of childcare responsibilities (Solomon 2010). Thus, despite the barriers to policy utilization, having policies supports workplace flexibility for those individuals who desire to be involved caregivers.

OUR STORY

North Dakota State University, categorized as Research University/Very High Research Activity by the Carnegie Commission on Higher Education, did not have a formal childbirth policy for faculty prior to April 2012. We played a key role in helping our employer, North Dakota State University (NDSU), adopt policies that provide for paid leave for women faculty who give birth and permit modified duties for faculty who experience various life events. The process began in a college and led to the adoption of university policies for parental leave and workload adjustments for other major life events. We were ultimately successful, despite numerous roadblocks along the way. The process took us five years. The rest of the chapter identifies the lessons that we learned through the process of developing and advocating for childbirth leave and modified-duties policies. Our hope is that these lessons can help others who might seek institutional changes.

A Brief History of the Problems for Female Faculty at NDSU

A 2006 report on gender equity among professors by the American Association for University Professors (AAUP) confirmed something that women faculty at NDSU had known for a while; their situation on campus was far from optimal. In fact, the report showed that NDSU had the second lowest percentage of female tenured faculty members in the country (Wilson 2006). A Chronicle of Higher Education article published the following year focused specifically on the many barriers that female faculty at NDSU identified, including a lack of paid maternity leave (Wilson 2007).

The Chronicle article indicated that the university president was not aware that gender inequity and a campus climate that did not support women was an issue. However, as a faculty member who had been part of the faculty group Women in Science, Math, Engineering, and Technology, the first author can state with certainty that the concern had been discussed with the university administration by multiple individuals many times. The response from administration representatives had been that it was "impossible" to provide for paid maternity leaves, that it was in fact "illegal," and that departments did a good job of "working something out" with women who gave birth during the semester. However, faculty members who were working on the institutional application for an NSF ADVANCE grant heard numerous individual stories that suggested that for many women, their departments were not able or not willing to "work it out." In fact, the arrangements for women in different departments were highly variable, ranging from department chairs who gave women a semester's teaching relief to a chair who expected the woman to return to the classroom three days after giving birth. Lack of accommodations for childbirth and adoption were identified by faculty who sought employment elsewhere as one of their reasons for leaving NDSU. The need for a university-wide policy that provided an equitable and consistent approach for all women faculty was apparent.

Perhaps because of the attention generated by the Chronicle articles, the university committed to addressing the campus challenges for female faculty, and this raised hopes that issues with childbearing would be addressed. However, administrators continued to claim that it was "impossible" and "illegal." Many women on campus became increasingly frustrated by the lack of institutional action, and feelings of anger and hopelessness began to set in.

Lessons Learned

Next, we will identify the lessons we learned as we sought to address the issues that were highlighted in the Chronicle articles.

Lesson One: You may have to start small—even if you cannot change the institution, you may be able to make changes at a more immediate level (e.g., college, department). Late in 2008, in the midst of general feelings of frustration, the first author asked the Dean of her college (the second author) if it were possible for their college (Human Development and Education) to have a policy outlining shared expectations for all the departments in the college related to childbirth/adoption, as no action was being taken at the university level. The Dean agreed that this was important and sanctioned the formation of a Family Friendly Policies Task Force (later renamed the Work-Life Balance Task Force). The policy originally adopted in our college became the basis for a university-wide policy several years later.

The mission of the task force was more broadly defined than to simply develop a childbearing leave policy for the college. We sought to make the college a good workplace for all employees by developing shared definitions of families and of managing work/family. Polices were developed to support these definitions. An anonymous vote by college employees was conducted for all policies developed by the task force to decide whether the policies should be officially adopted by the college. Members of the task force included several faculty (tenure-line and non-tenure track), staff, and one department head (Note: NDSU has a unique departmental administrative structure: department heads are hired through a national search, and department chairs are selected internally from faculty in the department, and often (but not always) have limited terms). The task force identified a number of potential policies for implementation and assigned members to research each one.

Lesson Two: Understand that your institution may be part of a larger whole, and that you have to make sure any policies you write are consistent with other policies. Two of the policies that were developed by the task force were a Childbearing Leave policy and a Modified Duties policy. Employees on campus had repeatedly been told that having a childbearing leave policy would be against state law. Policies for state universities are like an onion— many layered. NDSU, like many state institutions, is a part of a university system that has its own set of policies. Additionally, university employees are state employees and the state has its own set of policies. Thus, university-level policies cannot contradict either the State Board of Higher Education (SBHE) policies or the policies for North Dakota state employees. Anyone seeking to change policies at their school needs to have a good understanding of their policy hierarchy and ensure that they are well informed about any policies at any other level that would be relevant.

Lesson Three: Just because others say it is impossible, do not believe that without really looking into it yourself. In our case, we did learn that there was a SBHE policy that specifically said "family leave was an unpaid leave" (SBHE Policy 607.4) and that family leave for higher education employees conforms to FMLA parameters. Most state employees, including twelve-month faculty members and higher education administrators, earn paid sick leave and paid annual leave as state-funded benefits. Faculty employed less than twelve months a year, who constitute a majority of the tenure-line faculty, do not earn these state-funded benefits. The SBHE gives each institution the right to "adopt policies governing paid sick or dependent leave for faculty and members of the academic staff" (SBHE Policy 607.4, 2004). NDSU's policy regarding faculty sick leave, which did not mention pregnancy or childbirth, does not guarantee a specific amount of leave in the event of illness:

> Although there is no formal sick leave policy or provision for such faculty, the understanding is that they have the opportunity to reschedule their commitments or make appropriate voluntary arrangements with their colleagues during times when sickness makes it impossible or unwise for them to meet their professional obligations. This does not guarantee any certain amount of paid sick leave hours or days to faculty members whose regular term of appointment is less than 12 months, but the flexibility it provides seems to meet the needs of most faculty members. Where extended illness or disability is involved, however, the amount of such informal sick leave shall be limited to a maximum of two weeks for each year of academic service to NDSU, unless an exception is approved by the Provost. In any event, the University's TIAA-CREF disability insurance provides salary benefits after six months of disability. (NDSU Policy 320)

The vagueness of the sick leave policy about the parameters of the benefit is one of the many reasons that women experienced such inequities in the amount of time off after giving birth. Any woman giving birth who had been employed fewer than three years at NDSU could not justify a six-week medical leave using this policy. Furthermore, the phrase "does not guarantee" means that no department is obligated to provide this flexibility. Additionally, because the policy did not specifically mention pregnancy or childbirth, people unfamiliar with the Pregnancy Discrimination Act would have been unaware these events must be covered under the sick leave policy. However, our hope that we could develop a workable policy grew when we realized that the "institutional flexibility" provided by the SBHE could be utilized to develop a paid leave for childbearing as a form of sick leave. The key seemed to be to avoid calling anything "family leave," so as to avoid running afoul of the state law specifying that family leave is unpaid.

Lesson Four: Do your homework. You are not reinventing the wheel, just inventing or modifying it at your institution. There are excellent models of good family policies out there; use them! The next step was to dream about what was possible. This step actually involved a lot of legwork. We read countless policies at other institutions, as well as analyses that highlighted what made those policies work or not work. The resource that was the most helpful to us came from a document on family-friendly policies that was developed by the Center for the Education of Women and funded by the Sloan Foundation (Smith and Waltman 2006). While we were reasonably sure we could cover childbirth for women under the sick leave policy, until we did our homework, we were not sure what we could do for male faculty with a partner giving birth or for faculty members adopting children. The members of the task force shared a common philosophy that children and families benefit from having involved parents, regardless of the parent's gender. We also had all directly experienced the substantial period of household disruption that ensues with the addition of new children. We were committed to having a policy that could be utilized by any faculty member who had a child entering his/her family. What we ultimately decided would work best at our institution was to separate childbirth from the rest of these situations and develop two distinct college policies.

The childbearing leave policy guaranteed at least six weeks off with pay to recover from childbirth during the period of "medical disability." The second policy provided for modified duties, and it specified a semester of 100 percent employment at 100 percent pay, but with a renegotiation of duties to provide more flexibility. The Modified Duties policy that was passed in the college was as follows:

> Modified duties without reduction of salary. A person taking modified duties will still be at a 100 percent workload and 100 percent salary; however the nature of the responsibilities for this time period will be adjusted. Modified duties will be negotiated with the department head and approved by the dean. Modified duties can include, but are not limited to, a revision of workload for up to the equivalent of a semester, which may include relief from teaching courses and committee assignments. [1]

A value that was important to us was to ensure that the policy fit for the whole range of family formations, including those of gay and lesbian faculty members. The language we used to define eligibility was "An academic appointee who becomes a parent through childbirth or adoption of a child (by either him/herself or his/her partner in a committed relationship)." Additionally, we were concerned that the timing of the birth or adoption relative to the academic semester might create challenges. We included the following provision: "When a period of modified duties immediately follows childbearing leave, that period may be extended to the end of a semester to accommodate teaching schedules as necessary."

We were concerned about the potential for faculty members who took Modified Duties to be penalized in their annual evaluation. Thus, we included a provision that specified the faculty members, the department head or chair, and the dean would meet to develop agreed-upon goals for the period of Modified Duties. The document outlining the agreement would be included in the report faculty submit for evaluation each year. We included this to try to prevent some of the problems we knew people had encountered when extending the probationary period for tenure and promotion. Unless policies specifically require that a period of reduced or altered responsibilities are not counted against someone, some committee members will do so. Both policies were voted on by the tenure-line faculty members and passed with a substantial majority. It is worth noting that the vote was not unanimous, which was troubling but not surprising.

Lesson Five: Even people who want to see change can have unrealistic expectations about what is possible—broader coverage, more people cov-

ered, etc. You have to educate people about the limits of what is possible and why. The description provided here might make this process sound like it was easy; it was not. Even though as a committee we had some shared values, we all approached this from different perspectives: as parents who thought "what would I have liked," as promotion and tenure committee members who thought "how will this impact an evaluation," as feminists who objected to describing childbirth as creating a "period of medical disability," as advocates for healthy families who wanted to see mothers in a position to breast-feed on demand for eighteen full months, as a department head who thought "how will I implement this, and what about someone who is full-time on a grant," etc. The biggest challenge within our group seemed to be figuring out how to write the policy to cover enough people for long enough to make members of the committee feel it was minimally acceptable, while still working within the bounds of what was permissible given the constraints imposed by other policies. Also of concern was the possible creation of terrible inequities between faculty members with families and staff members with families. While having no policy for faculty was not equitable, writing a "platinum policy" for faculty while staff had a "nickel policy" would have also been unfair and would have likely led to resentment. However, the policies that govern twelve-month staff are dictated by the state and thus are not flexible. An important consideration for the task force was not to create an unfair level of privilege.

Lesson Six: Work with the university's general counsel to ensure the policy will stand up to scrutiny. Unfortunately, no one on the committee was a lawyer. This meant a lot of effort went into trying to interpret the language of policies that had been written or refined by lawyers. Terms (e.g., dependent-care leave) can have very specific meanings in the legal and policy worlds, and these meanings can vary by institution or by state. We were fortunate that the General Counsel for our university was willing to review the policies we had developed and point out areas that needed additional clarification. This was very valuable as it helped ensure that the policy adopted by the college was actually feasible given existing policies.

At the beginning, it was also important that we came to the General Counsel with an initial policy proposal that laid out elements that we wanted to see in the policy. It is all too easy to expect institutional officials to read one's mind, but perhaps not entirely fair. Having faculty members directly involved in the creation of the policies ensured that people who understood the nature of faculty work obligations had input, and getting input from the General Counsel ensured that we did not try to move forward with a policy that could not be implemented. Taking this step was a big part of the reason that our college-level policy was later able to be used as a basis for the university policy.

Lesson Seven: Having a policy, not just "guidelines" is important for there to be fairness in application across individuals. It is important to note the term "policy," as it was very intentional, implying "must be implemented when the situation warrants." While our college was creating and implementing a policy, another college on campus was working to address the same issues for faculty, but used the term "guidelines" rather than policy. It became apparent that having "guidelines" meant that if it were inconvenient, the accommodations outlined for childbearing did not have to be provided. While the effort was laudable, it still resulted in inequitable application for women with the same family situation (e.g., if the department head could not adjust funding to have someone else teach a course). Women may be reluctant to ask for accommodations; the absence of a formal policy guaranteeing accommodations can only serve to exacerbate that reluctance. Thus, although more than one college was attempting to provide clarity for faculty who had family-related demands, it was clear that a broader institutional-level solution was needed to prevent the same kinds of unfair variations in accommodations that had historically been seen in different departments.

Institutionalizing the Policies: The Commission Steps Forward

One of the central missions of the NDSU Commission on the Status of Women Faculty, which had been formed through the NSF ADVANCE grant that NDSU was awarded, was to encourage the recruitment, retention, and advancement of women faculty. The first author was invited to join the commission in 2010, and the second author had been an ad hoc member since the commission's inception. The commission used the College of HDE policies as a basis for the university policies for childbearing leave and modified duties that they brought forward. There were some changes made to the HDE policies. For example, we shifted the definition of eligible family members to fit with the FMLA definitions. This shift was made possible because of a recent clarification of the FMLA definitions to be more inclusive of parents who may not be legally or biologically related to the child (U.S. Department of Labor 2010).

Lesson Eight: Some policies intended to provide for parental leave can be written more broadly to cover general family or life issues. The College of Human Development and Education was the leader on campus for what was possible at the policy level. However, one additional feature that the modified-duties guidelines created in the other college was flexibility to cover situations beyond childbirth/adoption. Even though we tried to be broad by covering both men and women and both birth and adoption, we eventually realized that we could have also included issues that can occur throughout life, such as serious illness of the person or a family member. This became important when developing an institution-wide policy. Additional feedback was sought from multiple constituents, and the HDE modified-duties policy was revised to include a wider range of family circumstances.

Lesson Nine: Follow the Policy Through the Process. Adopting a new university policy requires the involvement of and approval by multiple committees, including the faculty senate. The initial attempt to move the policy toward institutional adoption resulted in what can only be termed a misfire. Although the commission members had a good understanding of why the policy was written the way it was, others on campus lacked that understanding. The language of the policy was modified during a committee meeting at which no one who understood the original rationale was present. The result was a policy that contradicted state board policies, and would ultimately not be viable. We decided at that point that any attempt to change policy required us to be more hands on. An individual was assigned to shepherd a new policy through the process, both as a way to advocate for the policy and to prevent well-intentioned but harmful changes along the way.

We finally succeeded in passing university policies for Childbearing Leave and Modified Duties policies in April 2012. The Childbearing Leave policy in effect at NDSU is as follows:

> Academic appointees (tenured and tenure-track faculty, professors of practice, and senior lecturers) with less than twelve-month appointments who give birth are eligible for childbearing leave during the period of medical disability. This is a temporary leave from all duties without reduction in pay during the time the faculty member is temporarily disabled because of pregnancy and childbirth. Childbearing leave begins on the actual delivery date and ends six weeks after (including university breaks), although individual circumstances may require extending this period. Any extension beyond six weeks (before and after delivery) shall require medical certification from the attending physician or midwife and is approved by the Provost. Unpaid leave that extends beyond the period of medical disability is available through FMLA. Eligibility for childbearing leave begins upon hiring (NDSU Policy 320.5, 2012).

The Modified Duties Policy is as follows:

> 6.1. Who is eligible: An academic appointee (tenured and tenure-track faculty, professors of practice, and senior lecturers) who 1) becomes a parent through childbirth, adoption, or foster placement of a child (as defined by the Family and Medical Leave Act (FMLA); 2) has a health condition that makes them unable to perform their regular duties but does not necessitate a reduction in workload; or 3) who will be caring for a child, spouse/partner or parent who has a serious health condition (as defined by FMLA). Additional modifications for longer-term conditions may be made in accordance with the Americans with Disabilities Act and NDSU Policy 100.1.
> 6.2. Definition: "Modified duties" means a change to duties and goals without reduction of salary for a limited period of time. A person taking "modified duties" will still be at a 100 percent workload and 100 percent

salary; however the nature of the responsibilities for this time period will be adjusted. Modified duties will include a revision of workload for up to the equivalent of a semester (e.g., release from or reassignment of teaching courses, committee assignments, advising, or alteration of research duties). When a period of modified duties immediately follows childbearing leave, the modified duties may be extended to the end of a semester to accommodate teaching schedules as necessary. Modified duties must conclude within 12 months of a birth or adoption.

6.3. Process: Modified duties, goals, and duration will be negotiated by the individual requesting modified duties with the department chair/head and approved by the dean. If agreement cannot be reached between the faculty member, the department chair/head, and the dean, the negotiation will advance to the Provost.

6.4. Performance evaluation: Faculty members who use the modification of duties and goals must still submit an annual report when it is due in their department. The time period in which duties were modified, as well as the specific modifications in place, must be included in the annual report. The report must also include the agreed upon goals and a statement about how those goals were accomplished, but must not disclose confidential medical information. Those reviewing and evaluating the document should take this into account and adjust expectations accordingly. Acceptance of modified duties does not change the candidate's responsibility for meeting the department's PTE standards by the end of the probationary period, whether that period has been extended or not. A period of modified duties is not a necessary condition for an extension of the tenure probationary period. A period of modified duties also does not require that the individual extend the tenure probationary period. (NDSU Policy 320.6)

Our involvement in this process has been both challenging and rewarding. Initially, it seemed as if it should be a relatively simple matter to develop a workable policy; it was not. It seemed as if a reasonable and legal policy would be readily adopted once it was developed; it was not. Ultimately, it took five years from the time that HDE Work Life Balance Task Force began its work to have a university-wide policy adopted. Our work on this issue is still not done, as we are continuing to monitor implementation. Our experiences with this have taught us a lot, and we hope our lessons are informative for others who are considering undertaking policy change.

Remaining Needs

The two policies that were adopted at NDSU showcase the steps toward managing work/family that we were able to accomplish without strong support from central administration. A strength of these policies is that they were developed with substantial input from the people whose job category is most affected by them; yet they are still limited in many ways. Currently departments (with the assistance of their college dean) are responsible for identifying funding to cover courses affected by utilization of the policies. Some departments and colleges have little flexibility in their budgets, thus adhering to these policies may increase resource strain in other areas. A centralized pool of funding that deans could draw upon to implement the policies would be a tremendous asset in the push to have the policies become widely accepted. Faculty members are generally reluctant to impose upon their already busy colleagues. They may be reluctant to ask for modified duties if there is a perception that departments and colleagues will suffer for faculty members' responsibility adjustments. Asking for such accommodations may be particularly challenging for untenured faculty. Additionally, strong administrative support at all levels is needed if these efforts to acknowledge that faculty members have lives outside of work are to be successful. Everyone from the university president down to the department heads and chairs needs to be aware of, and vocally support, the policies for them to become part of the institutional culture. Whether this will happen remains an open question. Although the policies on our campus are new, we are aware of multiple cases where the childbearing leave or modified-duties policies have been used; a hopeful sign is that this usage cuts across all the colleges on campus.

What to call these policies remains an open question. Although the term "family-friendly" continues to be used regularly, our task force shifted part of our name from family-friendly to work/life balance. The term "family-friendly" is potentially a bias-laden term. Talking about "family" activates a mental image of what a family is. Although parents with children are often included in that image, many other family forms are not automatically included. Thus, the term presumes that only certain kinds of people need accommodations for their personal lives. Yet the reality is that all faculty members have some element of a personal life outside of the workplace. Few individuals are completely isolated from relations with and responsibility toward other humans. Perhaps the term we should be using to describe the institutional policies that we design to create a more humane workplace is "people friendly." Ultimately, we all stand to gain at various points in our life cycle if our institutions are humane for everyone.

Certainly the policies outlined in this chapter are not the only policies needed to create a people friendly workplace. For example, academic men and women have reported that mandatory meetings and faculty obligations that extend outside of the bounds of the traditional workday create challenges in their personal lives (Colbeck and Drago 2005; Solomon 2011). One possibility is to create institutional policies that limit the time of day during which meetings can be held. The more policies institutions have that support the notion that work and personal life are both important, the more our institutions will become intertwined with the overall rhythm of faculty lives.

Our academic institutions serve as second homes for most faculty members. Most faculty members spend more of their waking hours physically present at, or otherwise engaged in the work of, these institutions. Creating policies that help to ensure the institutions faculty members devote themselves to are humane in times of faculty need serves as a way to close the loop in what can sometimes be experienced as a one-way street. Faculty put in long hours and the work they engage in can cut into the space that might otherwise be reserved for personal obligations. Being a faculty member is generally a labor of love; yet loving one's job does not mean that faculty should not have lives outside of these institutions. The image of the "ideal faculty member" needs to change from the image that was dominant when most faculty were men who had stay-at-home wives to manage the details of daily living. The world is changing; if academic institutions do not keep pace with those changes, they will eventually pay the price through the loss of the many talented women and men who seek to effectively manage their work and the other facets of their lives.

CONCLUSION

People often suggest that the phrase "May you live in interesting times" is intended as a curse. The rapidly changing face of the family and of the workplace might be considered to be interesting times. The challenges of shifting toward a new mode of being at the institutional level might feel like a curse for those who are endeavoring to help this shift along. The fact remains, however, that the opportunity to creatively shape institutions to accommodate the totality of faculty members' lives across the course of their careers provides a chance to leave a legacy for those who will come after us. Our experiences suggest that change is possible, even when an institution has been historically slow to meet the changing needs of the faculty. Perhaps one day, faculty members may take it for granted that their personal lives and work lives can operate in tandem, in a flexible and livable manner. Such is the hope if we are to continue to retain the best and brightest at our institutions.

NOTE

1. While a period of modified duties must be made available to those who qualify, qualified employees may also choose, at their sole discretion, to reduce their workload and expectations to a level less than full-time but greater than half-time, with a corresponding reduction in pay for a period not to exceed one semester (Work-Life Balance Task Force, 2009).

REFERENCES

American Council on Education. N.d. "Making the Business Case: The Imperative for Supporting and Promoting Workplace Flexibility in Higher Education." Retrieved September 28,

2013 (http://www.acenet.edu/news-room/Pages/Making-the-Business-Case-for-Workplace-Flexibility.aspx).

Anderson, Donna M., Betsy L. Morgan, and Jennifer B. Wilson. 2002. "Perceptions of Family-Friendly Policies: University Versus Corporate Employees." *Journal of Family and Economic Issues* 23:73–92.

Bailey, Martha J., Brad Hershbein, and Amalia R. Miller. 2012. "The Opt-in Revolution? Contraception and the Gender Gap in Wages." *American Economic Journal: Applied Economics* 4: 225–54.

Cancian, Maria, and Deborah Reed. 2009. "Family Structure, Childbearing, and Parental Employment: Implications for the Level and Trend of Poverty." *Focus* 26:21–26.

Colbeck, Carol L., and Robert Drago. 2005. "Accept, Avoid, Resist: How Faculty Members Respond to Bias Against Caregiving and how Departments can Help." *Change: The Magazine of Higher Learning* 37:10–17.

Drago, Robert, Carol Colbeck, Kai D. Stauffer, Amy Piretti, Kurt Burkum, Jennifer Fazioli, Gabriela Lazarrot, and Tara Habaseich. 2005. "Bias Against Caregiving." *Academe* 91: 22–25.

Education Portal. N.d. "How Much Does a Doctorate Degree Cost." Retrieved September 28, 2013 (http://education-portal.com/articles/How_Much_Does_a_Doctorate_Degree_Cost.html).

Haas, Linda, and C. Phillip Hwang. 2008. "The Impact of Taking Parental Leave on Fathers' Participation in Childcare and Relationships with Children: Lessons from Sweden." *Community, Work, and Family* 11:85–104.

Higher Education Recruitment Consortium. N.d. "How Much are Annual Membership Dues." Retrieved September 28, 2013 (http://www.hercjobs.org/prospective_member_institutions/prospective_member_institutions_faqs/).

Hollenshead, Carol S., Beth Sullivan, Gilia C. Smith, Louise August, and Susan Hamilton. 2005. "Work/family Policies in Higher Education: Survey Data and Case Studies of Policy Implementation." *New Directions for Higher Education* 130:41–65.

Kotila, Letitia E., Sarah J. Schoppe-Sullivan, and Claire M. Kamp Dush. 2013. "Time in Parenting Activities in Dual-Earner Families at the Transition to Parenthood." *Family Relations* 62:795–807.

Leonard, D. J. 2013. "Blame the Institution, Not Just the Fathers." *Chronicle of Higher Education.* Retrieved September 28, 2013 (http://chronicle.com/article/Blame-the-Institution-Not/140405/).

Mason, Mary Ann, Nicholas H. Wolfinger, and Marc Goulden. 2013. *Do Babies Matter: Gender and Family in the Ivory Tower.* New Brunswick, NJ: Rutgers University Press.

NDSU Policy 320. (2012) "Faculty Obligations and Time Requirements." Retrieved September 28, 2013 (http://www.ndsu.edu/fileadmin/policy/320.pdf).

Reddick, Richard J., Aaron B. Rochlen, Joseph R. Grasso, Erin D. Reilly, and Daniel D. Spikes. 2012. "Academic Fathers Pursuing Tenure: A Qualitative Study of Work-Family Conflict, Coping Strategies, and Departmental Conflict." *Psychology of Men and Masculinity* 13:1–15.

Rhoads, Steven E., and Christopher H. Rhoads. 2012. "Gender Roles and Infant/Toddler Care: Male and Female Professors on the Tenure Track." *Journal of Social, Evolutionary, and Cultural Psychology* 6:13–31.

Salle, Margaret W. 2013. "Gender Norms and Institutional Culture: The Family-Friendly versus the Father-Friendly University." *The Journal of Higher Education* 84:363–96.

Smith, Gilia C., and Jeane A. Waltman. 2006. Designing and implementing family-friendly policies in higher education. Retrieved September 28, 2013 (http://www.umich.edu/~cew/PDFs/designing06.pdf).

Smithson, Janet, and Elizabeth H. Stokoe. 2005. "Discourses of Work-Life Balance Negotiating 'Genderblind' Terms in Organizations." *Gender, Work, and Organization* 12:147–68.

Solomon, Catherine Richards. 2011. "'Sacrificing at the Altar of Tenure': Assistant Professors' Work/Life Management." *The Social Science Journal* 48:335–44.

———. 2010. "'The Very Highest Thing is Family': Male Assistant Professors' Work/Family Management." Pp. 233–55 in *Interactions and Intersections of Gendered Bodies at Work, at*

Home, and at Play, Vol. 14, *Advances in Gender Research*, edited by V. P. Demos and M. T. Segal. Bingley, UK: Emerald Group Publishing Limited.

Spalter-Roth, Roberta, and William Erskine. 2006. "Resources or Rewards? The Distribution of Work-Family Policies." American Sociological Association Department of Research and Development (www.asanet.org).

SBHE Policy 607.4. Sick and Dependent Leave; Family Leave. Retrieved September 28, 2013 (http://www.ndus.edu/makers/procedures/sbhe/default.asp?PID=185andSID=7).

U.S. Department of Labor: Wage and Hour Division. News Release Number: 10–0877–NAT. 2010 "US Department of Labor Clarifies FMLA Definition of 'Son and Daughter': Interpretation is a Win for all Families No Matter What They Look Like." Retrieved September 28, 2013 (http://www.dol.gov/opa/media/press/WHD/WHD20100877.htm).

U.S. Equal Employment Opportunity Commission. N.d. "The Pregnancy Discrimination Act of 1978." Retrieved September 28, 2013 (http://www.eeoc.gov/laws/statutes/pregnancy.cfm).

Weigt, Jill M., and Catherine Richards Solomon. 2008. "Work-family Management among Low-wage Service Workers and Assistant Professors in the USA: A Comparative Intersectional Analysis." *Gender, Work, and Organization* 15:621–49.

Wilson, Robin. 2006. "AAUP Report Blames Colleges for Gender Inequity Among Professors." *The Chronicle of Higher Education*. November 3, retrieved September 28, 2013(http://chronicle.com/article/AAUP-Report-Blames-Colleges/8774/).

———. 2007. "At North Dakota State, Women are Few and Far Between." *The Chronicle of Higher Education*. November 2, retrieved September 28, 2013(http://chronicle.com/article/At-North-Dakota-State-Wome/11174/).

Wolf-Wendel, Lisa E., and Kelly Ward. 2006. "Academic Life and Motherhood: Variations by Institutional Type." *Higher Education* 52: 487–521.

Work-Life Balance Task Force. 2009. Policies for Childbearing Leave, College of Human Development and Education, North Dakota State University.

Chapter Eight

Changing Work/Life Policy in Institutions of Higher Education

A Case Study

Leslie E. Tower

Work/life conflict may be defined as concerns about insufficient time to take care of family responsibilities because of work responsibilities (Blair-Loy and Wharton 2004). Limited legal supports and adherence to gender roles tend to lead to work/life conflict, particularly for women. Furthermore, work/life conflict may be more pronounced in demanding careers, such as academe. Stress in the academy tends to be related to a number of variables including work overload, role conflict, faculty interaction, academic advancement, and aging considerations (Hendel and Horn 2008). Such stressors are related to the fact that both men and women faculty report working long hours, fifty or more hours per week (Jacobs and Winslow 2004). In comparison to managers in the U.S. workforce, women and men professors worked about fourteen and nine hours more, respectively, per week than managers (Jacobs and Gerson 2004). Work/life conflict is of particular importance for women faculty.

EMPLOYMENT PATTERNS OF WOMEN IN THE ACADEMY

Across the academic career, women are less likely to follow the ideal academic career trajectory. Upon earning a PhD, women may not even enter the tenure track (Mason, Goulden, and Frasch 2009). When they do seek academic positions, post-PhD women who are either married or have children under six years old are significantly less likely than their male counterparts to attain tenure-track positions (Wolfinger, Mason, and Goulden 2008) and significantly more likely than men to become adjunct professors (Wolfinger, Mason, and Goulden 2009). A woman may accept lower status academic positions, such as adjunct professor, in lieu of tenure-track positions for a host of family formation reasons including supporting her partner's career until their children are school age; participating in stimulating part-time work; keeping a foot in the door within academe in case she decides to pursue a tenure-track position in the future; earning extra family income; or combining two or more of these (Webber and Williams 2008; Wolfinger et al. 2009). Hence, higher education has a tremendous untapped talent pool of women because many opt out of tenure-track positions for a variety of family-related reasons.

Talented women are also being lost due to discrimination against women and mothers. Faculty women who are successful in tenure-track positions are significantly less likely to marry and have children (and more likely to divorce) than their male counterparts and non-tenure track women post-PhD (Mason and Goulden 2004a). Furthermore, these limited hiring and promotion pools tend to systematically exclude women, not merely the least qualified candidates (Center for WorkLife Law 2012; Frasch, Mason, Stacy, Goulden, and Hoffman 2007).

Why do these trends endure? One theory relates to family formation (Webber and Williams 2008; Wolfinger et al. 2009). The customary six-year tenure clock tends to tick in time with a woman's biological clock (Armenti 2004; Jacobs and Winslow 2004). According to Wolfinger et al. (2009, 1613), "More than most vocations, academia does not really offer any good time to have children." By the time women (and men) complete their education and training, they are in their thirties. Post-PhD women who are either married or have children under six years old, are significantly less likely to attain tenure-track positions and significantly more likely than men in the academy to become adjunct professors (Wolfinger et al. 2008, 2009). If women wait until post-tenure to have a child, they are likely reaching the end of their fertility window.

The ideal career path for an academic has been characterized as attaining a tenure-track position and rising through the ranks of associate professor and professor. A tenure-track position provides approximately six years for a faculty member to make a significant contribution in research and teaching to her or his field in order to achieve tenure. The award of tenure conveys status and provides job security, as there is an expectation of lifetime employment to the recipient. If a tenure-track candidate does not earn tenure, she or he typically loses her or his job at that institution.

For women who achieve tenure, their bid for promotion to full professor may be delayed or dashed (Barrett and Barrett 2011; MLA 2009; Valian 1998). Geisler, Kaminski, and Berkely (2007) coined the term "13+ Club" for faculty who have not been fully promoted in the customary six years for tenure and six more years for promotion to full professor and report that women are 2.3 times less likely than men to have been fully promoted. Researchers have uncovered gendered explanations for the lag. Valian (1998) suggests that small setbacks that women face because of their sex, a slightly higher service load for example, compound over time and result in significant disparities in career progression. Women may spend more time engaged in non-research activities or "institutional housekeeping," such as service, teaching, or mentoring; while men may spend more time engaged in research (Bird, Litt, and Wang 2004; Misra, Lundquist, Holmes, and Agiomavritis 2011; MLA 2009; Valian 1998). Gender is also relevant when women are unable to work after hours as much as their male counterparts because of family responsibilities. Furthermore, because women faculty are more likely than men faculty to have an employed partner (Wolfinger, Goulden, and Mason 2010) managing the demands of home and work responsibilities make work/life conflict central to the lives of women professors.

However, work/life conflict may be minimized by changes in policies. If talented women are opting out of tenure-track positions or not being successful in faculty ranks, then policy is needed to support them to achieve career success as well as family satisfaction. This chapter considers the organizational change literature and, through the use of a case study, suggests strategies to improve work/life policies in institutions of higher education.

WORK/LIFE POLICIES

Work/life policies offer protections, supports, and benefits to employees that allow them to make real choices about how they manage their work and personal responsibilities. But, few U.S. laws confer protections, supports, or benefits related to family (e.g., childbirth and childcare). The seminal piece of legislation related to childbirth is the Family and Medical Leave Act of 1993. It offers job protection for up to twelve weeks of unpaid leave, for qualified life events, including childbirth or adoption (Family and Medical Leave Act of 1993; Gerstel and McGonagle 1999). Other beneficial work/life policies, paid maternity leave or publicly subsidized day care (Blau 2003), for instance, are not available to most U.S. citizens. But, these work/life benefits may be more prevalent in the academy.

Tower and Dilks (2014) surveyed the websites of ADVANCE Universities (N = 124), institutions awarded a National Science Foundation (NSF) ADVANCE grant. They report that 29 percent of ADVANCE universities allowed faculty to use accrued sick or disability payments for parental leave, 5 percent offered four weeks of paid parental leave, 16 percent offered six to eight weeks of paid parental leave, 36 percent offered six to eight weeks of paid parental leave plus teaching release for the semester. About 10 percent offered only unpaid leave through the Family and Medical Leave Act (FMLA). Universities receiving the prestigious NSF ADVANCE grants did not offer generous paid parental leave. Additionally, while 64 percent of ADVANCE Universities have an affiliation with a childcare center that offers infant care, only 2 percent guarantee a spot for faculty children and only 24 percent offer a discount (Tower and Dilks 2014). While work/life programs may be offered in the academy, availability of them tends to be uneven. Lack of work/life policies or accessibility to the policy continues to be a challenge for many faculty parents.

Polices may be mandated by government or voluntarily implemented by organizations. The apparent lack of political will and a sluggish economy makes it unlikely that sweeping policy change will occur at the federal or state levels (Alkadry and Tower 2013; Williams 2010). Williams (2010) makes the case that organizations should take it upon themselves to adapt to the changing realities of the workforce in order to optimize organizational effectiveness. Institutions that fail to support work/life policies are likely to see an increase in turnover because workplace satisfaction impacts one's intentions to leave an institution (Rosser 2004). This may result in a failure to attract and retain talented faculty (Mason and Goulden 2004b) or costly turnover in personnel (Betts and Sikorski 2008; Hailu, Mariam, Fekade, Derbew, and Mekasha 2013; Schloss, Flanagan, Culler, and Wright 2009).

In sum, influenced by discrimination against women and mothers and the support of traditional gender roles, women faculty disproportionately exit the academy or follow an alternative academic career trajectory. Work/life policies may help alleviate work/life conflict, allowing more women faculty to join, stay, and advance in the academic ranks. Achieving this benefits not only the women, but also their institutions, colleagues, and students. To achieve the most effective and inclusive work/life policies, faculty must advocate and affect the change they desire.

ORGANIZATIONAL CHANGE IN HIGHER EDUCATION

Attracting, retaining, and advancing women in the academy can be aided by implementing work/life policies. Several organizational change theories informed faculty in one U.S. university in the process of implementing a generous parental leave policy—Evolutionary/Environmental, Teleological, Life Cycle, Dialectical/Political, Social Cognition, and Cultural. In order to optimize change, Kezar (2001) suggests drawing on a combination of activities from the six prevailing theories used to understand organizational change in higher education. Table 8.1 outlines these theories.

This chapter describes ten activities that were informed by organizational change theories used within higher education—(a) Evolution/Environmental (e.g., understanding who and how decisions are made); (b) Teleological (e.g., aligning policy goals with the university's strategic plan, modeling by, perhaps, new administration, identifying cost/benefits of proposed policies); (c) Life Cycle (e.g., understanding the developmental stage—renewal and expansion—in shaping goals such as policies that will attract the next generation of scholars); (d) Dialectical/Political (e.g., cultivating policy champions and alliances with campus leaders and organizations); (e) Social Cognition (e.g., educating stakeholders of policy benefits); and (f) Cultural (e.g., modifying the physical environment to reflect new values) (Kezar 2001). Much has been written about the paucity of and need for work/life policies in higher education, particularly to help women advance at the same rates as men (for example, Gardner 2013; Terosky, O'Meara, and Campbell 2014; Welch, Wiehe, Palmer-Smith, and Dankoski 2011). But, less has been writ-

Table 8.1.   Change theories utilized in higher education

Evolutionary/ environmental	While academia may be viewed as having much independence, observing the external environment, such as accreditors, legislature, funders, and peers is important because of their increasing influence. Analyzing the organizational system as well as creating new structures may be helpful to the change process.
Teleological	Change may occur in a linear and planned fashion. Using strategic planning is one such systematic approach. This theory also focuses on leadership's ability to affect change, efficacy, cost containment, and an evaluation-modification loop.
Life cycle	These theories emphasize the attitudes, feelings, behaviors, and motivations of the organizational actors.
Dialectical/ political	In Dialectical Theories, facilitating change may happen through interest groups, informal change processes, persistence, mediation, and politics. In Political Theories, the shared governance system, between sometimes conflicting professional and administrative values of its players is examined. It is useful to build coalitions, understand power relationships, and use negotiation to achieve change.
Social cognition	Academics tend to identify with the university's image, yet decisions are made diffusely throughout and even outside the formal academic hierarchy; therefore, understanding various groups' interpretations as well as various perspectives is important to planned change. This may include educating organizational players.
Cultural	Academics tend to strongly identify with the organization, its values, and its history. Therefore, activities that would create new rituals as well as communicate beliefs and values to modify culture and subcultures are important.

ten about *how* to change work/life policies. This chapter documents a successful strategy and process used to achieve paid parental leave for faculty.

METHODS

One institution of higher education, EG University, is the basis of this case
study. The institution studied here is a large, land-grant, Research High University. This case study may be categorized as "change process research"
(Gilgun 1994, 373) as the focus here is on what the change agent(s) did to
affect change. Throughout the seven years of the case study, beginning in the
early 2000s, I logged my observations, conversations with decision makers,
other stakeholders, and so on, documenting information such as content,
action items, next steps, impressions, and interpretation of events. Artifacts
related to the process were also collected (e.g., institutional policies available
on the Internet, minutes from meetings, and survey findings). As a social
work professor, who teaches and researches policy, the motivation to engage
in policy-practice around work/life issues was inspired by frustration from
the uneven, and at times punitive, treatment faculty experienced, including
myself.

FINDINGS AND DISCUSSION

The following section consists of a description of 10 strategies used to obtain
paid parental leave at a case institution of higher education. One exception is
Strategy 6 which details a related work/life support program for lactating
mothers.

1. Understanding the Institution

Nearly every theory of organizational change applied to institutions of higher
education begins with a process of understanding the particular institution
and how decisions are made and by whom. Understanding an institution
means understanding its hierarchy and culture. In general, the structure of
governance at U.S. universities is comprised of both external and internal
entities. Each state has a postsecondary education planning commission
(McGuinness 2002). For the state in which EG University is located, the
Higher Education Policy Commission (HEPC) has power over the university
system. In addition, there is an institution-specific governing board: Board of
Governors. Governing boards, similar to their corporate counterpart of
boards of directors, typically deal with issues such as general management of
the university.

EG University has a president and administrative team (e.g., Policy Development Officer, Chief of Staff, Legal). The faculty is organized hierarchically with a chief academic officer (e.g., Vice President of Academic Affairs and Provost) who reports to the president. Deans of colleges report to the provost. Colleges contain departments or schools with divisions and programs. Similar to other public institutions, EG University has a Faculty Senate, that serves as a platform for faculty governance. EG University also has a student government organization, to represent student interests, and a staff group, to represent staff. In researching the hierarchy of EG University, stakeholders were identified and located within it to get a clear picture of the hierarchy, the power structure, and politics that influence decision making. In general, university stakeholders include such groups as the governing board, president, senior administrators, faculty, staff, students, parents, donors, competitors, community members, regulators, non-governmental regulators, financial intermediaries, and other partners (Benneworth and Jongbloed 2010; Burrows 1999).

It is also important to understand the institutional climate. EG University is a large, land grant, Research High University based on a top-down governance style that appeared to rely on a durable "good ol' boys network." Further, the university is underfunded, resulting in a zero sum mentality, pitting stakeholders against each other (e.g., faculty vs. staff). These norms contributed and other political events translated into low faculty morale.

During the period of the case study there was turnover of the university president and provost that had a positive impact on morale. A new provost and president were hired who appeared committed to moving the institution forward on many fronts, including meeting the metrics to move the institution into the Carnegie Foundation's classification of "Research Very High University." This quest and strategy to get there have been more inclusive than previous administrations' efforts, well-publicized, and visible (e.g., hiring one hundred new tenure-track lines consistent with goals of the strategic plan). The administrators have been successful in various attempts to increase funding to the institution, for example, working with legislators, offering supports to increase external dollars, and steadily increasing the student body.

2. Peer Comparisons

Faculty or staff who wish to advocate for a policy would benefit from understanding Evolutionary Theories, which argue for researching the external environment or how one's institution compares, on the issue, to peer institutions. University administrators rely on this analysis on a regular basis (e.g., financial and budgetary analyses). Peer analysis is useful to university leadership to make informed and thorough decisions (Anderes 1999).

Universities tend to keep more than one list of peers. EG University, for example, has several lists of peer institutions, including, Higher Education Policy Commission (HEPC) peers, Mission-based Peers (i.e., land-grant institutions), and Carnegie Classification foundation (Research University High). When selecting either a list of peers or universities from a particular peer list, it is important to provide a rationale for why particular universities are selected for peer comparison. I found it to be more powerful to select peers with similar institutional resources (vs. very well-funded peers) to show, for example, that generous parental leave policies are possible within less well-funded institutional environments.

Table 8.2 compares paid leave and teaching release at such peer institutions. Work/life policies were found on provosts' websites, work/life websites, human resources, on-line faculty handbooks, or some combination (Bristol, Abbuhl, Cappola, and Sonnad 2008). Some universities may restrict public access to human resource policy on the Internet (Tower and Dilks 2014). When I could not find the information I sought, I called the provost's office to ask for or clarify data.

During this search, I identified a model parental leave policy as a starting point for drafting what became EG's policy. EG University's Parental Assignment Procedure for tenure-line faculty was modeled after GHI State University's policy. Using peer comparisons to inform leadership and other stakeholders was imperative. I have used this strategy in advocating for

Table 8.2.   Parental leave policies for nine-month faculty, circa 2009

Peer Institution	Accrued sick leave after birth	Other accrued leave	Paid parental leave	Teaching release?
EG University	Do not accrue	No	No	Proportional pay cut, per course reduction
ABC University	Do not accrue	Up to 6 months	1 semester	1 semester
University of DEF	Do not accrue	No	6 weeks paid leave	Determined at College (e.g., TT: 1 semester release; Lecturer: 2 course release)
GHI State University	Do not accrue	No	1 semester	1 semester
University of JKL	30 days	Up to 4 months	No	1 semester

subsequent work/life policies at EG University, such as lactation support and currently with tuition remission.

3. Gathering Additional Data

While peer analysis was important, additional data was needed to make a case for parental leave. Good sources of data used at EG University included data from: the Institutional Research (IR) Office; an exit survey and climate survey; reports from a survey conducted by the Collaborative on Academic Careers in Higher Education (COACHE) at Harvard University; and of course, peer comparisons.

For example, in 2009, a team composed of researchers began developing a National Science Foundation (NSF) ADVANCE Institutional Transformation (IT) proposal. The principal goal of an ADVANCE IT grant is to comprehensively increase gender equity in academic science, technology, engineering, and mathematics (STEM) disciplines. In preparation for the proposal, IR data was obtained that showed, for example, the number of women faculty by rank and field. A potentially important source of data is the institution's Institutional Research Office or the equivalent. IR offices routinely provide data to decision makers about the institution. IR websites may offer some data but data not provided should be requested.

A member of the ADVANCE team developed and administered an exit survey to women who had recently left the institution. Data from a campus climate survey that had been conducted was also included. Surveys help demonstrate the need for work/life policies and make policy development easier to accomplish when data and other research on work/life policies are available to strengthen the proposal (Hollenshead, Sullivan, Smith, August, and Hamilton 2005).

Finally, EG University participated in COACHE. COACHE conducts tailored satisfaction surveys on tenure-line faculty. COACHE has had more than 150 institutions participate in its program (COACHE 2008). Analyses are compared with national and peer groups; data are disaggregated by such variables as gender, race/ethnicity, and rank.

Triangulating these data clearly showed that women faculty at EG University struggled to manage academic expectations and their personal lives. When faculty were asked on the climate survey how important paid parental leave was for recruiting or retaining quality faculty, 65 percent (532) of all faculty and 72 percent (319) of women faculty found it to be "important" or "extremely important." Having multiple respectable data sources showing similar information appeared to be a powerful tool.

4. Describing the Benefits to the Institution and the Target Group the Policies are Intended to Impact

For a policy or program proposal to move forward, Teleological approaches to change would suggest clearly articulating what change is sought, while Dialectical approaches suggest agenda setting. I developed a Parental Leave Policy Proposal. The Policy Proposal (i.e., the first draft of the policy that was ultimately implemented) described the parental leave benefit, the eligibility criteria (e.g., full-time, nine-month female and male faculty, who do not accrue leave), the purpose and intent of the policy (e.g., to give new parents uninterrupted time to recover from childbirth and bond), and the benefits to the institution (e.g., higher retention rates of faculty).

I also identified the potential benefits for implementing paid parental leave policy at EG University. First, a formal leave policy provides equity across colleges and departments, as it would be clear for chairs and would alleviate the need for a faculty member to "negotiate" the terms of leave. Second, the policy is cost-effective, as faculty often continue their research agendas (and service responsibilities) while on leave, even if the policy states such activity is not expected (Yoest 2004). Further, faculty who feel they are treated fairly or generously in their workplace tend to have higher morale and higher productivity which benefits the institution (Callister 2006; Sima 2003). Third, family-friendly policies are increasingly seen as key to recruiting, retaining, and advancing high-quality faculty (Welch et al. 2011). Reduced turnover results in lower direct recruitment costs (e.g., position advertisements, travel of candidates, recruitment packages). Reduced turnover also results in lower indirect costs of faculty recruiting (faculty time to select and host candidates on campus) and protecting new faculty (work released from new faculty such as lighter service responsibilities, is shifted to other faculty, who will carry a heavier service burden, potentially taking him/her away from other important activities). Fourth, generous benefits are related to a positive institutional reputation. Elite universities currently offer twice as many work/life policies as other universities (Hollenshead et al. 2005), contributing to the desire to work for them. Fifth, it is the "right thing to do." It is easier for an institution, rather than an individual, to bear the costs of work/life support.

5. Estimating the Costs

It was vital to estimate the costs of the current practice and the costs of the proposed policy. Before the policy change, EG had both (a) a formal policy—proportional salary reduction per course released, and (b) an informal policy—colleague collegiality to pick up duties and cover courses one could not complete due to birth or bonding time. Under informal practices, colleagues or departments absorbed the additional expenditures. Having a policy that places financial responsibility on the college or provost level, however, may be less likely to disadvantage smaller departments or departments with higher percentages of women, such as social work, education, or nursing.

Costs were also estimated for the proposed policy of giving faculty six weeks of uninterrupted time to recover from childbirth (eight weeks after a cesarean section) and bond with their children. Allowing all new parents this release permits both parents to participate in caregiving and bonding. Costs were also estimated for one semester of teaching release for faculty parents who provide at least 50 percent of the caregiving. Average number of births in a year, average number of courses tenure-track faculty teach, and payment rates for a course to be taught by a replacement individual were all taken into consideration in cost estimation.

6. Acting Within One's Control

In order to fully illustrate the point of acting within one's control, I must diverge from the parental leave policy illustration for a moment and discuss prior advocacy work conducted around lactation support at EG University. When I began advocating for work/life policies, I realized that I needed a stakeholder group to sponsor my work. A stakeholder group lies within some formal structure of the institution. I applied to join EG University's Council for Women's Concerns (CWC) because their mission was consistent with my policy change goals. The council reported to the EG University Office of Social Justice. That hierarchal structure was one way to be heard by senior administrators. But, when they were not interested in using institutional resources toward these goals, I used my position as chair of the newly formed Climate Committee to offer support within my control. To support breastfeeding mothers, I developed an informal network of employees who were willing to donate their office space (e.g., private office, lab, or conference room) to women who needed a private place to express milk. Beginning in 2006, each semester, I sent out emails to the university list-serve asking for volunteers to join the "Lactation Network." This also served as a reminder to the university community that the network existed. The council developed a page on their website that listed employees willing to be part of the network. As years went on, the Lactation Network appeared on institutional materials, indicating that the university recognized the network. This ultimately led to the creation of a formal Lactation Program with dedicated, accessible lactation rooms and more generous benefits than the Affordable Care Act requires. The reputation and relationships I built in developing and disseminating information about the Lactation Network was part of developing policy alliances, as discussed in section 7.

7. Cultivating Policy Champions and Alliances

From Political and Dialectical standpoints, it is important to build relationships with institutional actors with the power to make or influence institutional change. The president, provost, deans, committees on the status of women, and faculty senate committees (e.g., faculty welfare) often play critical roles in work/life policy development in postsecondary institutions (Hollenshead et al. 2005). I provided updates to stakeholders with whom I had developed relationships and formed alliances with new stakeholder groups. For example, I began attending meetings of a faculty senate committee, the Welfare Committee. I was subsequently elected to be a senator from my college and became a member of this committee the following year. Later in the process, the Welfare Committee became an important supporter of the policy.

Stakeholder support appeared to be important in the change process. From a review of organizational change literature, Galambos, Dulmus, and Wodarski (2005) recommend developing a method for continuous feedback from stakeholders. Even with constituent participation, resistance to change tends to be universal among stakeholders who feel change will threaten their own interests. One strategy for minimizing resistance is to introduce change through a pilot project or to introduce the program on a limited basis (Child 2005). Parental leave for faculty at EG University was originally piloted on nine-month tenure-track faculty, and then expanded to include additional nine-month faculty groups (e.g., Teaching Professors).

Social Cognition Theory reminds us that while stakeholders may have very different interpretations about the environment, education about the policy change process can shape perceptions. For example, the first "EG University Parental Work Assignment Procedure" document indicated that it was one of many phases of policy development to come. It specifically named the four constituency groups recognized (i.e., twelve-month faculty, faculty with less than twelve-month contracts, faculty at affiliated campuses, and staff) that could expect future policy development. It also explained that nine-month tenure-track faculty was the first group to be addressed because these positions do not accrue sick or vacation leave, unlike twelve-month faculty and staff.

Teleological theory informs us that it is essential that stakeholders understand, "What is in it for them." Therefore, communication is necessary. Leslie and Manchester (2011) suggest de-gendering work/life conflict as a strategy to increase the support of such initiatives. They reframe work/life conflict as both a men's and women's issue, recognizing differences in men's and women's experiences. The language used to communicate policy change is key to the change process; how a policy is framed impacts how people think about and ultimately support or don't support it (Marshak and Grant 2011).

8. Policy Change Is Not Linear

The process of achieving a generous parental leave policy was not linear. It took seven years, spanning four presidents and two provosts. In the early years of advocating for work/life policies, many upper-level administrators were not supportive of work/life policies discussed herein (i.e., the issue was not interpreted as urgent enough to dedicate institutional resources at the time).

Resistance to change, a concept often highlighted in Dialectical Models, from administrators or colleagues can be a challenge. Key personnel were educated using peer comparisons to show EG University was behind its peers (see strategy 2), data sources demonstrating that faculty wanted the paid parental leave at EG University (see strategy 3), a list of the ways EG University and nine-month faculty would benefit from having paid parental leave (see strategy 4), and a cost estimate of implementing the policy (see strategy 5). The EG University Parental Leave Workgroup also conducted a conference call with GHI's Human Resource Director. This appeared to be an important turning point for the Workgroup (comprised of mostly high-level administrators and some faculty) becoming comfortable with such a generous policy as upper-level administrators at EG University heard about the benefits of such a policy from a colleague of similar rank at a peer institution. The outcome of the Parental Leave Workgroup was a draft of a generous parental leave policy.

Over time, changes in the university's administration and funding of the NSF ADVANCE grant contributed to the establishment of a paid parental leave policy. However, a change in leadership or a prestigious grant may not be necessary to affect change. According to Evolutionary Theories, change happens over time because the environment demands it (Kezar 2001). In time, leadership may change from being unsupportive of work/life policies to supportive. Administrators may be swayed by changing public support, recognizing best practices, changing institutional goals (e.g., to recruit and retain more talented women faculty), or a policy change campaign.

9. Considering Implementation

A cornerstone of Teleological Theories is to insure that policy is having the consequence that was intended, hence the interest here in policy implementation. Ryan and Kossex (2008) identified four implementation attributes that ought to be considered when implementing work/life policies: supervisor support, communication quality, universalism, and negotiability.

Supervisor support. Support by a chair is critical to policy utilization by faculty members. According to Ryan and Kossex (2008), chairs (a) have the power to approve the use of the policy (e.g., course releases), (b) impact how well the policy is disseminated within the department, and (c) remove or erect barriers that impact policy utilization (e.g., the time of day faculty meetings are scheduled). In the *Cornell Couples and Careers Study*, supervisor support was associated with less work/life conflict (Valcour and Batt, 2003).

At EG University, a faculty member is required to complete the "Request for Parental Work Assignment" form in consultation with their chair. The form is sent up the chain of command for approval: chair, dean, and provost. Supervisor support or lack of support for the policy may be measured by the assignment agreed to on the form, if it is even approved at all. If the assignment reflects that a faculty member will return to the classroom during the semester, or if a faculty member is assigned to teach an online course as a substitute for classroom teaching, then the purpose of the policy has not been met. Alternatively, should a chair (or dean) not approve the teaching release, as stipulated in the policy, there is a place to check "not approved" box, along with the reasons for denial. This allows the form to move up the chain of command. In either of these circumstances the form should be flagged at the provost level and sent back down to the faculty member or chair for a better outcome.

Communication quality. It is vital to regularly disseminate information to faculty and administrators about work/life policies. Broadly communicating policies will help them be seen as legitimate and routine (Quinn, Lange, and Olswang 2004). It is also important to have an institutional commitment to educating employees (Galambos, Dulmus, and Wodarski 2005). At EG University, several venues were used to educate individuals about the new policy, including new faculty orientations; forums; informational sessions for faculty, deans, chairs; and promotion and tenure committees.

The EG ADVANCE Center also initiated a work/life educational campaign. The provost sent an email to all faculty about the new parental leave policy. In consultation with the provost's office, the ADVANCE Center developed case examples of simulated faculty usage of it. ADVANCE team members gave informational sessions to faculty (voluntary) and chairs (at a mandatory retreat), where the cases were utilized. The provost's website was updated and expanded to include work/life policies, including the new policy, and their applicable forms. The Internet allows faculty to anonymously research policy before going public with a request, which is important in any negotiation process.

Researchers have found that many faculty initially learn about policies from their departments; chairs' understanding of the policy may lead to inconsistent implementation of it (Quinn et al. 2004; Ryan and Kossex 2008). For instance, a new chair and dean had not been at EG University during the communication campaign and constructed parental assignments that were initially inconsistent with the policy. It is critical to communicate information about policies on a regular basis because of the regular turnover of chairs and deans as well as their influence on the process and influx of new faculty. Such communication also avoids the risk of faculty members missing out on a policy because they were not aware of it and the resentment that would likely follow (Hollenshead et al. 2005; Smith and Waltman 2006).

Universalism. The degree to which employees are eligible to use a policy impacts its implementation. Policies open to employees regardless of rank, location, sex, sexual orientation, or other demographic group are more inclusive than policies with restrictions. Universalism is related to workplace climate and research has shown that workplace climate affects the usage of work/life policies. Faculty may fear career repercussions if they utilize a work/life policies in some climates (Hollenshead et al. 2005).

Workplace culture that supports the use of work/life policies is necessary for the policies to be fully utilized (Mesmer-Magnus and Viswesvaran 2006). In fact, a culture that includes supportive language around work/life balance, or in how employees are treated or work is organized, may have more of an impact on a worker's perceptions of his or her own work/life balance and job than any work/life policy (Saltzstein, Ting, and Saltzstein 2001). But, if a workplace does not support the usage of such policies, it is helpful to have a powerful supervisor who may be able to protect the employee from perceived or real career penalties (Blair-Loy and Wharton 2002).

As previously discussed, the Parental Work Assignment Procedure at EG was developed in phases, as there are differences between the constituency groups to which the policy applies. For example, unlike twelve-month faculty and staff, nine-month faculty do not accrue sick or vacation leave. This made the development of a policy for this group more urgent than for a group that could draw on paid leave. There are numerous additional distinctions, such as the cost of the policy for these groups and the dissimilar work responsibilities. While policies vary between groups because of these differences, consistency was sought to achieve universalism so that all individuals within a group are treated similarly.

Negotiability. Negotiability relates to how much of a policy needs to be negotiated by an individual wishing to utilize the policy in order to receive the maximum that the policy allows; the perceived fairness of the negotiation impacts the utilization of the policy (Ryan and Kossex 2008). The policy states: "The University and its colleges and schools expect that faculty members eligible for a Parental Work Assignment will routinely use this benefit. Such use shall not adversely affect the faculty member's standing or salary in any manner . . ." (Parental Work Assignment Procedure 2011, 3). The purpose of this statement in the policy is important to the potential negotiated outcomes for faculty because it communicates the university's intent that faculty regularly and fully use the policy without any retribution for doing so. But, this statement alone is not enough to ensure consistency of its use.

Communication and supervisor support are important to address the potential unevenness of the policy's implementation across departments.

10. Evaluating, Correcting, and Improving

Teleological Theories advocate for the evaluation and modification of the policy to reach the policy goals. After policy implementation, evaluating the policy helps to understand what about the policy is working or not working and why. Continuing with the above example about faculty utilization of the Parental Work Assignment Procedure, the ADVANCE Center suggested that an entity external to the provost's office (the ADVANCE evaluators) should review the procedure usage. Alternatives to this group might have been the Office of Social Justice or the formation of a new task force for this purpose. At EG University, the forms are reviewed in the aggregate by the AD-VANCE evaluators, with identifying information redacted. This evaluation process has the benefit of protecting the privacy of the faculty using the policy as well as having fresh eyes review it.

The purposes of the evaluation include (a) report patterns of procedure usage to the provost's office and ADVANCE Center, (b) offer recommendations for possible revisions to the procedure, or (c) recommend increased education about the procedure if it is not being fully utilized as intended. Smith and Waltman (2006) suggest that is also important to understand faculty perceptions in terms of pros and cons, usage and non-usage, and whether the policy positively impacts recruitment and retention.

Another implementation issue is whether there are unintended consequences of the policy. As an example, the most common work/life policy provided by universities, particularly at research universities, is a stop the tenure clock policy (Hollenshead et al. 2005). This policy allows a faculty member to pause the tenure clock or extend the probationary period to accommodate certain life circumstances. Because of women's biology (overlap of the pre-tenure period with their biological clock) and gender (women tend to provide caregiving to relatives), women tend to use this policy more frequently than men. The intent of this policy is to allow faculty to continue their career trajectory, without derailing it because of increased family demands. This can be an important career-saving policy. Nevertheless, when women use this policy more than men, it creates a systematic pay gap between men and women faculty, which may be perceived as a career penalty for women (Gerten 2011). The pay differential created by this career-saving policy is an unintended consequence of the policy. Modifying the stopping the tenure clock policy, without the unintended consequence of systematically lowering women's pay would be beneficial to promoting gender equity in academia.

CONCLUSIONS

Policy change illustrated herein is aimed at improving social justice for faculty, allowing improvements in attracting, retaining, and promoting women faculty. A case study is used to illustrate organizational change strategies implemented to achieve a generous parental leave policy. The ten proposed strategies rely on components of organizational change models prominent in higher education literature. First, *understanding the institution* is an important starting place. Nearly every theory of organizational change applied to institutions of higher education begins with a process of understanding the particular institution. Second, *peer comparisons* and third, *gathering data* help to understand the external environment in comparison to the internal environment (Evolutionary Theories). Fourth, *describing the benefits to the institution and the target group* the policies are intended to impact is suggested by Teleological approaches (clearly articulating what change is sought) and Dialectical approaches (agenda setting). Fifth, *estimating the costs* is important for an organization to implement policy.

Sixth, according to Evolutionary Theories, change happens over time because the environment demands it. Sometimes this happens from the bottom up, or *acting within one's control*. Seventh, *cultivating policy champions and alliances* is predominant in Political and Dialectical standpoints—it is important to build relationships with institutional actors with the power to make or influence institutional change. Social Cognition Theory reminds us that while stakeholders may have very different interpretations about the environment, education about the policy change process can shape perceptions.

Eighth, *policy change is not linear.* And resistance to change, a concept often highlighted in Dialectical Models, can be expected. Ninth, *considering implementation*, a cornerstone of Teleological Theories, helps insure policy is having the consequences that were intended. Tenth, Teleological Theories remind of the importance of *evaluating, correcting, and improving policy* to reach the policy goals. In conclusion, policy change within a complex institution, such as a university or university system, may take a great deal of time, preparation, determination, and inclusivity. By highlighting some of the author's institutional change praxis, this article demonstrated tactics for preparing a campaign to improve work/life policy in higher education, with the goal of social justice.

A case study of a process for creating paid parental leave in an academic institution is applicable to faculty, staff, and students interested in making work/life policy changes at their institutions of higher education. While this chapter focused on affecting change related to work/life policies, Gerten (2011) argues for policies to go beyond gender and parental status; "career-friendly policies" that support all faculty are needed. After all, Solomon

(2010) concludes that childless faculty and fathers also experience work/life conflict.

ACKNOWLEDGMENT

Partial support for this work was provided by the National Science Foundation's ADVANCE IT Program under Award HRD-1007978. Any opinions, findings, and conclusions or recommendations expressed in this material are those of the author(s) and do not necessarily reflect the views of the National Science Foundation.

Thanks to Anna Greta Hrafnsdottir for her research assistance, which was made possible by the Beatrice Ruth Burgess Center for WV Families and Communities. Thanks also to Rachel Stoiko for her research assistance. Thanks to the wonderful people at WVU, Melissa Latimer, Kasi Jackson, and C. B. Wilson, for their helpful comments.

REFERENCES

Anderes, Thomas. 1999. "Using Peer Institutions in Financial and Budgetary Analyses." *New Directions for Higher Education* 107:117–23.

Alkadry, Mohamad G., and Leslie E. Tower. 2013. *Women and Public Service: Barriers, Challenges, and Opportunities.* Armonk, NY: M.E. Sharpe.

Armenti, Carmen. 2004. "May Babies and Posttenure Babies: Maternal Decisions of Women Professors." *The Review of Higher Education* 27:211–31.

Barrett, Lucinda, and Peter Barrett. 2011. "Women and Academic Workloads: Career Slow Lane or Cul-De-Sac?" *Higher Education* 61:141–55.

Benneworth, Paul, and Ben W. Jongbloed. 2010. "Who Matters to Universities? A Stakeholder Perspective on Humanities, Arts and Social Sciences Valorization." *Higher Education* 59:567–88.

Betts, Kristen S., and Bernadine Sikorski. 2008. "Financial Bottom Line: Estimating the Cost of Faculty/Adjunct Turnover and Attrition for Online Programs." *Online Journal of Distance Learning Administration* 11.

Bird, Sharon, Jacquelyn Litt, and Yong Wang. 2004. "Creating Status of Women Reports: Institutional Housekeeping as 'Women's Work.'" *NWSA Journal* 16:194–206.

Blair-Loy, Mary, and Amy S. Wharton. 2002. "Employees' Use of Family-Responsive Policies and the Workplace Social Context." *Social Forces* 80:813–45.

———. 2004. "Mothers in Finance: Surviving and Thriving." *Annals of the American Academy of Political and Social Science* 596:151–70.

Blau, David M. 2003. "Child Care Subsidy Programs." Pp. 443–516 in *Means-Tested Transfer Programs in the United States*, edited by R. A. Moffitt. Chicago: University of Chicago Press.

Bristol, Mirar N., Stephanie Abbuhl, Anne R. Cappola, and Seema S. Sonnad. 2008. "Work-Life Policies for Faculty at the Top Ten Medical Schools." *Journal of Women's Health* 17:1311–20.

Burrows, Joanne. 1999. "Going Beyond Labels: A Framework for Profiling Institutional Stakeholders." *Contemporary Education* 70:5–10.

Callister, Rhonda R. 2006. "The Impact of Gender and Department Climate on Job Satisfaction and Intentions to Quit for Faculty in Science and Engineering Fields." *Journal of Technology Transfer* 31:367–75.

Center for Work Life Law. 2012. "Effective policies and programs for retention and advancement of women in academia." http://worklifelaw.org/wp-content/uploads/2013/01/Effective-Policies-and-Programs-for-Retention-and-Advancement-of-Women-in-Academia.pdf

Child, John. 2005. *Organization: Contemporary Principles and Practice*. Hoboken, NJ: Wiley-Blackwell.

COACHE. 2008. "Membership Benefits." (http://isites.harvard.edu/icb/icb.do?keyword=coacheand tabgroupid=icb.tabgroup100716).

DeBeauvoir, Simone. 1952/ 1989. *The Second Sex*. New York: Vintage Books.

Family and Medical Leave Act of 1993, 29 U.S.C. §§ 2601–2654.

Frasch, Karie, Mary Ann Mason, Angy Stacy, Marc Goulden, and Carol Hoffman. 2007. "Creating a Family Friendly Department: Chairs and Deans Toolkit." UC Faculty Family Friendly Edge (http://ucfamilyedge.berkeley.edu).

Friedan, Betty. 1963/2001. *The Feminine Mystique*. New York: Norton.

Galambos, Colleen, Catherine N. Dulmus, and John S. Wodarski. 2005. "Principles for Organization Change in Human Service Agencies." *Journal of Human Behavior in the Social Environment* 11:63–78.

Gardner, Susan K. 2013. "Women Faculty Departures from a Striving Institution: Between a Rock and a Hard Place." *Review of Higher Education* 36:349–70.

Geisler, Cheryl, Debbie Kaminski, and Robyn A. Berkley. 2007. "The 13+ Club: An Index for Understanding, Documenting, and Resisting Patterns of Non-Promotion to Full Professor." *NWSA Journal* 19:145–62.

Gerten, Annette M. 2011. "Moving Beyond Family-Friendly Policies for Faculty Mothers." *Affilia* 26:47–57.

Gerstel, Naomi, and Katherine McGonagle. 1999. "Job Leaves and the Limits of the Family and Medical Leave Act." *Work and Occupations* 26:510–34.

Gilgun, Jane F. 1994. "A Case for Case Studies in Social Work Research." *Social Work* 39:371–81.

———. 2010. "Reflexivity and Qualitative Research." *Current Issues in Qualitative Research* 1:1–8.

Hailu, Alemayehu, Damen Haile Mariam, Daniel Fekade, Miliard Derbew, and Amha Mekasha. 2013. "Turn-over Rate of Academic Faculty at the College of Health Sciences, Addis Ababa University: A 20-Year Analysis (1991 to 2011)." *Human Resources for Health* 11:1–12.

Hendel, Darwin D., and Aaron S. Horn. 2008. "The Relationship Between Academic Life Conditions and Perceived Sources of Faculty Stress Over Time." *Journal of Human Behavior in the Social Environment* 17:61–88.

Hollenshead, Carol S., Beth Sullivan, Gilia C. Smith, Louise August, and Susan Hamilton. 2005. "Work/Family Policies in Higher Education: Survey Data and Case Studies of Policy Implementation." *New Directions for Higher Education* 130:41–65.

Jacobs, Jerry A., and Kathleen Gerson. 2004. The Time Divide: Work, Family, and Gender Inequality. Cambridge, MA:Harvard University Press.

Jacobs, Jerry A., and Sarah E. Winslow. 2004. "Overworked Faculty: Job Stresses and Family Demands." Annals of the American Academy of Political and Social Science 596:104–29.

Kezar, Adrianna J. 2001. "Understanding and Facilitating Organizational Change in the 21st Century: Recent Research and Conceptualizations." *ASHE-ERIC Higher Education Report*, 28:1.

Kemp, Susan P., and Ruth Brandwein. 2010. "Feminisms and Social Work in the United States: An Intertwined History." *Affilia* 25:341–64.

Leslie, Lisa M., and Colleen F. Manchester. 2011. "Work-Life Conflict is a Social Issue Not a Women's Issue." *Society for Industrial and Organizational Psychology* 4:414–17.

Marshak, Robert J., and David Grant. 2011. "Creating Change by Changing the Conversation." *Organizational Development Practitioner* 43:2–7.

Mason, Mary Ann, and Marc Goulden. 2004a. "Do Babies Matter (Part II)? Closing the Baby Gap." *Academe* 90:10–15.

———. 2004b. "Marriage and Baby Blues: Redefining Gender Equity in the Academy." *Annals of the American Academy of Political and Social Science* 596:86–103.

Mason, Mary A., Marc Goulden, and Karie Frasch. 2009. "Why Graduate Students Reject the Fast Track." *Academe* 65.

McGuinness, Aims C. 2002. "Reflections on Postsecondary Governance Changes." Education Commission of the States (http://www.ecs.org/clearinghouse/37/76/3776.htm).

Mesmer-Magnus, Jessica R., and Chockalingam Viswesvaran. 2006. "How Family-Friendly Work Environments Affect Work/Family Conflict: A Meta-Analytic Examination." *Journal of Labor Research* 27:565–74.

Misra, Joya, Jennifer H. Lundquist, Elissa Holmes, and Stephanie Agiomavritis. 2011. "The Ivory Ceiling of Service Work." *Academe* 97:2–6.

Modern Language Association of America (MLA). 2009. "Standing Still: The Associate Professor Survey." Report of the Committee on the Status of Women in the Profession. (http://www.mla.org/pdf/cswp_final042909.pdf).

NSF. 2009. "ADVANCE at a Glance." (www.nsf.gov/crssprgm/advance/nides.jsp)/

Parental Work Assignment Procedure (2011) http://wvufaculty.wvu.edu/r/download/98343.

Quinn, Kate, Sheila E. Lange, and Steven G. Olswang. 2004. "Family-Friendly Policies and the Research University." *Academe* 90:32–34.

Ryan, Ann Marie, and Ellen E. Kossex. 2008. "Work-Life Policy Implementation: Breaking Down or Creating Barriers to Inclusiveness?" *Human Resource Management* 47:295–310.

Saltzstein, Alan L., Yuan Ting, and Grace H. Saltzstein. 2001. "Work-Family Balance and Job Satisfaction: The Impact of Family-Friendly Policies on Attitudes of Federal Government Employees." *Public Administration Review* 61: 452–67.

Saulnier, Christine F., and Mary Swignonski. 2006. "As Feminists in the Academy." *Affilia* 21:361–64.

Schloss, Ernest P., Daniel M. Flanagan, Cheryl L. Culler, and Anne L. Wright. 2009. "Some Hidden Costs of Faculty Turnover in Clinical Departments in One Academic Medical Center." *Academic Medicine: Journal of the Association of American Medical Colleges* 84:32–36.

Sima, Celina M. 2003. "The Role and Benefits of the Sabbatical Leave in Faculty Development and Satisfaction." *New Directions for Institutional Research* 105:67–75.

Smith, Gilia C., and Jean A. Waltman. 2006. "Designing and Implementing Family-Friendly Policies in Higher Education." University of Michigan, Center for the Education of Women (http://www.cew.umich.edu/sites/default/files/designing06.pdf).

Solomon, Catherine Richards. 2010. "'The Very Highest Thing is Family': Male Untenured Assistant Professors' Construction of Work and Family." Pp. 233–55 in *Interactions and Intersections of Gendered Bodies at Work, at Home, and at Play*, Vol. 14, *Advances in Gender Research*, edited by V. P. Demos and M. T. Segal. Bingley, UK: Emerald Group Publishing Limited.

Stake, Robert E. 1994. "Case Studies." Pp. 236–47 in *Handbook of Qualitative Research*, edited by N. K. Denzin and Y. S. Lincoln. Thousand Oaks, CA: SAGE.

Terosky, Aimee L., KerryAnn O'Meara, and Corbin M. Campbell. 2014. "Enabling Possibility: Women Associate Professors' Sense of Agency in Career Advancement." *Journal of Diversity in Higher Education* 7:58–76.

Tower, Leslie E., and Lisa M. Dilks. 2014. "Work-Life Satisfaction Policy in ADVANCE Universities: Assessing Levels of Progressiveness." Unpublished Manuscript.

Valcour, P. Monique, and Rosemary Batt. 2003. "Work-Life Integration: Challenges and Organizational Responses." Pp. 310–31 in *It's About Time*, edited by P. Moen. Ithaca, NY: Cornell University Press.

Valian, Virginia. 1998. *Why So Slow? The Advancement of Women*. Cambridge, MA: MIT Press.

Webber, Gretchen, and Christine Williams. 2008. "Mothers in "Good" and "Bad" Part-Time Jobs: Different Problems, Same Results." *Gender and Society* 22:752–77.

Welch, Julie L., Sarah E. Wiehe, Victoria Palmer-Smith, and Mary E. Dankoski. 2011. "Flexibility in Faculty Work-Life Policies at Medical Schools in the Big 10 Conference." *Journal of Women's Health* 20:725–32.

Williams, Joan C. 2010. *Reshaping the Work-Family Debate: Why Men and Class Matter.* Cambridge, MA: Harvard University Press.

Wolfinger, Nicholas H., Marc Goulden, and Mary Ann Mason. 2010. "Alone in the Ivory Tower." Journal of Family Issues 31:1652–70.

Wolfinger, Nicholas H., Mary Ann Mason, and Marc Goulden. 2008. "Problems in the Pipeline: Gender, Marriage, and Fertility in the Ivory Tower." *Journal of Higher Education* 79:388–405.

———. 2009. "Stay in the Game: Gender, Family Formation and Alternative Trajectories in the Academic Life Course." *Social Forces* 87:1591–1621.

Yoest, Charmaine. 2004. "Parental Leave in Academia." Report to the Alfred P. Sloan Foundation and the Bankard. Fund at the University of Virginia, February, 2004. (http://www.faculty.virginia.edu/familyandtenure).

Chapter Nine

Understanding Family and Medical Leave at a Large Public University

Stacey Oliker and Amanda I. Seligman

Understanding the operation of family and medical leave at a large public institution, like the one where we teach, was harder than we expected. Our work on the issue emerged from our personal experiences with childbirth and maternity leave and grew from conversation with others in a network of colleagues at the University of Wisconsin–Milwaukee (UWM), the second research university in the large UW System. We originally had planned to convene a forum on parental leave and advocate for improvements in the university's policy. We encountered administrative obstacles to conducting the forum. So, when a small group of us found ourselves in a meeting with the UWM Provost, who charged us to form a task force on family and medical leave at UWM and report back to her, we agreed to do that first.

Between January of 2008, when we received our initial charge, and September 2010, we studied family and medical leave law at four regulatory levels that apply to our public institution: federal and state laws; administrative policy at the level of the University of Wisconsin system; and policy and practice on our campus. We learned quite a bit about the implementation of the Family and Medical Leave Act (FMLA) policy, what faculty and staff members actually knew about it, and how they experienced it. We immediately discovered much that we had not anticipated. We learned that leave pursuant to childbirth is bound up in a broad and complex set of policies and practices. Because what we thought was "maternity" leave turned out to be a subset of "family and medical leave" governing all of the institution's employees, we found that the treatment of faculty and staff were interrelated, with significant effects on employees' perceptions of the fairness of leave administration. We also discovered that both broad policies and system-wide and campus administrative practices affected how family and medical leaves actually turned out.

University employees who arrive at a moment when they need family or medical leave must navigate complicated rules and practices, often in haste. We learned about them at a more deliberate pace, initially as leave seekers and then over almost two years, as researchers and authors of a long internal report. The task force examined practices explained on the websites of other universities, formed an advisory board, spoke with experts in the field, interviewed the campus staff primarily responsible for administering leaves, conducted an online survey of and interviews with UWM employees, and contacted colleagues working on similar issues at other UW system campuses. Although we spoke to administrators to learn more about leave policies and practices, we conducted our analysis and wrote our report without administrative input. Our final report, which remains publicly available through the UWM provost's website, included forty-five distinct recommendations for improving leave policy at the level of the UW system and improving leave administration by a variety of relevant parties at UWM itself (Kramer et al. 2010).

This chapter recounts what and how we learned and our assessment of the advantages and disadvantages of our approach. We describe the implementation of leave at UWM and our findings on faculty and staff experience and assessment of leave policy. The same complexities that make the opportunities for leave hard for employees to understand also make the creation of change a difficult, onerous, and long-term task. As a consequence, we conclude that reforms to the administration of family and medical leave at UWM, and perhaps other similar institutions, need to take place at multiple levels: policies at the institutional, system, and state government level all must be addressed; the distinctive needs and workloads of faculty and staff must be balanced; and administrative practices also need reform. Finally, we speculatively discuss organizing and advocacy.

LITERATURE REVIEW:
LEAVE AND WORK FLEXIBILITY IN THE ACADEMY

Most of the existing scholarship about family and medical leave at American universities focuses on the experiences of and implications for women faculty members. In 1975, Arlie Hochschild identified the "clockwork of male careers" as creating a time crunch for academic women, wherein the early-career years of intense devotion to work are often also the years of intense maternal investment. Forty years later, the apparent solution to that contradiction is that women with PhDs who are married or mothers of young children are less likely than comparable men to pursue and, when they do, be hired on the tenure track (Mason et al. 2013).

Once they have tenure-track jobs, women, but not men, often forgo marriage and parenting (Mason et al. 2013). When they do marry, women faculty members do considerably more housework and childcare than their male counterparts (Jacobs and Winslow 2004; Suitor et al. 2001). Women scientists who are married with young children are seriously disadvantaged in achieving tenure (Mason 2013). Such disadvantages likely lead to women faculty having fewer children, and fewer than they want, in comparison to their male faculty counterparts. Earnings are lower for women faculty who are parents, as well. Thus, these personal, professional, and economic costs indicate why the issue of making academia more supportive of families and creating a fairer field of competition for women has become a prominent topic of discussion among faculty (Lester and Sallee 2009; Mason et al. 2013).

Today, researchers have easy access to online information on family-related policies at various colleges and universities. We know, for example, that academic institutions increasingly focus human resource efforts and leadership support on "family-friendly" benefits like parental and sick leave, work flexibility, and tenure clock reform (Lester and Sallee 2009). In general, it is elite research universities that have developed the most extensive family supports. In a stratified sample of colleges and universities, the premier research universities were most likely to offer benefits like paid or extended leave, modified duties, reduced appointment, or tenure clock stoppage to faculty members. Most schools fund leaves via sick or disability leave provisions. A quarter of the 255 schools in the sample offered faculty members a maternity leave, separate from sick, disability, or vacation leave (Drago and Davis 2009; Hollenshead et al. 2005). Of the sixty-two schools in the Association of American Universities, more than half provide at least six weeks of some type of paid leave for researchers who are mothers, but far fewer offer paid leave for fathers (Mason et al. 2013). Though some of the schools in the surveys cited leave policies that apply to all employees, we were unable to find data on which of them did or on policies for non-academic university employees.

Despite the availability of leave policies, researchers consistently find that only a small proportion of faculty members actually take leave when they are eligible. Both quantitative and qualitative studies suggest that faculty underutilization of family benefits is driven by the wish to avoid discrimination, as well as their more altruistic concerns about the needs of students and departments (Drago et al. 2006; Hollenshead et al. 2005). Faculty in the sciences and medicine, especially, voice concerns about grants and grant-writing obligations (Lundquist et al. 2012; Mason et al. 2013; Villablanca et al. 2011; Williams and Ceci 2012).

Faculty men, like men in the general population, take leave less often than women do (Armenia and Gerstel 2006; Drago et al. 2006; Klerman et al. 2012; Lundquist et al. 2012; Villablanca et al. 2011). There is a debate, however, about whether leave for faculty men levels the playing field or whether it augments their competitiveness. Even on leave, men divert more time from childcare to scholarship than women on leave do (Lundquist et al. 2012). Though the effect of fathers' as well as mothers' leaves on gender equality is well worth further study, it is difficult to imagine how women with families could compete as equals in academia if their colleagues who are fathers do not share caregiving at home. In addition to making caregiving easier for fathers and changing a culture that is suspicious of caregiving, institutional encouragement of paternal leave taking may provide resources of power, in information and legitimacy, for their partners to draw upon in delegating caregiving to academic men. Such changes could, of course, reduce gender disadvantage but preserve the disadvantage of family-invested faculty, but when more men are giving care, the routes to tenure and promotion are likely to diversify.

None of the research we encountered studied university staff members. We cannot assume, though, that experiences and perspectives among the latter are the same as faculty. But like the national workforce, university staff includes salaried and waged, white- and blue-collar workers. Thus, we use recent nationally representative studies of leave among U.S. employees speculatively here to suggest patterns we might find among university staff members. The 2012 Department of Labor FMLA survey of worksites and employees shows that the most common reason for leave is an employee's illness. Most leaves are less than eleven days and are taken continuously, rather than intermittently (Klerman et al. 2012). Women are one third more likely to take leave than are men, their leaves are longer, and they also more often report they needed but did not take leave. Seventy percent of men who take parental leave take less than eleven days of leave, while only 23 percent of women take such short leaves (Klerman et al. 2012).

The 2012 National Study of Employers found shrinking leave allowances and wage coverage and fewer work-reduction options among employers over the previous seven years, a period of widespread economic instability. Large workplaces and nonprofits, which include universities, tend to have more family-friendly practices than other workplaces. A majority of employers pay at least partially for maternity leave time, but only a quarter pay anything for paternity leave. Paid maternity leaves are generally employer-funded through temporary disability insurance. Employers who offer this insurance usually provide paid sick leave, as well. Workers with partially paid or unpaid leave face economic difficulties and often shorten their leaves (Matos and Galinsky 2012).

In sum, the literature describes FMLA-related policy and practices more clearly for faculty members than for university staff. Compared to forty years ago, when Hochschild examined "the clockwork of male careers" to explain gendered work/family conflict among faculty, there is greater availability of and pay for leave. Yet the constraints of the conventional career are still evident in the academy, in gendered patterns of parental leave use, childbearing, child rearing, domestic work, tenure-track entrance, and particularly for scientists, tenure. And, while we know little about these patterns among academic staff, faculty patterns are similar to those in the U.S. workforce, in general. Still unsettled is whether lengthy desired leaves for care disadvantage (predominantly women) faculty who take them and whether if men took more leave, it would help women in the workplace. The research we report next focuses on a distinctive but common academic setting. We explore leave policy and practices and the experiences and interpretations of both faculty and staff members on one large campus of a public university system.

METHODS

The goal of our research[1] was to learn about FMLA policy and how it was implemented and perceived at UWM. To this end, we used qualitative and quantitative methods of research. Our methods included the study of documents, interviews with people who implemented family and medical leave policy, an online survey of all employees, and a small number of interviews with faculty and staff members who had used or declined leave. The documents we read included official policy statements, both paper and online educational materials produced or distributed by the campus Department of Human Resources, and reports from an equity task force that were previously conducted in the UW System. We also studied documents from other institutions and the federal government that were accessible online. Our interviews with personnel who administered the family and medical leave included the Director of Human Resources, a few HR staff members, the nine personnel representatives (PReps) representing UWM colleges and schools, and a handful of other involved administrators. We also interviewed people involved in previous system-level reports. For interpretation of our findings and recommendations, we drew on knowledge of family change, of organizations (including the academy), and of the dynamics of gender inequality.

To construct the employee survey, we drew on institutional expertise and task force members' informal discussions with staff and faculty about family and medical leave policy. The provost emailed all university employees with a request for participation and a link to the survey, which was administered online. We exceeded the routine requirements of the Institutional Review Board to assure confidence in confidentiality among participants. Respondents indicated whether or not we could use verbatim answers to open-ended questions, without identifying details. Respondents to the survey were able to indicate their willingness to participate in a confidential follow-up interview. To protect the confidentiality of respondents, we intentionally excluded some kinds of information that would have been helpful to our analysis. We do not know respondents' college or department, or their precise rank or position, only their occupational classifications. Lacking funds to conduct more than a few in-person interviews, we emailed "self-interviews" to those who were willing to write out answers to our follow-up questions. The qualitative responses were wider ranging than the survey responses, touching on individuals' rationales, meanings, reactions, consequences, and emotions, and they helped us interpret survey data.

Out of 5,725 survey notifications emailed, 1,111 were returned, an almost 20 percent response rate. This is a respectable proportion of a population for an online survey, but we never expected to generalize our case study findings. Nor could we justify weighting the data statistically, to make it representative of UWM, despite large numbers of responses across occupational categories. Survey researchers tend to bracket the fact that people respond most often to surveys whose topics interest them—either positively or negatively—but we believed we could not ignore this source of self-selection into the sample. The speedy return of surveys suggested that many respondents were indeed interested in the topic. Given our intention to learn about the needs and experiences of people who might ever consider parental leave, this did not trouble us.

Groups of people who were underrepresented in our survey included men (except for leave takers who were faculty and academic staff men) and employees in jobs that did not involve work on computers (for example, custodians and grounds staff). Our analysis here includes three categories of occupation: tenure-track faculty (whether tenured or probationary), permanent academic staff (almost all of them non-teaching professionals, for example, non-teaching scientists), and classified staff (such as office administrators, custodians, groundskeepers, and their supervisors), both union represented and non-represented. We eliminated higher-level administrators and limited-term employees (LTEs, teaching or otherwise) from our sample for this analysis because of their low response rates. LTEs' low response rates may stem from mistaken beliefs that FMLA was one of the many university benefits they were ineligible to claim.

Despite plentiful responses, many survey questions were missing answers, and this meant entire surveys had to be excluded from some quantitative analyses. We imputed missing cases when possible, but the pervasiveness of missing responses across variables often impeded the use of valid predictor variables. Thus, missing data may present a limitation to the reported findings. Since we are not attempting to generalize or argue beyond our data, missing data seems to us less problematic than it would be otherwise.

In the end, our multi-method approach yielded new knowledge we could analyze and integrate. We had a rich variety of survey and interview accounts by employees who used or chose not to use leave, and opinions and suggestions for change from the broader sample. We can identify patterns of experience and belief that might generate policy discussion at UWM and other settings as well. And our extensive qualitative examination of implementation patterns enables new insights in an understudied area of family and medical leave and work flexibility.

IMPLEMENTATION OF LEAVE AT UWM

One of our first questions when we began our work was what rules governed family and medical leave administration at UWM.[2] We learned that there were multiple relevant sets of rules. First, the well-known federal Family and Medical Leave Act establishes the minimum standards to which large employers like UWM must adhere. Second, the Wisconsin Family and Medical Leave Act, which is quite similar to the federal FMLA, also provides for leave. When employees take leave, the university uses whichever relevant provision from federal or Wisconsin FMLA is more generous, but otherwise leaves run concurrently. The University of Wisconsin system also promulgates policies governing leave for personnel. Additionally, UWM makes its own administrative policies and procedures. Finally, UWM faculty governance policies affect the impact of leave on the tenure clock. When we issued our report in 2010, union contracts with classified state employees also governed the rights of represented staff members; but in 2011 the governor and legislature ended unionized representation for state employees.

At UWM, the central actors in family and medical leave are administrators called Personnel Representatives—PReps, for short. PReps are employed by a school, college, or division within UWM, rather than by the Department of Human Resources (HR). In some units, deans and associate deans are also involved in the administration of FMLA requests from employees. When faculty and staff develop a plan for leave, their formal process is supposed to begin with their PRep, dean, or associate dean. The PReps are charged with helping employees file their paperwork. Staff in the Department of Human Resources, for their part, consult with employees and PReps and review and approve leave notices.

The decentralization of the primary expertise in the administration of family and medical leave outside of HR has advantages and disadvantages. The most important advantage almost certainly is that PReps and employees may work together before the need for leave arises. PReps told us with great conviction that housing their expertise in units, rather than centralizing it in HR, enables better provision of services to employees. Because PReps' offices are usually geographically close to the employees they assist, they have the opportunity to develop relationships that facilitate the application for leave at delicate times in employees' lives. Additionally, because leave is implemented with the help of administrators rather than departments, untenured faculty members do not have to request advice from colleagues who will later vote on their tenure applications. In practice, faculty members often begin to develop their plan for leave by consulting with colleagues or their chair, but they are permitted to bypass their departments.

The decentralized approach to leave administration also offers disadvantages that differentiate administrators' ability to serve faculty and staff. Because PReps serve multiple functions for their units, they bring varied expertise and interest in leave issues to their work. They also have different amounts of time available to work on leave issues. Additionally, because the units vary considerably in size, PReps gain different levels of experience working with leave issues. In a large unit, such as the College of Letters and Science, PReps may deal with multiple leave applications in any given week, cultivating expertise in the policy. In a small unit, with many fewer staff and few women on the faculty, years may pass without a leave application. To keep PReps up to date, the Department of Human Resources offers monthly informational meetings for the PReps. Importantly, these meetings also facilitate relationships among the PReps. When we asked PReps what they would do in complicated or unfamiliar leave situations, some said that they would ask the appropriate person in HR, but others indicated that they would ask another PRep. Having variably knowledgeable PReps who take varying routes to information gathering has the potential to create different outcomes for employees with similar needs for leave. Employees' accounts confirmed these discrepancies. HR cannot mandate attendance at its informational meetings, potentially exacerbating differences in PRep familiarity with policy and practices.

As we deliberated on our findings, we wondered whether we should recommend centralization of personnel functions as a route to creating more uniform—and therefore fairer—outcomes across campus. Our interviews with administrators and faculty who negotiated their leaves, however, led us to believe that decentralization offers significant advantages. We discovered that the discretion exercised by PReps and college officials provides them considerable latitude for creativity and sensitive responses to particular situations. The decentralized context allowed for substantive, as well as formal, fairness, for example, in cases that fall outside historical practices, such as recognition of the need for leave to care for a same-sex partner.

Some of the recommendations that we included in our final report were practices already in use in some units and that we believed should be spread across the university. The latitude that compassionate administrators enjoyed in testing the limits of the system functionally enabled UWM to expand the practice of leave giving without undergoing a slow and conflict-ridden change in policy articulation. We argued that with better communication of best practices, these discretionary acts could spread across units and build consensus for formal policy change. Decentralized decision making, we maintained, is the best practice, at least at this early stage of policy development in our university.

The important role of the PReps was not initially apparent to us, despite our collective decades of experience as UWM employees. Like leave seekers, only as we were deep into our investigation did we come to understand that it was PReps who were central to leave administration. This is one reason we recommend below that future leave researchers and advocates conduct a careful study of the implementation process at their institution, rather than attempt another rigorous survey of employee experience. UWM employees who responded to our survey also found a variety of paths to taking leaves—and, we learned, did not always begin with the PReps.

RESPONDENTS' ACCOUNTS

We asked respondents about their reasons for needing leave and their patterns of leave taking in the past five years, how they gathered information about their options, and how they assessed the process and the leave. Over half of our respondents experienced one or more conditions that might have made them eligible for coverage under FMLA. We label this group, to which assignment did not depend on the respondent's knowledge of eligibility for leave, "apparently eligible." We found it useful to examine this group's responses, along with the responses of those who took leave or considered but ultimately declined it.

The findings presented here largely dovetail with what is already known about the use of family and medical leave. Not everyone who is eligible for leave takes it, with more women and staff than men and faculty using the available benefits. In this analysis, we also emphasize the obstacles that leave seekers encountered and how employees' perceptions of disparities in leave-granting practices informed respondents' opinions about treatment of faculty and staff. Here, we summarize respondents' answers to forced-choice survey questions, open-ended survey questions, and a small number of emailed and in-person interviews. In addition to asking about leave, we asked about three possible adaptations of work for FMLA–eligible employees at UWM, which could supplement or substitute for leave. In our term, "leave or adaptation," adaptation refers to two options respondents took: "work reduction," working fewer paid hours, or "reassignment," generally substitute work that could be done at home. The latter option appears to have been available mostly to faculty members. These options, along with stopping the tenure clock, are among the choices referred to as "flexibility" in the literature. We use the phrase "new child" to refer to reasons for leave involving birth, adoption, or fosterage.

Finding Information

By far, the most common complaint we heard from respondents was related to gathering knowledge about their choices for leave or related options. Among those who took leave or other options, when they ranked themselves on a five-point scale of how well informed they were about options before deciding what to do, 31 percent ranked themselves low (1 or 2). Forty-six percent of respondents who had *not* taken leave (but were apparently eligible or who considered themselves eligible) also ranked themselves as less knowledgeable about options.

Most respondents in our sample sought to remedy the gaps in their knowledge by consulting several different sources of information. According to forced-choice questions about sources, employees consulted chairs or supervisors, colleagues, unit personnel representatives (PReps), the HR website, and HR staff, in that order of frequency. Respondents ranked the helpfulness of their main sources of information similarly—with a mean of 3.4 out of 5 points—though fewer than half of respondents ranked chairs and supervisors as very helpful. Among the small number of faculty respondents who consulted deans and associate deans, a majority ranked associate deans very helpful. Respondents ranked deans as less helpful than associate deans.

In open-ended answers, respondents most often described confusion about relevant information and inaccuracy in information provided to them about their leave options. Some respondents were stymied by a seemingly impenetrable organizational structure: "I didn't even know which questions to ask to find out all the possibilities." Others experienced the hazards of decentralized expertise: "The [business manager] in our dep[artmen]t gave me conflicting information [from] what the division [personnel] rep provided. That was all worked out, but it was confusing, frustrating and scary." Another respondent, perhaps learning about options from our survey, wrote, "HR reps [and] the PRep were not forthcoming about options—reassignment, workload reduction, intermittent leave, etc., were NEVER mentioned." A third explained, "College personnel rep kept referring me to HR who kept referring me to the [college] personnel rep. When I finally got some answers, most turned out to be wrong." Administrative personnel apparently misunderstood union-negotiated benefits: "[I] had to show the rep that the collective bargaining agreement allowed a member to take up to six months unpaid leave for child birth—she first stated that the 6 month leave was not an option." Some respondents praised their PReps or other sources of information, especially colleagues, but both average ratings and as many as half of respondents, depending on the interview or survey question or the respondent subgroup, indicated unsettling confusion and dissatisfaction with information on leave options.

Likelihood of Taking Leave or Adaptation for any FMLA-Qualified Reason

The survey asked about eligibility or leave in the five years before the survey. Among those who were *apparently FMLA-eligible*, 57 percent took leave (or work reduction or reassignment). Sixty-nine percent of those who had a new child took leave, 59 percent of those who had a serious illness that impeded work did, and 30 percent of those whose child or close kin needed care also did. When they were apparently FMLA-eligible for leave, 37 percent of men and 59 percent of women took leave, but this difference mostly stems from gender differences in leave taking for a new child.

Among those apparently eligible for leave, and controlling for age, occupation, and gender, those welcoming a child were far more likely to take leave than those who were caring for an adult or child (p < .006). Likewise, those respondents needing leave for their own illness were more likely to take leave than were caregivers (p < .001, p < .01). Controlling for age, gender, and reason for apparent eligibility, union-represented classified staff were over three times more likely than faculty to take leave, and unclassified staff (nonteaching professionals, not administrators) were two and a half times more likely than faculty to take leave (p < .000, p < .002). Eighty percent of those who took an FMLA-related option chose leave of absence. Few chose other adaptations: 14 percent took reduction in hours, 4 percent received work reassignment, and some combined two options.

In addition to asking about apparent eligibility, we also asked whether respondents considered themselves eligible but did *not* take leave or adaptation. With above mentioned controls in place, faculty members, men, and those whose need did not involve a new child were more likely to decide against leave after considering it (p < .02, p < .003, p < .006). Represented classified staff members were least likely to opt out of leave, once they considered taking it (p < .002). We asked those who considered but decided against leave to indicate all the reasons for their decision, choosing from a lengthy list of possible explanations. Four reasons predominated: "it would negatively affect my job/work" (50 percent); "I could not afford the unpaid part of the leave" (49 percent); "I did not know enough about my eligibility" (32 percent); and "I did not want it" (21 percent). Far fewer chose answers like "people in my department or unit [or 'of my gender'] do not take leave," "I would have had to take the whole semester off," or ". . .was not approved."

Faculty and staff reported similarly. Men were more likely than women to answer that they did not want leave, but small cell sizes rule out a significance test.

Respondents elaborated on reasons for choosing against leave in open-ended questions. The most common answer about not taking leave was that the employee managed to use short-term sick leave alone to accommodate needs, without bothering to file FMLA paperwork. Classified staff members also voiced concerns about job security and supervisors' resentment, writing "retaliation by management to other workers was observed" and "in this economy, who is going to jeopardize their position and ask for time off?" Unclassified staff more often invoked harm to the work unit, for example, "I believed . . . my department would only receive a 75 percent position in future budget years." Faculty members, for their part, worried about missing time from their courses or, if they took a full semester of leave to keep courses stable, the amount of income they would forgo, since they would be paid and accrue benefits for only part of the semester. (For both faculty and staff, policies often limit the amount of paid leave that can be used.) Though faculty members recalled their tenure concerns or department disapproval in open-ended questions, only a few offered this as a specific reason for not taking leave, explaining, "I was pre-tenure then," and "I did not choose to take leave because I wanted to be in good standing." The literature suggests that in-depth interviews are more likely than surveys to elicit these reasons (Drago et al. 2006; Mason 2013).

Likelihood of Taking Parental Leave When Eligible

Logistic regressions with controls in place for age and occupation show that among those who had welcomed a new child in the past five years, women were four and a half times more likely than men to take leave ($p = .000$). Again, gender differences in leave taking lie here, not in other FMLA-related reasons for leave. Among women, parental leave taking did not differ by occupation, but male faculty appeared less likely than men in other university jobs to take leave when a new child arrived (small cell sizes for men rule out significance testing). Among faculty, women were about twice as likely as men to take leave for a new child ($p < .01$).

Continuous or Intermittent Leave and Proportion Paid

In our open-ended questions, as in other studies, supervisors complained most about effective operations when employees whose FMLA-relevant conditions call for intermittent leave (for example, for a recurring health condition). Most leaves by our respondents (as among U.S. employees) were continuous rather than intermittent (cf. Klerman et al. 2012). Having a new child most often entails continuous leave (p < .008); leaves for one's own illnesses also tend to be continuous (but the numbers are small). Across jobs, but especially among classified staff, employees complained about the frequent documentation required for and during leave. People with ongoing or chronic illnesses resented the time and expense required for frequent doctors' updates. Among those who took leave, men appear to be eight times as likely as women to have their leaves fully paid, rather than partially paid (but cell sizes are small). We lack data on length of leave, but national data suggests that this gender difference may be driven by men's shorter leaves for a new child or care for another family member (Klerman et al. 2012). Since the UW system provides cumulative sick leave, few leaves were completely unpaid. Only 9 percent of leaves were completely unpaid (this group was disproportionally faculty); faculty leaves tended to be fully paid, staff leaves fully or partially paid.

Satisfaction with Leave and Adaptations

Respondents who took leave were generally quite satisfied with leaves, but many were also critical of their options and the process of securing leave. Survey questions registered high satisfaction: on a five-point scale, the mean satisfaction score was four, and there were no statistically significant differences in satisfaction among various groups. In open-ended questions, the same respondents who described positive experiences tend also to list negative ones. For example, a faculty member offered both: "It was all very easy and smooth," and "I was given different/incorrect information from different people." A classified staff member greatly benefitted from her leave, but added, "The only negative experience . . . was what I felt was harassment from a supervisor upon returning to work."

Classified and academic staff members submitted more open-ended accounts than faculty members did and many described negative experiences. Classified staff especially emphasized problems with supervisors' disapproval or unhelpfulness: "I was told by my department chair I wasn't eligible for a leave. I was also told that I shouldn't receive a contract for the time I would be on leave . . . something to the effect of 'Why should we pay you if you aren't going to be here?'" Another respondent wrote, "I felt a great deal of fear about my future and whether I would indeed have a job at the end of the process." Among occupational groups, classified staff more often described financial harm as a result of leave, probably because their lower-paying jobs left them more vulnerable in periods of unpaid leave and benefits.

Staff members who worked alongside faculty members were also aware that their own FMLA-related needs were handled more bureaucratically than were those of faculty members, who often negotiated the terms of accommodation with associate deans or deans, frequently with the support of chairs: "I think faculty are offered options that are not available to other employees . . . and that this 'classist' treatment is unfair." Faculty members sometimes secured leave arrangements only for their teaching, and they were paid to continue research and service while on leave. Faculty members' success in such negotiations depended very much on their college or having department personnel who were supportive of family leave. So some faculty members joined staff in expressing resentment about uniformity across occupational positions.

Faculty and academic staff were often dissatisfied with a lack of "transparency" in the process. The term usually indicated a lack of uniformity in support and options across units and employees' sense that they lacked knowledge of others' negotiated arrangements: "because faculty negotiate separately with their deans, I had the sense that I had to figure out how to strengthen my negotiating position." Sometimes, transparency referred to recurrent but unacknowledged disadvantages for faculty and academic staff members who used leave or other supports. One faculty member who described leave as an "incredibly positive experience," continued with, "I have seen friends and colleagues be very uncertain about the arrangements available, and while several have ended up with an acceptable solution, there is no doubt that the overall impression is that the system is neither transparent nor inherently structured in a way that supports the mother." Another emphasized, "transparency of the process is crucial as is institutional awareness that no stigma or hidden penalties be associated with such decisions on the part of employees."

A few faculty members, however, acknowledged concerns about uniformity, while suggesting that uniformity in administration, at this time, might reduce offerings to their lowest common denominator: "There very much needs to be a procedure for this, but I am concerned that if a specific procedure is put in place it will be more restrictive than the current 'haphazard' methods of managing maternity leave."

Several faculty members expressed dissatisfaction with using sick leave for parental leave, arguing that paid parental or care leave should be separate from sick leave. One reason for dissatisfaction was that using paid sick leave for family leave depletes access to necessary time for illness and, when sick leave is unpaid, wages. As one respondent told us, "The options appear to be very limited for paid leave. . . . The solution of using all of your paid sick leave is very short-sighted, as once you come back to work it is likely that you will have a sick child every once in a while, but won't have any sick leave." Pre-tenured faculty and staff who had not had much time to accumulate sick leave faced consequences that separate paid parental leave could remedy.

In addition, faculty members were most likely to frame paid parental leave, separate from sick leave, as an issue of gender equity. In the UW system, accumulated unused sick days are very valuable, as they can be used to subsidize health care in retirement. Recognizing the long-term effects of using up sick leave for maternity, one respondent wrote, "It is also difficult to swallow that women need to use this sick time while men generally choose not to, which means at retirement time, men are more fully covered by health insurance than are women who had children." Another respondent pointedly told us, "I think it is a disgrace that women are deemed 'sick' when they take maternity leave."

UWM employees' accounts combined expressions of appreciation for leave and the people and processes that generated them with criticisms of the limits of leave policy and unfairness in implementing it. This pressed us toward recommendations for extending and elaborating policy to enable employees to be productive workers and to enable women, who continue to be primarily responsible for caregiving, to gain economic equality (both short- and long-term) and to compete with men in the workplace. Once we began to think about the implications of our findings for advocacy on behalf of family-friendly workplace policy, we had to take account of the different positions of privilege from which members of the organization viewed leave, where faculty are advantaged over staff and men's opting out of leave privileges them in the long run.

RECOMMENDATIONS, IMPACT, AND THOUGHTS ABOUT ADVOCACY

After issuing our report, with its many recommendations, to the provost, the university community, and system-wide, we assessed our impact and considered effective forms of advocacy.

Task Force Recommendations

Having learned that both policy and procedures affected how employees experienced leave, we organized our recommendations to *address various levels of UWM and UW system authority*, advocating policy knowledge and innovation and *building a campus culture that supports family and medical leave*. The detailed list of recommendations is available in the report. Here, we include those that may be useful to other advocates, especially those in public universities. When we began our work, we believed that the main thrust of our recommendations would be about changing policies that led to unfair practices. After two years of research in our institution, we learned that we needed also to *pay attention to practices of implementation*, as well as the staff charged with that task. Further, as discussed above, we discovered the need to *consider discrepancies between faculty and staff experiences* in a state benefits system, even though this substantially complicates creating fair policies. Our recommendations in this section and the next one include best practices now appearing repeatedly in the literature cited above such as automatic but revocable tenure stoppage, and others specific to our kind of institution. For example, for most public universities that are part of state systems, only state law, prompted by system-level advocacy, will produce a distinct paid parental leave policy that is separate from sick and vacation leave coverage. The nationwide climate of suspicion of public workers makes this demand worth registering, though unlikely to be addressed in the foreseeable future.

At the campus level, we recommended that administrators and faculty members *publicize creative practices* pioneered by deans, PReps, and departments, in order to expand knowledge of innovation and build widespread consensus for supportive leave policies. To establish legitimacy, this process should *start with support at the highest level of administration.* We also recommended *using a principle of substantive fairness* in decision making; for example, in cases involving leave for employees who are providing primary care in family or family-like relationships that are not currently recognized by state law. Another example is tying adaptations involving pay for work at home to work description, rather than reserving it for faculty. Specific positions or tasks might permit some clerical or technical work at home when they do not require close supervision or working with others. Though many of our respondents asked for consistent policies across units, we argued that rigorous systematization, at this early stage of policy development, would routinize insufficient practices. We suggested that we could craft better policy with some *flexibility for innovating, modeling, refining, and publicizing practices.* Then, dissemination of refined practices may be useful to colleagues at other institutions, as well.

Several of our recommendations addressed the financial implications of leave for faculty and departments. As a stopgap measure for faculty when winning paid parental leave for state workers is unlikely, we recommended that the system *permit semester-long use of available sick leave after the arrival of a child to release faculty from teaching responsibilities,* in order to assure stable courses for students. Also, we recommended *university-level funding of departments' expenses for adjunct faculty* who replace faculty members on leave, so that remaining faculty are not overburdened. We recommended *funding for replacing classified staff members taking leave,* using a pool of variously skilled replacement workers or reimbursing departments who can "lend" skilled staff as replacements. Such measures would reduce the burden on remaining employees when their coworkers take leave, reduce requests made to employees while on leave, and ease the amount of catch-up work required when employees return to the workplace.

Assessing Impact and Considering Advocacy

Though the provost welcomed our recommendations, realizing most of them will require active and persistent advocacy by faculty and staff. As we assess our impact and consider strategies for change, we frame them using our own case, rather than provide a list of general recommendations for readers, as a way of acknowledging the hypothesis-generating results of case study. We address three available avenues of influence: administrative initiatives, research, and "grassroots" or interest-group advocacy, inviting readers to consider what might best inform their organizing strategies, especially in large public university settings.

The impact of our task force's work on the campus has been modest. Our campus-wide survey and later our report briefly raised awareness of family leave policy on campus. Our colleagues on faculty and staff thanked us. Colleagues who find our report online occasionally seek us out for informal advice before they notify their PReps and departments. The provost circulated our report campus-wide and invited us to present our findings to deans. The Department of Human Resources now includes an online FMLA "Toolkit" that provides formal guidance about federal and state policies and a flowchart for how employees can file a leave notice. Our recommendations directly informed the chancellor's marquee "Best Place to Work" Initiative's recommendations and the provost agreed to hire an ombudsperson.

The new "Best Place" administrative initiative at UWM holds the promise of institutionalizing the formulation, enactment, and monitoring of family-friendly policy change. Though it is too soon to assess their impact, we observe that the committee operates in the absence of a grassroots effort of the kind that we had hoped to spark. Our own administrative task force experience suggests that regardless of composition, there may be limits to the effectiveness of administrative initiatives that substitute for, rather than complement interest-group advocacy. Advocates should *recognize that structurally, the accountability of administrative initiatives flows upward.* Responsiveness to faculty and staff stakeholders is diffused through individual contacts with them. Organized grassroots advocacy, however, might galvanize and focus responsiveness more dependably, and it can better adapt to the opening and closing of windows of opportunity for policy.

Our project began with our interest in advocacy and support for family-friendly policies among faculty and staff. But the lengthy research we undertook, as an unfunded administrative task force, drained our energies for organizing. Moreover, our report coincided with a series of recessionary cutbacks and a statewide, then nationwide, backlash against public workers. The possibilities for successful organizing, advocacy, and policy making evaporated. We think advocacy and organizing are likely to be essential, though, so we speculatively add further recommendations.

Our findings converge with a fast-growing body of research-based knowledge on family-related policy in colleges and universities. So, if we were beginning now, we would not want to strive for the legitimacy conferred by rigorous research on the experiences of faculty and staff at our university. Instead we would amplify existing knowledge by generating employee accounts through focus groups and public forums—our original plan, before we were recruited as a provost's task force. We would *focus research on understanding policies and explaining patterns and variations in their implementation.* So, we would again interview PReps and HR personnel, whose knowledge of formal benefit implementation and informal practices undergird our independent organizational assessment. This knowledge is essential for achieving effective local change. We would *study the particularities of policy and policy making in our institution and our state university system,* and through early contact *with others working on the issue in other public systems, learn from and disseminate best practices.* In systems where benefits apply to all schools, *alliances with others at the premier state research institutions* may be especially fruitful, since, in general, this tier already offers the most supportive family-work policies (Drago and Davis 2009; Hollenshead et al. 2005). Elite state schools, which pay faculty less than private peers, may be well disposed toward policies that make them more competitive in recruitment. The tack of collaborating with the elite state school to meet standards of its private peers could facilitate new policy and practices for others in the system. In state systems, where many policies apply to all employees, we would *attend to both converging and distinct interests of faculty and staff in research and organizing,* as well. The recent history of unsuccessful attempts to organize faculty members, even amid the backlash against public workers, suggests the difficulty of prospective organizing efforts. Yet, even when thoroughgoing policy change may be difficult to achieve, social media promise to lower the transaction costs of communication and organizing, especially in university contexts. It may be possible to calibrate strategies of education and mobilization and to quickly take advantage of opening policy opportunities. Continuing cultural change in ideals of involved fatherhood and egalitarian marriage may make widespread workplace mobilization more plausible than ever, even if the actual domestic division of labor is still changing slowly (Gerson 2002; Lundquist et al. 2012; see Solomon 2010, 2014).

Reform in this arena requires understanding how "the devil is in the details" (Frasch et al. 2009). Reforming formal policy is one thing; addressing cultural change and unintended consequences are two others. Our task force analyzed how practices that privilege faculty in substantively fair leave negotiations might translate into general employment practices that extend leave adaptations to other employees. For example, the "sunk" and replacement costs of personnel, the amount of necessary face-to-face time with others at work, and the amount of close supervision required all affect how much work an employee who is eligible for leave can accomplish successfully at home, thereby extending leave time. Using substantively fair criteria also extends the possibilities for wage replacement, work reduction, and reassignment. Such reasoning makes for good policy and also shapes the possibilities of successful organizing in a workplace where one's position shapes one's ideas about change.

At UWM the bedeviled details are the arenas of action that begin in the department (actually, in family patterns) and ascend. Understanding the system, which was our goal, is only the first part of the task for improving family and medical leave implementation at the university. The next step for advocates would be to craft a nuanced proposal for change in multiple arenas, with a realistic eye toward the opportunities and obstacles present in a state system with multiple levels of policy authority. Then, we would circulate the proposal beyond local policy circles, revise, and begin the hard part: organizing for change.

NOTES

We gratefully acknowledge Kate Kramer, the third member of the Provost's Task Force on Family Leave; Terry Batson and Nancy Mathiowetz, for advice on survey construction and data analysis for the original report; and Matthew McCarthy, for data analysis for this paper. We thank Erin Anderson and Catherine Richards Solomon for fine editing.

1. Our research does not examine how the end of the union's recognition might have affected family and medical leave issues for classified staff. Regrettably, we also could not extend our research to graduate students.

2. When we began our work, department executive committees were routinely expected to confirm leave requests made under FMLA. The University of Wisconsin system has a strong faculty governance tradition in which executive committees possess authority over personnel decisions. This practice, however, has reportedly been discontinued since the release of our report.

REFERENCES

Armenia, Amy, and Naomi Gerstel. 2006. "Family Leaves, the FMLA and Gender Neutrality: The Intersection of Race and Gender." *Social Science Research* 35:871–91.

Drago, Robert, Carol L. Colbeck, Kai D. Stauffer, Amy Pirretti, Kurt Burkum, Jennifer Fazioli, Gabriela Lazzaro, and Tara Habasevich. 2006. "The Avoidance of Bias Against Caregiving: The Case of Academic Faculty." *American Behavioral Scientist* 49:1222–47.

Drago, Robert, and Kelly Davis. April 14, 2009. "Parental Leave and Modified Duties Policies across the Big Ten." Retrieved July 9, 2013 (http://wiseli.engr.wisc.edu/uwpgms/Big10parentalleavefinal.pdf).

Frasch, Karie, Angelica Stacy, Mary Ann Mason, Sharon Page-Medrich, and Marc Goulden. 2009. "Creating Family-Friendly Departments for Faculty at the University of California." Pp. 88–104 in *Establishing the Family Friendly Campus,* edited by Jamie Lester and Margaret Sallee. Sterling, VA: Stylus.

Gerson, Kathleen. 2002. "Moral Dilemmas, Moral Strategies, and the Transformation of Gender: Lessons from Two Generations of Work and Family Change." *Gender and Society* 16:8-28.

Hochschild, Arlie Russell. 1975. "Inside the Clockwork of Male Careers." Pp. 47–80 in *Women and the Power to Change*, edited by F. Howe. New York: McGraw-Hill.

Hollenshead, Carol H., Beth Sullivan, Gilia C. Smithy, Louise August, and Susan Hamilton. 2005. "Work/Family Policies in Higher Education: Survey Data and Case Studies of Policy Implementation." *New Directions for Higher Education* 130:41–65.

Jacobs, Jerry A., and Sarah E. Winslow. 2004. "Overworked Faculty: Job Stresses and Family Demands." *The Annals of the American Academy of Political and Social Science* 596:104–29.

Klerman, Jacob, Kelley Daley, and Alyssa Pozniak. 2012. *Family and Medical Leave in 2012: Technical Report for the U.S. Dept. of Labor.* Cambridge, MA: Abt Associates. Retrieved May 16, 2013 (http://www.dol.gov/asp/evaluation/fmla/FMLATechnicalReport.pdf).

Kramer, Kate, Stacey J. Oliker, and Amanda I. Seligman. 2010. *Provost's Task Force on Family Leave: Report on Policy and Practice.* http://www4.uwm.edu/acad_aff/climate/fmla/fmla_report.pdf.

Lester, Jaime, and Margaret Sallee, eds. 2009. *Establishing The Family-Friendly Campus: Models for Effective Practice.* Sterling, VA: Stylus.

Lundquist, Jennifer H., Joya Misra, and KerryAnn O'Meara. 2012. "Parental Leave Usage by Fathers and Mothers at an American University." *Fathering* 10:337–63.

Mason, Mary Ann, Nicholas H. Wolfinger, and Marc Goulden. 2013. *Do Babies Matter: Gender and Family in the Ivory Tower.* New Brunswick, NJ and London: Rutgers University Press.

Matos, Kenneth, and Ellen Galinsky. 2012. *2012 National Study of Employers.* New York: Families and Work Institute. Retrieved May 16, 2013 (http://familiesandwork.org/site/research/reports/NSE_2012.pdf).

Misra, Joya, Jennifer H. Lundquist, and Abby Templer. 2012. "Gender, Work Time, and Care Responsibilities among Faculty." *Sociological Forum* 27:300–23.

Solomon, Catherine Richards. 2014. "'I Feel Like a Rock Star': Fatherhood for Stay-at-Home Fathers." *Fathering* 12:52–70.

———. 2010. "'The Very Highest Thing is Family': Male Untenured Assistant Professors' Construction of Work and Family." Pp. 233–55 in *Interactions and Intersections of Gendered Bodies at Work, at Home, and at Play*, Vol. 14, *Advances in Gender Research*, edited by V. P. Demos and M. T. Segal. Bingley, UK: Emerald Group Publishing Limited.

Suitor, J. J., Dorothy Mecom, and Ilana S. Feld. 2001. "Gender, Household Labor, and Scholarly Productivity among University Professors." *Gender Issues* 19:50–67.

Villablanca, Amparo C., Laurel Beckett, Jasmine Nettiksimmons, and Lydia P. Howell. 2011. "Career Flexibility and Family-Friendly Policies: An NIH-Funded Study to Enhance Women's Careers in Biomedical Sciences." *Journal of Women's Health* 20:1485–96.

Williams, Wendy M., and Stephen J. Ceci. 2012. "When Scientists Choose Motherhood." *American Scientist.* Retrieved June 3, 2013 (http://www.americanscientist.org/issues/id.14801,y.0,no.,content.true,page.1,css.print/issue.aspx).

Chapter Ten

Life Happens

The Vilas Life Cycle Professorship Program at the University of Wisconsin-Madison

Jennifer Sheridan, Christine Maidl Pribbenow, Molly Carnes, Jo Handelsman, and Amy Wendt

Life as a faculty member can be all-consuming. Teaching, research, service; advising and consulting; conferences and research travel; papers, books, and grants; reviewing and editing—all of these activities require a tremendous amount of time. On average, faculty members work fifty-five to fifty-seven hours each week, with little difference in the average number of hours worked by faculty rank (Jacobs and Winslow 2004; Savoy and Sheridan 2011; Sheridan and Winchell 2003; Sheridan and Winchell 2006; Shollen et al. 2009). Thus, full-time faculty members work many more hours than the typical forty-hour "full-time" workweek and they maintain this grueling pace for decades, staying in the professoriate for twenty or more years (WISELI 2006).

Despite the high time demands of this profession, most faculty members do manage to have personal lives. They may find partners, have children, care for aging parents, get divorced, and manage their own and others' health issues. Often, faculty members are the "responsible" ones in their families and, in addition to caring for their own immediate family, often manage care for adult siblings, aunts and uncles, nieces and nephews. In a past era when most faculty members were male, heterosexual, and married, they relied on the unpaid labor of their wives for much of this caregiving. For such faculty members, only their own health might have interfered with their all-consuming job. Now, however, given broad societal changes in families and in the workplace, faculty are more diverse and are much less likely to have such a helpmate. Faculty, both men and women, are more likely than in the past to have a partner or spouse who works outside the home (Jacobs and Gerson 2004; Moen and Roehling 2005), or to be raising children as a single parent (Jacobs and Gerson 2004). Even in more "traditional" families with a full-time female caregiver at home, the gendered division of labor around care-giving has changed—fathers devote more time to their children (Bianchi et al. 2006; Sandberg and Hofferth 2001; Yeung et al. 2001) and are engaged in the care of aging parents (Mason, Wolfinger, and Goulden 2013; Rossi and Rossi 1990).

Many researchers investigating the culture of academia uncover a silence or even fear around openly acknowledging one's personal life when at work. They report that faculty are often afraid to tell their colleagues about a new baby, parental care issues, or other personal matters. Faculty, for example, will report that they went through a divorce and their colleagues did not find out for years, or that they did not apply for a tenure clock extension because they feared their colleagues would think they were "weak" (Drago et al. 2005; Palepu and Herbert 2002; Pribbenow et al. 2010; Ward and Wolf-Wendel 2004; Ward and Wolf-Wendel 2008) .

What happens when something goes wrong in a faculty member's person-al life? What if she can't be in her laboratory at all hours because she is recently divorced and is suddenly a single parent? The probability of divorce is especially high during the pre-tenure years (Mason, Wolfinger, and Goul-den 2013). What if research projects are delayed because a faculty member must travel overseas at regular intervals to care for an aging parent? Eighteen percent of faculty members report having parental care duties (Sheridan and Winchell 2003). What if he misses a grant deadline because of a heart attack or cancer? Approximately one in seven men report heart disease by age sixty-four and one in twelve women are diagnosed with cancer by age sixty-four (National Center for Health Statistics 2011). What if, in addition to a personal crisis, the faculty member is at a critical career juncture, i.e., going up for tenure, or promotion? How much greater is the negative impact of the personal event when it occurs at such a critical juncture, particularly in the academic environment where discussing such issues is taboo? In this paper, we describe a program implemented at the University of Wisconsin-Madison (UW-Madison) designed to address this problem. Using data obtained from several sources—program evaluation data, institutional data, climate survey data, and data from program applications—we will show the value of the program to all faculty on campus, and the benefits to the university for supporting such an initiative.

VILAS LIFE CYCLE PROFESSORSHIP PROGRAM

Recognizing that "life happens"—that faculty members sometimes experience events in their personal lives that can interfere with their research productivity for a period of time, and that these events can be particularly devastating if they come at a critical career juncture, the UW-Madison implemented a grant program to assist faculty in such times of crisis. With support from the National Science Foundation's ADVANCE Institutional Transformation program (National Science Foundation 2001), a new "Life Cycle Research Grant" program was introduced to Biological and Physical Sciences faculty in 2002. After five years, the funding for the program changed and the program expanded its scope to include faculty in all disciplines at UW-Madison. At that time the program's name changed to the "Vilas Life Cycle Professorship" (VLCP) to reflect this new funding. The VLCP program provides funds to faculty members who are experiencing a life event that interferes with research productivity *and* who are at a critical career juncture in their professional lives; both criteria must be satisfied to be eligible for the grant (WISELI 2009). Annually, the program awards an average of $279,000 in total to twelve faculty members. Individual awards are capped at $30,000, and awards are constrained to last for only one year with no carryover or extensions. Faculty may apply for the award more than once, if a new life event has occurred; however, new applicants are given priority for the funding.

Several ADVANCE institutions have implemented similar programs, usually using a name that includes "transitional support" (e.g., University of Washington (Riskin et al. 2007), Cal Poly Pomona (2010), Utah State University (2004), University of Michigan (2012)). The programs vary in their target population (e.g., women only or both men and women; STEM faculty or all faculty; off-track faculty included or not) and the amount of funds available (some are capped at $5,000 or $10,000; one went as high as $38,000). Some of the programs are exclusively for life cycle events impacting research, and others include additional award criteria such as "increasing retention or promotion of women" or "childcare expenses . . . incurred during fieldwork." Most of these programs have not continued beyond their ADVANCE funding.

The VLCP is one program that obtained institutional support subsequent to the ADVANCE-funded pilot period. It meets the ADVANCE goal of promoting the participation and advancement of women in STEM, because although the program is open to all faculty, women faculty apply for and receive the grants in much greater proportion than their presence in the faculty (Table 10.1). This likely reflects the fact that despite substantial changes in family and work, the responsibility for managing these responsibilities still rests most heavily on women (Drago et al. 2005; Jacobs and

Winslow 2004; Mason, Wolfinger, and Goulden 2013). Faculty from racial-ethnic minority groups also apply for and receive grants in slightly greater proportion to their presence on the faculty. Assistant professors are much more likely than faculty at other ranks to apply for and receive funding. Faculty in the Physical Sciences apply in much lower proportion to their presence on the faculty, while Social Studies and especially Arts and Humanities faculty are more likely to be both applicants and recipients.

The VLCP grant applications are reviewed by a four-person volunteer committee representing each of the four broad disciplinary areas of Biological Sciences (BIO), Physical Sciences (PHY), Social Studies (SOC), and Arts and Humanities (A&H). The applications are reviewed not on the basis of the research proposed, although a research project must be specified because the funds must be applied toward research. Rather, the review committee makes the assumption that all faculty at UW-Madison are doing outstanding and sound research and reviews the applications using two different criteria. First, the applicant must be experiencing a "life event" that is disrupting his or her research progress. A "statement of need" is the basis for this evaluation. Second, the applicant must be at a "critical career juncture" that is placing his or her career at some risk. As part of evaluating the "critical career juncture," the review committee reviews the applicant's curriculum vitae or biosketch and their current and pending grants, including startup fund balances.

The types of "life events" that disrupt a faculty member's research sufficiently to motivate them to apply for this funding typically include: (1) personal health (37.0 percent), (2) parental caregiving (18.8 percent), (3) a child's health (14.4 percent), (4) divorce (10.5 percent), (5) a spouse or partner's health (6.6 percent), and (6) complications from childbirth (3.9 percent)—see Table 10.2. One type of life event has been determined to be ineligible for the award when it occurs in the absence of other factors: childbirth/adoption. When initiated, the program originally included the birth or adoption of a child as an eligible life event, but it soon became clear that this event was actually too normative to be considered for the grants. Compared to the often sudden, unexpected, and traumatic events such as suffering a heart attack or having one's child diagnosed with leukemia, the addition of a child into a family seemed more manageable given other support provided by the university, such as tenure clock extensions. In addition, such cases had the potential to overwhelm the applicant pool. Given the number of applicants experiencing more devastating life events, normative childbirth/adoption was excluded as an eligible life event unless accompanied by significant complications, such as an order of extended bedrest during pregnancy or postpartum depression.

Some applicants described events affecting their research that could not be classified as "life events." Many factors beyond faculty members' control

Table 10.1. Demographic characteristics of VLCP applicants and recipients

Demographic characteristic	Total faculty[a]		Applicants		Recipients	
	Number	*Percent*	*Number*	*Percent*	*Number*	*Percent*
Female	644	29.4%	122	67.4%	88	73.9%
Male	1550	70.6%	59	32.6%	31	26.1%
Racial-ethnic minority[b]	357	16.3%	c	~20%	c	~20%
Racial-ethnic majority[b]	1837	83.7%	c	~80%	c	~80%
Assistant professor	487	22.2%	75	41.4%	52	43.7%
Associate professor	404	18.4%	41	22.7%	25	21.0%
Professor	1304	59.4%	59	32.6%	38	31.9%
Permanent PI/ academic staff[d]	48	N/A	6	3.3%	4	3.4%
Biological sciences (BIO)	715	32.6%	65	35.9%	41	34.5%
Physical sciences (PHY)	495	22.6%	22	12.2%	12	10.1%
Social studies (SOC)	575	26.2%	49	27.1%	39	32.8%
Arts & humanities (A&H)	409	18.6%	45	24.9%	27	22.7%

Source: Data obtained from VLCP applications and institutional data sources.

Note: Total faculty (N = 2194); Applicants (N = 181); Recipients (N = 119). Some percentages may not total 100% due to rounding.

[a] "Total faculty" is the mean annual headcount from 2003-2012.

[b] "Racial-ethnic minority" faculty are those whose ethnic group code is listed as black, Asian, American Indian, Hispanic, or two or more races in university records. "Racial-ethnic majority" faculty are listed as white or have missing data on the race indicator.

[c] Race/ethnicity codes from university human resources data cannot be assigned to individual applicants' records due to confidentiality issues. The percentages reported are approximations based on knowledge of the applicant population and information revealed in the applications.

[d] Academic staff are assigned a divisional affiliation (BIO, PHY, SOC, A&H) based on their research areas.

or related to events in their work life can disrupt research (e.g., a server crash led to loss of data; a fire led to the loss of important research resources; a stint as department chair halted a research program). While such events can indeed harm research productivity at critical career junctures, it is not the intent of this program to provide support in the face of such events and therefore they were excluded from consideration. The VLCP remains a safety net for faculty experiencing problems in their personal lives that affect research productivity; as such, it enables faculty at UW-Madison to better manage their personal and professional lives.

The types of "critical career junctures" considered are varied, as noted in Table 10.3. The most common and obvious is the tenure juncture. Faculty in their third to fifth year on the tenure clock are especially vulnerable when a research setback occurs, and such cases receive priority for funding. Early in the tenure process (years one and two), faculty may have time to get back on track following a life event, especially if they have startup funds available or take a tenure clock extension, for which they would be eligible given the event they are experiencing. Unfortunately, a life crisis occurring later in the process (year six) can sometimes make it impossible to "save" the tenure decision at that point with only a year of funding, and so these cases are not often a priority relative to applicants with two or more years left on their clock. For associate professors, the next career juncture is the promotion to

Table 10.2.   Life events of VLCP applicants and recipients

	Applicants		Recipients	
Event	*Number*	*Percent*	*Number*	*Percent*
Own health	67	37.0%	47	39.5%
Parent health	34	18.8%	19	16.0%
Child health	26	14.4%	20	16.8%
Divorce	19	10.5%	13	10.9%
Partner health	12	6.6%	9	7.6%
Childbirth complications	7	3.9%	6	5.0%
New baby[a]	7	3.9%	2	1.7%
Other	9	5.0%	3	2.5%

Source: Data obtained from VLCP applications.

Note: Applicants (N = 181); Recipients (N = 119). Some percentages may not total 100% due to rounding.

Note: Most applicants indicate only one life event. In the cases where more than one is offered, only the primary event or the first mentioned are included.

[a] The two awarded in this category had multiple life events, with "New baby" being the primary event. Applicants whose only life event was a new baby are not eligible; see text.

full, but surprisingly this is not the "critical career juncture" that most tenured associate professors identify when applying for the award. Instead, they describe a "loss of momentum," or a missed grant deadline that will lead to a layoff or loss of valuable staff, further reducing the chances that future grant applications will be successful; in short, they foresee a negative spiral of events that would occur if not interrupted immediately. For full professors, determining the critical career juncture is less clear, and faculty applicants are expected to articulate what that juncture is and why it is imperative to receive the funding now. For all tenured professors, the critical junctures most often cited are: (1) revive stalled research/regain "momentum" (14.4 percent); (2) finish incomplete project (9.4 percent); (3) reestablish funding/collect preliminary data (8.8 percent); or (4) new research focus (7.2 percent).

Use of Funds

Use of the Vilas Life Cycle Professorship funds are partly constrained by the stipulations of the funding source, the Vilas Trust. Because of the way the trust was originally established in the 1903 will of William F. Vilas, the funds may be used only for "research purposes"—not for faculty salary or to support the teaching mission of the university.[1] Thus, the grants are used most commonly to support people who will assist the faculty applicant in conducting the research—staff, graduate and undergraduate students, and postdoctoral researchers. Including the fringe benefits and tuition associated with the funding of these employees, approximately 75 percent of all the funding distributed through the VLCP program is for personnel expenses. In the Biological Sciences, professional staff members (e.g., lab managers, research specialists) are the most commonly requested resource, while other disciplines more often ask for graduate student support. Funds for supplies are frequently requested in all fields, while the Arts and Humanities faculty more frequently request funds for research-related travel. Arts and Humanities faculty also rely on undergraduate student hourly employees more often than other faculty.

METHODS

The Vilas Life Cycle program has been evaluated each year since its inception. In the first two years, face-to-face interviews were conducted with grant recipients. Beginning in 2005, awardees were asked to complete an email questionnaire regarding their experiences with the program, and to report on their research progress within one year of the end of the receipt of the grant. Approximately 98 percent consented and responded to this request, which

Table 10.3. Critical career junctures of VLCP applicants and recipients

	Applicants		Recipients	
Critical career juncture	*Number*	*Percent*	*Number*	*Percent*
Tenure/promotion to associate	73	40.3%	52	43.7%
Revive stalled research/regain "momentum"	26	14.4%	15	12.6%
Finish incomplete project	17	9.4%	14	11.8%
Reestablish funding/collect preliminary data	16	8.8%	11	9.2%
New research focus	13	7.2%	8	6.7%
Promotion to full	12	6.6%	9	7.6%
Loss of staff	7	3.9%	5	4.2%
Missed grant deadline	5	2.8%	3	2.5%
Not clear	5	2.8%	0	0.0%
Continue work	3	1.7%	0	0.0%
Build new lab	2	1.1%	1	0.8%
Other	2	1.1%	1	0.8%

Source: Data obtained from VLCP applications.
Note: Applicants (N = 181); Recipients (N = 119). Some percentages may not total 100% due to rounding.
Note: Most applicants indicate only one critical career juncture. In the cases where more than one is offered, only the primary juncture or the first mentioned are included.

was approved by UW-Madison's Institutional Review Board for Human Subjects Research.

Recipients responded to questions about how the grant affected them, both personally and professionally:

- To what use did you put the grant funds?
- To what extent did the grant assist you in making significant progress in your research?
- What would you have done if you had not received the grant?
- If your life event negatively influenced your career path, to what extent did the funds help you re-align with that path?
- Were you ever at risk for leaving UW-Madison? If so, to what extent did the funds help you to stay at UW-Madison?
- How is your receipt of this grant perceived by others?

Responses to the interview and survey questions were coded into themes and reported in an annual report that was posted to the program website and distributed to UW-Madison administrators and the Vilas Trustees. Even though a different set of VLCP recipients respond to the evaluation survey each year, response themes have remained consistent throughout the decade in which this program has been administered. The following major benefits of the VLCP are drawn from ten years of evaluation reports.[2] Direct quotes reflecting each of the themes are provided, as is the year in which that grant recipient was surveyed/interviewed. We include multiple quotes from across the decade to show the consistency of these themes.

OUTCOMES

Faculty at UW-Madison value the Vilas Life Cycle Professorship program to a great extent. Not surprisingly, recipients of the grants are enthusiastic about the importance, value, and uniqueness of the program. Words like "lifesaver," "one of a kind," "totally unique," "lifeline," "immensely valuable," "fantastic," and "absolutely essential" repeatedly occur in evaluations of the program. At the same time, faculty who are not recipients of the program also rave about its presence at the UW-Madison. Applications to the program (whether funded or not) will often cite the faculty member's gratefulness that the program exists. Some faculty send unsolicited emails after a call for proposals is announced, thanking the university for supporting such a program. Data from the 2006 *Study of Faculty Worklife at UW-Madison*, a campus-wide faculty climate survey, showed that 96.5 percent of faculty who had heard of the program thought it was valuable; only three[3] of seventeen campus-wide programs related to diversity and work/life management were deemed more valuable (Sheridan and Winchell 2006).

Provided Psychological Support

Many of the faculty who apply for the VLCP report feeling desperate. At a time when they face immense pressure in their personal lives due to a life event, their research suffers and they have the added stress of not performing up to the expectations of their job. At a research-intensive university such as the UW-Madison, faculty members know that their value is measured primarily by their scholarly output—papers, books, grants, performances, artistic displays. Untenured faculty fear the loss of their jobs if that scholarly output is not up to departmental or university standards. Tenured faculty fear they will become "dead weight" in their departments and lose their labs, research programs, and the respect of their peers as a result. Many of the faculty applicants describe their situations as a "downward spiral":

> There are times when it seems very difficult to balance family and research and to try to excel at both. In academics it can be very difficult to catch up

once you have slipped behind. The long term stress of this can become debili-
tating and I was getting close to that point. (2006)

Without this funding, I would have had to let my specialist go (and thereby her
organizational skills and productivity) and drastically reduce the size of our
mouse colony. . . . Loss of these assets would have initiated a powerful downward spiral in my research program. Even if these losses had been for a
relatively short period, the need to train a new person would have been a
substantial drag on productivity and morale. (2011)

Receiving the VLCP funding provides not only a financial boost, but a
psychological one for faculty who receive the grants. Surprisingly, being
chosen to receive the funds was in itself a motivating factor in reviving a
stalled research program:

[The grant] kept my hope up . . . I was desperate. I was desperate because I
knew I was lacking hands to work in the lab, not lacking ideas. But the
situation with my family just totally put everything on hold, I wasn't able to
concentrate enough to do everything. [My daughter] was hospitalized so much
and she needed so much, and we didn't have immediate family around us. . . .
So, the grant actually gave me a little bit of hope that I would keep my
momentum. Otherwise, I think it would be a downhill spiral. At that moment,
the grant pulled me up, so that prevented me from sliding further down in my
career path. I was really afraid I wouldn't be able to make it to tenure, or even
to extend my contract. (2004)

[I felt] an enormously beneficial personal sense that I have the backing and
support of this university during an ongoing period of crisis, rather than being
a faculty member who has been written off as an unproductive loser. (2010)

The positive feedback I received regarding my research and my value to the
UW campus was incredibly important during that time in my tenure process.
This sense of positive acknowledgment—and what it signaled to others—
fueled my drive to succeed. (2012)

Ensured Career Progression

One of the main goals of the VLCP is to assist faculty with their career
progression, as evidenced by the criterion that a recipient must be at a critical
career juncture. Recipients of VLCP awards do report that the awards have
assisted them in their career progression:

My [issue] was related to the fact that I couldn't get things done as fast as I
wanted to and therefore, I was denied full professor. . . . Right now I've got so
many things in the works that I'm hoping that they're going to look at [my
promotion package] differently when I go up. [The grant] really helped this

process . . . I'll probably go up again next spring. (2004, note: this recipient was promoted.)

I think my tenure application was at risk because the pace of my scholarship had slowed down. The combination of this grant and an extension of my tenure clock has made a tremendous difference in my scholarship quantity and quality. I go up for tenure soon. I won't really know how much of a difference they've made until I get tenure (or not). However, I am feeling much better about my prospects. (2006, note: this recipient did achieve tenure.)

The key timing of the VLCP award allowed me to continue at a very critical juncture for me. Without it, I am convinced that I would have endured a personally frustrating and institutionally taxing period, and then have opted for an early retirement. Instead, my laboratory is flourishing today. (2011)

The critical career juncture of the tenure decision is especially positively influenced by the infusion of funding from the VLCP grants. The tracking data from applicants show that this program has been enormously successful in providing the resources that assistant professors in crisis need so that they may go on to achieve tenure. As shown in Table 10.4, a higher percentage of VLCP awardees achieve tenure than is seen in the faculty population more generally, and among VLCP applicants who are not awarded the grants. The grant is less successful in helping faculty get promoted to the full professor rank. Interestingly, far fewer faculty who apply for or receive VLCP grants take on leadership roles in the university, such as department chair, assistant or associate dean, an administrative role at the central university level (e.g., vice provost), or director of a research center. This may be because assistant professors are overrepresented in the VLCP applicant/recipient population (see Table 10.1), and thus they have had less time to mature into these roles.

Other kinds of career progression that occur for tenured faculty, aside from the promotion to full professor, are challenging to objectify and measure. Tenured faculty report a surge of "momentum"—a word that appears frequently in applications and evaluations from VLCP grant recipients, and report getting their research "back on track":

The grant came at a time when I was rearranging my whole life, and so . . . everything contributed to getting things back on track. (2004)

Given the stage in my career, this program was the second most important during my cancer and its aftermath. I say second only because the assistance of my department came at the height of the crisis. This program, however, made it possible for me to regain the momentum of my research. Though there are other grants and professorships offered at the UW, none takes into consideration these circumstances. (2005)

Table 10.4.   Career transition outcomes for UW-Madison faculty, 2003–2012

Outcome	All faculty			Awardees			Not awarded		
	Elig.	*Achieved*	*%*	*Elig.*	*Achieved*	*%*	*Elig.*	*Achieved*	*%*
Tenure/ promote to assoc.	1276	570	44.7	50	26	52.0	22	7	31.8
Promote to full	1027	488	47.5	50	17	34.0	21	9	42.9
Leader role[a]	2478	596	24.1	86	6	7.0	40	5	12.5

Source: Data obtained from institutional data sources.
Note: Academic staff removed. Faculty who applied or were awarded multiple times are removed from analysis.
[a] Only tenured faculty (associate and full professors) are eligible for leadership roles.

> The funds provided me with essential time and momentum. Time, in the sense of offering grant support for my research at a moment in my career when there was enormous stress on my work/life "balance" and I needed to attend to the life/home side. Momentum, in permitting me to hire an excellent doctoral student who completed qualitative data coding and analyses for me on two projects. Rather than being shelved for an extended period, I was able to keep going on both of those studies. (2012)

Faculty also report an ability to embark on new research directions that they would not have been able to accomplish without the support of the VLCP grant:

> During the time I had a PA [Project Assistant] funded by this program, a colleague offered me the opportunity to take on a completely new research project, using a not-yet-released public dataset, and complete with assistance from one of his graduate students. I would never have even considered taking this on were it not for having the Project Assistant supported by the Vilas Award helping me with my primary research agenda during this period. With a semblance of balance restored to my personal/professional life, I agreed to take the new project on. It was a great opportunity to pursue a new line of research that capitalized on my previous research experience while allowing me to explore a new direction for my research program. (2007)

> Surprising to me, the work accomplished during the time of the Vilas Life Cycle laid the foundation of a new theoretical framework to my research that I am now pursuing. (2007)

> This project marked a transition of my research from strictly [scientific method] to an integrated experimental and [scientific method] approach. Had we

failed, it would have proven especially challenging to persuade any funding agency that we are competent experimentalists. (2012)

ENHANCED FACULTY RETENTION

One of the goals of any program designed to improve work/life management in the university is increased faculty retention. The loss of a faculty member is expensive for institutions, both financially (Committee on Maximizing the Potential of Women in Academic Science and Engineering 2007) and in terms of non-fiscal costs such as loss of students or mentors (Williams and Norton 2008). Losing one's position is certainly disruptive to the career of a faculty member who leaves under circumstances related to a lack of productivity. Recipients of VLCP grants report that the receipt of the grant was a determining factor in their decision to stay at the UW-Madison:

> I didn't feel I could make it. So I probably would have started to draw a backup plan and apply [for] a teaching position within a year or so . . . I'm not drawing any backup plan now, because I'm very optimistic. But, if I didn't [get the grant] I probably would have abandoned the research position and go for teaching. (2004)

> Without the extra help made possible by this grant, I would probably have explored possibilities for either an unpaid leave of absence or a move to a job closer to my [family] in [another state]. The latter option was really starting to look like the best thing for me to do at the time, even though it would have almost definitely meant a downward move in my career trajectory. (2007)

> I was at risk for having to leave the university to go on long-term disability, and I believe having this funding helped me to continue making research progress so that I could qualify for tenure at UW-Madison. (2012)

We have analyzed the attrition of faculty members from 2003 through 2012, distinguishing as much as possible between those who left for reasons of retirement or unfortunately death, and those who left for other positions or left at ages younger than fifty-five. Those who "leave" may still be employed at the university, but in a nontenure-track position. As shown in Table 10.5, faculty who receive VLCP grants are slightly less likely to leave, compared to faculty who apply for the grants but are not awarded. Untenured faculty who receive the awards leave at about the same rate as other untenured faculty, while tenured faculty who apply for the VLCP (whether they receive it or not) leave at about half the rate as other tenured faculty. It may be that, due to the life event, they are even more tied to the Madison area than other faculty; more research is needed to explain this difference.

Benefits to the University

Recipients of the VLCP awards not only provide evidence of personal benefits emanating from a VLCP grant, they also articulate a variety of positive
outcomes for the university as a whole for investing in this unique grant
program.

Increased Grant Funding

Many faculty use their VLCP award to position themselves for future grant
funding. Many recipients specifically talk about how the infusion of a small
amount of funding via the VLCP results in dividends for the university in
terms of much higher amounts of outside grants:

> [With other grants] you're competing on a national level on everything, and I
> think that's fair, but you are at a disadvantage because you just don't have the
> time and energy at the same level as perhaps other people and so it just gives

Table 10.5.   Attrition of UW-Madison faculty, 2003–2012

	All faculty			Awardees			Not awarded		
Outcome	N^a	Left UW	%	N	Left UW	%	N	Left UW	%
Retire/death: All ranks	3184	527	16.6	111	5	4.5	54	4	7.4
Retire/death: Untenured[b]	1276	3	0.2	50	0	0.0	22	0	0.0
Retire/death: Tenured[b]	2478	524	21.1	87	5	5.7	39	4	10.3
Leave/off-track: All ranks	3184	488	15.3	111	13	11.7	54	7	13.0
Leave/off-track: Untenured[b]	1276	223	17.5	50	9	18.0	22	5	22.7
Leave/off-track: Tenured[b]	2478	265	10.7	87	4	4.6	39	2	5.1

Source: Data obtained from institutional data sources.
Note: Academic staff removed. Faculty who applied or were awarded multiple times are
removed from analysis.
[a] Ever employed at this rank. Untenured and tenured ranks add up to more than total due
to promotions (i.e., faculty could be counted as both untenured and tenured over the
period 2003–2012, if they received a promotion during that time).
[b] Rank at the time of the retirement/leave outcome, not at the point of entry to the
database.

you that little bit of, little extra money to get things pulled together—have another person, have more reagents, have more [of] whatever you need to have your grant be competitive. I also think it's a good idea because of the investment value. If I get my grant, it's going to pay off for the university several fold over. (2004)

[The Life Cycle grants] are a valuable investment for our university. Relatively small amounts of money can make huge differences at critical times. Funding in the biological sciences is so very competitive at present (~10 percent of grants are funded at NIH) that many research programs are ending. After funding has ended for a significant period and productivity drops, it is very difficult to regain NIH funding. Funding that allows labs to remain active over such periods makes it possible to regain funding. (2006)

The grant provided essential bridge funding. . . . I have since received an NIH R01 and a NARSAD Independent Investigator Grant! If it were not for the VLCP, I may have lost my lab, because I needed the extra support in order to apply for an R01. (2012)

Analysis of grant funding for VLCP applicants and awardees shows that, at the mean, most faculty recipients of the VLCP funding are indeed using the VLCP funds to leverage increased grant funding, three years after their VLCP grants end. Only in the Arts and Humanities is this not the case. VLCP applicants who did not receive an award have a much more difficult time reestablishing their funding (except the Social Studies faculty).

Increased Productivity of Faculty

Helping faculty reinvigorate their research programs is a boon to the university not only because of the increased grant funding, but also because it increases the overall productivity of the faculty:

I strongly think that the university benefits from the grant I received. In the current political climate, obtaining federal funding for the . . . sciences is extraordinarily competitive (one in ten grants are getting funded at present). A relatively small amount of money, at a time when it helped substantially for me to regain my competitive edge will, I hope, keep me in a pool of faculty that can support research programs. (2005)

[Had I not received the grant], I probably would not have been able to get much done beyond teaching my courses. I would not have received the additional funding from [funding institution], not been able to return to my [research] project, and not compiled data for [a different] project. (2007)

Investment in their/our careers at or after a point of crisis is both humane and efficient in terms of generating research progress and publications, attracting outside funds, and stabilizing and accelerating professional development. It is

Table 10.6.   Grant awards to VLCP applicants/awardees, 2002–2009

Division	Awardees	Mean grant awards, 3 years prior	Mean life cycle investment	Mean grant awards, 3 years post	Mean increase (decrease) in grant awards
			Awardees		
BIO	30	$609,964	$26,133	$1,360,686	$750,722
PHY	8	$275,016	$22,449	$429,685	$154,669
SOC	26	$97,987	$21,694	$178,082	$80,095
A&H	15	$12,378	$20,602	$1,443	-$10,935
			Not Awarded		
BIO	15	$824,410	$0	$391,920	-$432,490
PHY	5	$463,204	$0	$369,033	-$94,171
SOC	4	$6,686	$0	$100,748	$94,062
A&H	7	$95,548	$0	$39,067	-$56,481

Source: Data obtained from institutional data sources and VLCP award letters.

more efficient than losing faculty members who leave, or who become non-productive in research terms, then trying to refill tenure lines. (2010)

Increased Prestige/Reputation of the University

Some faculty remarked that the reputation of the university as a whole is enhanced because of the program. For some, this happens because retaining a faculty member at a vulnerable time could mean retaining a potential "star":

It's really unique to give [a grant] during a very difficult time of a person's career. And the person could turn out to be, in five years, a big star for the university . . . I'm not saying that I'm going to be a star, but I could be. And, and who is to say that the thirty-two thousand dollars[4] that was spent . . . it's really a drop in the bucket, but it really helps the most fundamental part of the university, which is research and teaching. If you can't keep faculty, you can't get good faculty to stay here, then you lose your prestige as a university. We come here because it's a prestigious university. We believe our colleagues are stars in the field. And if we don't have that belief, we wouldn't be here. So I hope the university will want to keep us here, and develop some mechanism to help us. (2004)

I believe this program is one of the most important on campus. Without question, it has helped the university keep and cultivate world-class scholars, as well as a more compassionate campus/departmental climate. (2012)

For others, the presence of the program itself speaks highly of the supportive working environment for faculty that the university creates:

> I consider the program an example of the University of Wisconsin at its most humane best, where the university provides resources to faculty going through a difficult period, to enable them to maintain the kind of research productivity that strengthens their careers, and strengthens the university as a whole. (2006)

> I have told others about the grant in the context of explaining why I think UW-Madison is such an exceptional institution. For example, I have mentioned it to job candidates as an illustration of how this institution takes seriously life cycle issues and is genuinely humane and supportive in not just accommodating but actively supporting faculty through periods where personal and professional life pressures may be unnaturally intense or exacerbated by unforeseen health issues. The distinction between "accommodation" and "support" that is embodied in this program is crucial, and it really sets it apart from the kinds of institutional responses to life cycle issues that are the current norm in American universities (not to mention other kinds of workplaces). (2007)

> I wish the UW talked about this program more, in fact. It's a selling point for our culture and an indication of the way that a progressive workplace can treat women if it wants to! Not that anybody, male or female, wants to be in a situation where they need the help this program gives—but lightning can and does strike us all. (2011)

Increased Loyalty of Faculty

By supporting faculty members at their most vulnerable moments, the VLCP program increases faculty loyalty to the university, improving the retention of faculty and the institution's reputation simultaneously.

> This program generates a feeling of commitment to this institution, and a desire and willingness to give back, to help ensure that others benefit from similar institutional support in the future. (2007)

> I heartfully can tell you that this program was the most significant help I ever received from the university, or any major national program. Its non-competitive nature, its generosity, and speed were absolutely crucial in helping me, and feeling valued by the university in its investing in my work—and person—as part of a long-term agenda, rather than a reward for past achievements, or future/ongoing projects. I am extremely grateful to VLCP, and will remember it as a major asset and support I have received in this institution. (2008)

> The fact that this resource was made available to me in a time of crisis definitely engendered in me a stronger loyalty toward UW-Madison. (2012)

Impact on Others

A final benefit of the VLCP is that the career boost provided by the funds not only help the faculty member who receives the grant, but very often boosts the careers of students and staff in the faculty member's research group. Many faculty comment on their gratefulness not only for reviving their own research programs, but also for saving the careers of the people who work with them:

> This award enabled me to keep a research specialist and postdoc, who would have been let go otherwise. The postdoctoral researcher also obtained independent funding for herself in 2007. Hence, two women in science directly benefited from the VLCP. (2006)

> I began to repopulate my lab by bringing in three undergraduates to work on various projects, especially ones relating to other species. Two of the undergraduates are still with me (one departed), and another has joined us this spring. (2012)

Negative Outcomes: Lingering Stigma

In all evaluations, VLCP recipients are asked whether there were any negative outcomes from receiving the grant. VLCP recipients report no negative outcomes of receiving the grant itself, but they do mention the lingering stigma associated with those personal life events that interfered with their research progress. Although some note that the presence of the program can help reduce that stigma, they forthrightly explain that the stigma remains:

> Initially, when I first was dealing with my life event, some of my colleagues were not very supportive, they didn't understand what was going on and they were criticizing me that I wasn't here on Saturdays. (2004)

> It is extremely valuable for those in need in terms of acknowledging faculty needs outside the box (e.g., emotional needs, practical needs involving family). It makes an attempt to legitimatize these things in an environment where any weakness is seen as potentially damaging. (2009)

> Just knowing that there were other faculty members who had benefitted from such support was important. Often, difficult situations that pose barriers to progression toward tenure are not discussed, due to a fear of raising red flags along a career path. Openness about the ways that life events might alter a path to tenure was invaluable. (2012)

PROGRAM IMPLEMENTATION AND RECOMMENDATIONS

The UW-Madison has had tremendous success implementing the Vilas Life Cycle Professorship program. The program is in its second decade, and faculty continue to value and support the program. In this section we highlight some of the elements of the VLCP program that recipient feedback indicates make it successful, using this evidence to provide recommendations to other campuses wishing to create similar programs for their faculty.

Importance of Confidentiality

Due to the private nature of the life event occurring for faculty, combined with the culture of avoiding discussion of personal issues within the academy, the promise of confidentiality for VLCP applicants is a crucial feature of the program. The assurance of confidentiality is stated in the program's Frequently Asked Questions and in the call for proposals:

> Applications will remain confidential within the review committee [and in] special cases, a Graduate School Dean or Associate Dean may be asked for technical advice regarding the research program; they will also regard the application materials as confidential. Graduate School Research Committees will review expenditures for awards, but will not have access to applications. (WISELI 2009)

Several recipients commented that they would not have applied if confidentiality had not been promised:

> The application process was straightforward, but very painful and difficult to complete because it involved writing about hurtful and difficult personal experiences, and forced me to objectively confront and evaluate the negative impact on my career of [my situation]. Although difficult to write, I found that the process helped me to realize that I wasn't a victim, and that I could jump start my research program again. I also knew that the proposal would be read and evaluated in the strictest confidence. (2007)

> The one disadvantage now, however, for applying for this grant in my department is that last year the department asked that people notify a departmental committee if they wished to apply for the grant. If I had to do that, I would have not applied, since I am not sure I would have liked to describe the details of my family and personal situation to a departmental committee. (2010)

Note that this last quotation indicates that the department is attempting to circumvent the confidentiality of the program. We cannot know what department this is, due to the confidentiality of responses to the evaluation studies; however, it is not a requirement of the VLCP program to have the permission of a department to apply. In fact, the VLCP program does not require a supporting letter from a department chair or anyone else, precisely because of confidentiality issues. It is the case that departments, especially financial personnel, will know that an award has been made, but will not know the reason for the award. As a further confidentiality measure, the UW-Madison grants office does not include faculty names in any searchable fields of the university's grants awards database. Any university implementing a grant program such as the VLCP should ensure that the application and review process are as confidential as possible. Consider not posting names of recipients, not requiring letters of support from chairs and/or other colleagues, and not sharing applications beyond a small evaluation committee that is committed to protecting the disclosures made in the applications.

Lack of "Red Tape"

The program is designed to make it as easy as possible to apply. The application itself is fairly straightforward and clear; the requirement for a "statement of need" is only three pages maximum; faculty do not need to write a very detailed account of their research study; faculty can send their documents in whatever format is most convenient for them; applications that are incomplete, incorrect, or not within the correct time frame are not turned back (although sometimes additional documents are requested or application review is postponed if necessary). Faculty appreciate the "full service" approach to administering the program. They are applying for the funding at a time of extreme stress; a burdensome application process would add to rather than reduce their problems.

> [The application process was] easy, and absolutely the best administrators I have ever come across in my three years in the university. (2007)

> The application was very straightforward and did not involve unnecessary work or "red tape." It was not onerous in any way. [The grant administrator] was immensely helpful in answering all of my questions as I prepared the application as well as after I received the award. (2012)

Faculty in crisis will have a difficult time using the program if the requirements for application or award are too demanding. We recommend making the process as simple and flexible as possible.

Importance of Funding for Research

Several faculty commented that the value of the program is in recognizing that when faculty are in crisis, they don't just need time, they need funding to get back on track. Several programs already in place at most universities—

extending the tenure clock, paid or unpaid leave—can buy a faculty member some time. But the infusion of additional research resources is key to a faculty member's ability to become a productive researcher again after a personal crisis:

> Stoppage of the tenure clock for women giving birth is nice but it doesn't support students, fund the lab, get more papers out or do any of the things that actually help one achieve tenure. Financial support can do all those things and thus can have a much larger impact on career success and satisfaction, which are necessary for retention. (2007)

Use of Funds (Salary Support vs. Other Research Support)

One area where the program falls short of truly providing faculty with the support they need for their research in times of personal crisis is in the restrictions on the use of the funds offered in the program. Per the terms of the Vilas Trust, funds cannot be used for faculty salaries—only for direct research costs (e.g., student assistants, lab equipment, research travel). However, what some faculty—especially faculty in the Arts and Humanities disciplines—really need is paid time to do their research. The inability to pay for a course buyout with these funds limits their usefulness to many of the UW-Madison faculty. For campuses considering the implementation of a program such as the VLCP, we would recommend finding a funding source that would allow funding of faculty salary.

> I applied for the money to give myself some time in the summer to work on research projects. And that was invaluable, because I was able to get a manuscript out. (2004—at the time, the funds could be used for salary.)

Another program element that contributes to its success, but about which recipients were not directly asked, is flexibility. The program, including the use of the funds, is designed to be as flexible as possible. Three different deadlines for proposals throughout the year ensure that faculty can time their awards in a way that is to their best advantage. The program only provides funds for one year, but the start/end dates of that year can be set to maximally benefit the recipient—it does not need to be tied to the fiscal year. The UW-Madison VLCP program unfortunately does not allow for no-cost extensions. If an institution is considering the implementation of a program like this, allowing for such extensions would be a good feature to add. Creating a program with maximum flexibility in the timing and use of funds not only makes the program more useful for faculty, but it allows for greater ability to change and adapt the program into the future as the research environment for faculty changes.

Evaluation of Program

In order to justify continued funding for a program such as the VLCP, continuous evaluation is imperative. We recommend surveying grant recipients about their experience with the program, tracking their promotional progress and productivity, and constantly monitoring the types of applications received and types of resources requested. These data not only help to convince administrators and philanthropists that the program is worth maintaining, but also helps all faculty appreciate the needs of their peers and makes the campus climate around work/life issues more accepting.

CONCLUSION

The VLCP at UW-Madison is a popular program with many positive outcomes. The investment of approximately $279,000 per year results in higher promotion rates and lower attrition rates for junior faculty at risk, increased grant productivity, and a stronger feeling of faculty loyalty to the university. It is a large investment to make in order to improve research productivity of faculty in crisis, but for a university willing to make the investment the return is large as well. We believe that one reason for the success of the VLCP is that faculty tend to apply for the program as a crisis is ending or after it has passed, and not actually during the height of the crisis. Thus, the timing is right to provide research funding to highly motivated faculty who are well-positioned to take maximum advantage of the funds.

ADVANCE programs that piloted similar "transitional support" programs, such as at the University of Washington, found similar positive outcomes (Riskin et al. 2007), yet were unable to secure the institutional resources to continue their programs. We hope that this thorough explanation of the costs and benefits of implementing this program at UW-Madison will encourage more universities to make the investment, thus improving the safety net for all faculty.

NOTES

1. Prior to the infusion of Vilas Trust funds to the program, faculty salary was an allowable expense; however, this was only available to faculty in the STEM disciplines at the time, and only one faculty recipient used the funding this way.

2. All evaluation reports are available online at: http://wiseli.engr.wisc.edu/vilas.php (WISELI 2009).

3. The top three were: family leave (98.3 percent valuable); tenure clock extensions (97.6 percent valuable); and new faculty workshops (97.0 percent valuable).

4. Prior to 2006 and the Vilas funding, awards were allowed to exceed $30,000.

REFERENCES

Bianchi, Suzanne M, John P. Robinson, and Melissa A. Milkie. 2006. *Changing Rhythms of American Family Life*. New York: Russell Sage.

Cal Poly Pomona: ADVANCE. 2010. "Cal Poly Pomona ADVANCE Transition Support Awards." Retrieved September 5, 2013 (http://www.csupomona.edu/~advance/documents/TransitionSupportAward.pdf).

Committee on Maximizing the Potential of Women in Academic Science and Engineering. 2007. *Beyond Bias and Barriers: Fulfilling the Potential of Women in Academic Science and Engineering*. Washington, DC: National Academies Press.

Drago, Robert, Carol Colbeck, Kai Dawn Stauffer, Amy Pirretti, Kurt Burkum, Jennifer Fazioli, Gabriela Lazarro, and Tara Habasevich. 2005. "Bias Against Caregiving." *Academe* 91:22–25.

Jacobs, Jerry A., and Kathleen Gerson. 2004. *The Time Divide: Work, Family, and Gender Inequality*. Cambridge, MA: Harvard University Press.

Jacobs, Jerry A., and Sarah E. Winslow. 2004. "The Academic Life Course: Time Pressures and Gender Inequality." *Community, Work, and Family* 7:143–61.

Mason, Mary Ann, Nicholas H. Wolfinger, and Marc Goulden. 2013. *Do Babies Matter? Gender and Family in the Ivory Tower*. New Brunswick, NJ: Rutgers University Press.

Moen, Phyllis, and Patricia Roehling. 2005. *The Career Mystique: Cracks in the American Dream*. Lanham, MD: Rowman and Littlefield.

National Center for Health Statistics. 2011. "Health, United States, 2010: With Special Feature on Death and Dying." Retrieved September 13, 2013 (http://www.cdc.gov/nchs/data/hus/hus10.pdf).

National Science Foundation. 2001. "ADVANCE: Increasing the Participation and Advancement of Women in Academic Science and Engineering Careers." Retrieved September 13, 2013 (http://www.nsf.gov/funding/pgm_summ.jsp?pims_id=5383andorg=NSFandsel_org=NSFandfrom=fund).

Palepu, Anita, and Carol P. Herbert. 2002. "Medical Women in Academia: The Silences We Keep." *Canadian Medical Association Journal* 167:877–79.

Pribbenow, Christine Maidl, Jennifer Sheridan, Jessica Winchell, Deveny Benting, Jo Handelsman, and Molly Carnes. 2010. "The Tenure Process and Extending the Tenure Clock: The Experience of Faculty at One University." *Higher Education Policy* 23:17–38.

Riskin, Eve A., Sheila Edwards Lange, Kate Quinn, Joyce W. Yen, and Suzanne G. Brainard. 2007. "Supporting Faculty During Life Transitions." Pp. 116–29 in *Transforming Science and Engineering: Advancing Academic Women*, edited by A. J. Stewart, J. E. Malley, and D. LaVaque-Manty. Ann Arbor: University of Michigan Press.

Rossi, Alice S., and Peter H. Rossi. 1990. *Of Human Bonding: Parent-Child Relations Across the Life Course*. New York: Aldine de Gruyter.

Sandberg, John F., and Sandra L. Hofferth. 2001. "Changes in Children's Time with Parents: United States 1981–1997." *Demography* 38:423–36.

Savoy, Julia N., and Jennifer Sheridan. June 6, 2011. "Results from the 2010 Study of Faculty Worklife at UW-Madison: Tenured and Tenure-Track Faculty." Page 9. Retrieved September 3, 2013 (http://wiseli.engr.wisc.edu/docs/Report_Wave3_2010TT.pdf).

Sheridan, Jennifer, and Jessica Winchell. 2003. "Results from the 2003 Study of Faculty Worklife at UW-Madison." Page 13. Retrieved August 30, 2013 (http://wiseli.engr.wisc.edu/docs/Report_Wave1_2003.pdf).

———. 2006. "Results from the 2006 Study of Faculty Worklife at UW-Madison." Pp. 7,12. Retrieved August 30, 2013 (http://wiseli.engr.wisc.edu/docs/Report_Wave2_2006.pdf).

Shollen, S. Lynn, Carole J. Bland, Deborah A. Finstad, and Anne L. Taylor. 2009. "Organizational Climate and Family Life: How These Factors Affect the Status of Women Faculty at One Medical School." *Academic Medicine* 84:87–94.

University of Michigan: ADVANCE. 2012. "Elizabeth C. Crosby Research Fund." Retrieved September 5, 2013 (http://sitemaker.umich.edu/advance/crosby_research_fund).

Utah State University: ADVANCE. 2004. "Transitional Support Pilot Program." Retrieved September 5, 2013 (http://digitalcommons.usu.edu/cgi/viewcontent.cgi?article=1551and

context=advance).

Ward, Kelly, and Lisa Wolf-Wendel. 2008. "Choice and Discourse in Faculty Careers: Feminist Perspectives on Work and Family." Pp. 253–72 in *Unfinished Agendas: New and Continuing Gender Challenges in Higher Education*, edited by J. Glazer-Raymo. Baltimore: Johns Hopkins University Press.

———. 2004. "Fear Factor: How Safe is it to Make Time for Family?" *Academe* 90:28–31.

Williams, Joan C., and Donna L. Norton. 2008. "Building Academic Excellence Through Gender Equity." *American Academic* 4:185–208.

Women in Science and Engineering Leadership Institute (WISELI). 2006. "Gender equity indicators, 2000–2012." Table 5a. Retrieved September 5, 2013 (http://wiseli.engr.wisc.edu/indicators.php).

———. 2009. "Vilas Life Cycle Professorships." Retrieved May 1, 2014 (http://wiseli.engr.wisc.edu/vilas.php).

Yeung, W. Jean, John F. Sandberg, Pamela E. Davis-Kean, and Sandra L. Hofferth. 2001. "Children's Time With Fathers in Intact Families." *Journal of Marriage and Family* 63:136–54.

Chapter Eleven

Discussion

Erin K. Anderson and Catherine Richards Solomon

Most contemporary workplaces are gendered institutions (Acker 1990). Employees are men and women, fathers and mothers, sons and daughters who have responsibilities in their workplaces and in their families (Lorber 2005). A long-held assumption is that "women workers have families and men workers have wives" (Lorber 2005, 71), but as rates of women's employment have increased and men's contributions to home and childcare have evolved, so has the likelihood that both women and men will have caregiving responsibilities. Unlike the practices in many nations, in the United States the negotiation of work and family responsibilities largely falls on individuals and individual families to develop strategies and make sacrifices in order to manage the public and private spheres of their lives in the absence of policies that aid these efforts.

The Family and Medical Leave Act (FMLA) was expected to be one such policy that could assist employees in attending to personal or family needs. Although somewhat controversial when initially passed, the FMLA has proven to be an important policy which helps employees balance their work and family responsibilities. In the twenty years since it was implemented, the U.S. Department of Labor estimates it has been used nearly one hundred million times (Fortman 2013). Concerns about employee absence and lost productivity for businesses appear to be unfounded; most employers who are subject to the FMLA report little difficulty in complying with the policy and fewer than 10 percent of worksites claim negative effects related to employee productivity, absenteeism, turnover, or business profitability (Simonetta 2013). Two significant drawbacks of the policy, however, are the fact that approximately 40 percent of Americans are not eligible for leave and that the policy has no provision for continued pay while an employee is on leave. Many employees report having to choose between taking needed leave and giving up needed income. Nearly half of the employees who reported not taking leave when they needed it have cited the inability to afford the leave as their rationale (Simonetta 2013).

Many American employers have responded to these concerns and developed family-friendly policies that extend beyond the requirements of the FMLA and offer employees greater flexibility in work schedules, sick leave, and parental leave (Hollenshead, Sullivan, Smith, August, and Hamilton 2005). These policies have largely proved to be cost effective in the corporate and nonprofit sectors and have resulted in a greater sense of community among employees, better workplace loyalty, higher morale, and lower rates of turnover. Thus, it appears that recognizing the employer's role in helping workers negotiate their family and workplace responsibilities is a benefit for business.

Academic institutions, however, have generally not kept pace with necessary changes in family-friendly policies. In 1974 the American Association of University Professors (AAUP) advocated for

> [a]n institution's policies on faculty appointments [to be] sufficiently flexible to permit faculty members to combine family and career responsibilities in the manner best suited to them as professionals and parents. This flexibility requires the availability of such alternatives as longer-term leaves of absence, temporary reductions in workload with no loss of professional status, and retention of full-time affiliation throughout the child-bearing and child-rearing years.

One of the greatest changes in academe in the past forty years has been the growth in the number of professional women. Yet, whether working toward graduate degrees, seeking tenure-track positions, or pursuing tenure or promotion, women continue to be more likely to face obstacles in the balancing of work and family responsibilities (AAUP 2001). As a result, women are more likely to occupy positions as instructors, lecturers, and unranked teaching positions, are less likely to be tenured or promoted to the rank of full professor, and have lower average salaries than their male colleagues (AAUP 2001; August 2006; Mason and Goulden 2002; West and Curtis 2006; Wolfinger, Mason, and Goulden 2009). In response to this persistent pattern, at the beginning of the twenty-first century the AAUP renewed the call for "the development and implementation of institutional policies that enable the healthy integration of work responsibilities with family life in academe" (AAUP 2001, 340).

The Center for the Education of Women (CEW) finds that the average number of family-friendly policies available to faculty per institution has increased since 2002, but that the academy still has work to do. The continuing necessity of colleges and universities to respond to the need for family-friendly policies is seen in the current state of affairs: 78 percent of institutions have formal, written policies to offer paid time off for new mothers during the period of disability; 65 percent grant tenure clock extensions; 44 percent permit unpaid dependent-care leave beyond the twelve-week FMLA period; 36 percent allow for paid time off for new biological fathers; 29 percent provide paid time off to biological mothers after the period of disability; and 21 percent have a modified-duties policy that does not reduce take-home pay (CEW 2007).

The research and case studies in this volume highlight the need for additional policy development as well as the possibilities for policy expansion. Three themes that emerge from the findings presented here are 1) the desire among faculty and staff to have policies available to them that allow them to perform their workplace roles while also managing their family needs, 2) the need for a greater variety of family-friendly policies, and 3) the importance of understanding how workplace culture and colleagues can influence the perception and use of existing policies.

Academics recognize one of the limitations of the twelve weeks of FMLA leave is that it does not correspond neatly with a typical fifteen-week college semester. Moreover, the unpaid leave federal policy allows is prohibitive for many college and university employees who cannot forgo their income during a leave period and may not have paid vacation or sick leave available to them. Such circumstances have prompted faculty at many institutions to engage in policy research and activism on their own behalf in an effort to create and implement workable solutions on their campuses. Looking to successful policies at other schools, as suggested by Randall and Johnson (chapter 7), Tower (chapter 8), and Oliker and Seligman (chapter 9), is imperative. In the words of Randall and Johnson, "You are not reinventing the wheel, just inventing or modifying it at your institution. There are excellent models of good family policies out there; use them!" The scholars featured here detail their obstacles and triumphs in assessing employee needs, collaborating with stakeholders and administrators, and designing and implementing policy. While it is obvious that a number of challenges might complicate this process, these success stories should encourage faculty and staff to envision the kind of policies they need and work toward their development.

There is also a clear need for a variety of family-friendly policies. Although a majority of academic institutions appear to offer some leave for faculty and staff when they become new parents (CEW 2007), family responsibilities that might interfere with workplace responsibilities exist across the life course. With changes in the gender demographics of faculty, delays in family formation, and a growing number of Americans sandwiched between caring for children and aging parents, managing work and family needs is increasingly complex. Aside from time needed for the recovery from childbirth and the care of newborns, college and university employees are likely to have continuing needs associated with child care, medical leave, and elder care, as well as various other life events. The research of Karasik, Berke, and Scheer (chapter 5) on elder care and Sheridan, Pribbenow, Carnes, Handelsman, and Wendt (chapter 10) on the resources provided through the Vilas Life Cycle Professorship is significant for highlighting work/life needs that are not often considered and how colleges and universities can support faculty and staff in these times of need, ultimately allowing employees to continue to contribute to the academic workplace.

Finally, the research presented here reinforces the fact that policies are important, but a workplace culture that allows one to feel they can utilize family-friendly policies is vital to their success. Surveys and interviews repeatedly reveal that faculty and staff often lack a full comprehension of the policies available to them or fear the professional consequences of using them. Solomon (chapter 2), Berheide and Linden (chapter 3), and Anderson (chapter 4) all conclude that colleagues and supervisors play substantial roles in the management of family needs while trying to fulfill professional duties. These patterns confirm the AAUP's conclusions about family and work in the academy, "institutional policies may be easier to change than institutional cultures" (2001, 344).

Collectively, these works demonstrate the continuing need for faculty, staff, and administrators to understand how their academic institutions work, how they could improve, and how they can work together to achieve work/life policy goals. The provision of work/life policies will aid institutions in attracting qualified personnel, retaining valued employees, and improving the teaching and research accomplished on college and university campuses. Many work/life policies may be controversial or difficult to design and implement, but academe can learn a lesson from the FMLA history: greater institutional support for the management of personal and professional responsibilities may ultimately prove to be beneficial for the academy.

REFERENCES

Acker, Joan. 1990. "Hierarchies, Jobs, and Bodies: A Theory of Gendered Organizations." *Gender and Society* 4:139–58.

American Association of University Professors (AAUP). 2001. "Statement on Principles of Family Responsibilities and Academic Work." Retrieved December 5, 2014 (http://www.aaup.org/file/Family_and_Academic_Work.pdf).

August, Louise. 2006. "It Isn't Over: The Continuing Under-Representation of Women Faculty." Center for the Education of Women. Retrieved August 1, 2012 (http://www.cew.umich.edu/sites/default/files/augustfemrep06_0.pdf).

Center for the Education of Women. 2007. "Family-friendly Policies in Higher Education: A Five-year Report." University of Michigan Research Brief.

Fortman, Laura. 2013. "The FMLA: 20 Years On and Keeping America's Families Strong." U.S. Department of Labor. Retrieved December 5, 2014 (http://social.dol.gov/blog/the-fmla-20-years-on-and-keeping-america percentE2 percent80 percent99s-families-strong/).

Hollenshead, Carol S., Beth Sullivan, Gilia C. Smith, Louise August, and Susan Hamilton. 2005. "Work/Family Policies in Higher Education: Survey Data and Case Studies of Policy Implementation." *New Directions for Higher Education* 130:41–65.

Lorber, Judith. 2005. *Breaking the Bowls: Degendering and Feminist Change*. New York: W. W. Norton and Co.

Mason, Mary Ann, and Marc Goulden. 2002. "Do Babies Matter?" *Academe* 88:21.

Simonetta, Jonathan. 2013. "Family and Medical Leave in 2012: Executive Summary." U.S. Department of Labor. Retrieved December 5, 2014 (http://www.dol.gov/asp/evaluation/fmla/FMLA-2012-Executive-Summary.pdf).

West, Martha S., and John W. Curtis. 2006. "AAUP Faculty Gender Equity Indicators 2006." Retrieved August 1, 2012 (http://www.aaup.org/NR/rdonlyres/63396944-44BE-4ABA-9815-5792D93856F1/0/AAUPGenderEquityIndicators2006.pdf).

Wolfinger, Nicholas H., Mary Ann Mason, and Marc Goulden. 2009. "Stay in the Game: Gender, Family Formation, and Alternative Trajectories in the Academic Life Course." *Social Forces* 87:1591–1621.

Index

About the Contributors

Erin K. Anderson, PhD, is assistant professor of sociology at Washington College, where she also contributes to the Gender Studies Program. Her research has looked at women participants in welfare to work programs, institutional patterns of gender socialization, constructions of gender identity, and experiences of gender role nonconformity. In these areas she has studied the state-designed Welfare to Work programs, the Girl Scout organization, stay-at-home fathers, and men who decide whether or not to utilize available family-friendly policies in their workplaces. She teaches in the areas of gender, family, and work.

Catherine White Berheide, PhD, is professor of sociology and principal investigator of the National Science Foundation ADVANCE grant, "SUN: Supporting Women Faculty in STEM at Liberal Arts Colleges," at Skidmore College. She has been studying the relationship between work and family since she coauthored an article in *Family Relations* (1988) and coedited *Women, Family, and Policy: A Global Perspective* (1994). Her most recent publication on the topic is a chapter on work-family conflict among college faculty in *Social Production and Reproduction at the Interface of Public and Private Spheres* (*Advances in Gender Research*, Volume 16, 2012). She is coeditor of *Gender Transformation of the Academy* (*Advances in Gender Research*, Volume 19, 2014).

Debra L. Berke, PhD, CFLE, is an associate professor and director of psychology programs at Wilmington University, where she oversees two undergraduate programs and two post-master's certificates. She teaches a variety of courses at the undergraduate level, including Research Methods in Psychology; Senior Seminar in Psychology; Families and Crisis; Human

Sexuality; Marriage and Family; Lifespan Development; and Adult Development and Aging, in both online and face-to-face formats. Her research interests include work and family, family policy, human sexuality, and the scholarship of teaching and learning. Dr. Berke has been a consultant for the Pennsylvania Commission on Crime and Delinquency and the state of Delaware. She has served as an officer in regional and national organizations, has been a guest editor for journals, and has numerous publications and presentations. Dr. Berke is also certified as a family life educator.

Molly Carnes, MD, MS, is professor of medicine, codirector of the Women in Science and Engineering Leadership Institute (WISELI), and director of the Center for Women's Health Research at the University of Wisconsin-Madison. Dr. Carnes has published extensively in the area of women in STEMM (science, technology, engineering, mathematics, and medicine), beginning with her first publication on the topic of work/life balance in academic medicine in 1996. Since then, she has published more than thirty articles or commentaries related to gender equity in academia. Her latest area of inquiry is investigating the potential for implicit gender bias to influence evaluations of grant proposals.

Jo Handelsman, PhD, is Frederick Phineas Rose Professor and Howard Hughes Medical Institute Professor in the Department of Molecular, Cellular, and Developmental Biology at Yale University. Her research focuses on the genetic and functional diversity of microorganisms in soil and insect gut communities. In addition to her microbiology research program, Dr. Handelsman is also known internationally for her efforts to improve science education and increase the participation of women and minorities in science at the university level. Dr. Handelsman was the senior author on the influential 2012 study "Science Faculty's Subtle Gender Biases Favor Male Students," which received national press attention and garnered her the distinction from *Nature* as "one of ten people who mattered in 2012."

Virginia Clark Johnson, PhD, is dean and professor of the College of Human Development and Education at North Dakota State University.

Rona J. Karasik, PhD, is a professor and director of the Gerontology Program at St. Cloud State University, where she teaches a variety of undergraduate and graduate gerontology courses on topics including dementia, health, housing, and aging in the community. Her work also includes publications and presentations in the areas of aging families; housing for older adults (including specialized dementia care); diversity (including disparities in later life); and pedagogy in higher education (e.g., service-learning, experiential learning, and anti-racist pedagogy). Her current research focuses on incorporating anti-racist pedagogy into the gerontological curriculum. Dr. Karasik is active in local, regional, and national educational initiatives regarding aging and holds fellow status in the Gerontological Society of America (GSA) and the Association for Gerontology in Higher Education (AGHE).

Rena Linden is a research assistant at the Population Reference Bureau. Previously she worked as a research assistant on the National Science Foundation ADVANCE grant, "SUN: Supporting Women Faculty in STEM at Liberal Arts Colleges," at Skidmore College, coauthoring an article examining gender differences in promotion at two liberal arts colleges in the Forum on Public Policy (2013).

Stacey Oliker, PhD, is professor of sociology at the University of Wisconsin-Milwaukee. She has studied low-wage care work, caregiving across social institutions, families during welfare reform, and friendship and social networks. Her books are *Best Friends and Marriage: Exchange Among Women* (University of California Press, 1989) and, with Francesca Cancian, *Caring and Gender* (Rowman and Littlefeld, 2000).

Christine Maidl Pribbenow, PhD, is an associate scientist at the Wisconsin Center for Education Research and the Evaluation Director of WISELI (Women in Science and Engineering Leadership Institute) at the University of Wisconsin-Madison. Dr. Pribbenow is the lead evaluator on many projects related to diversity in STEMM (science, technology, engineering, mathematics, and medicine), and has published her research on topics such as tenure clock extensions, training of faculty hiring committees, and departmental climate.

Brandy A. Randall , PhD, is associate dean of the College of Graduate and Interdisciplinary Studies and associate professor of human development and family science at North Dakota State University.

Scott D. Scheer, PhD, is a professor in the Department of Agricultural Communication, Education, and Leadership (ACEL) at the Ohio State University. His research focuses primarily on outreach education and youth development and has been published in a variety of academic journals and supported through externally funded grants. Dr. Scheer teaches undergraduate and graduate courses (both online and in the classroom) in areas of program development, evaluation, and human development. He has received national and university awards for teaching and service.

Amanda I. Seligman, PhD, is associate professor of history and urban studies at the University of Wisconsin-Milwaukee. Her books include *Block by*

Block: Neighborhoods and Public Policy on Chicago's West Side (Chicago: University of Chicago Press, 2005) and *Is Graduate School Really for You?: The Whos, Whats, Hows, and Whys of Pursuing a Master's or Ph.D.* (Baltimore: Johns Hopkins University Press, 2012).

Jennifer Sheridan, PhD, is the executive and research director of the Women in Science and Engineering Leadership Institute (WISELI) at the University of Wisconsin-Madison. A sociologist by training, she has published several articles on the advancement of women in STEMM (science, technology, engineering, mathematics, and medicine), including a 2010 piece demonstrating the effectiveness of using the literature on implicit bias to improve the hiring of women faculty in STEMM.

Catherine Richards Solomon, PhD, is professor of sociology and department chair in the Department of Sociology at Quinnipiac University in Connecticut. She studies how individuals construct work and personal lives that make sense to them—and how these constructions are shaped by gender and class. The majority of her scholarship focuses on professors' work/life management and she published this research in *Advances in Gender Research, Gender, Work, and Organization, The Social Science Journal*, and in *Disrupting the Culture of Silence: Women Navigating Hostility and Making Change in the Academy*, edited by Kris DeWelde and Andi Stepnick, and *People at Work: Life, Power, and Social Inclusion in the New Economy*, edited by Marjore L. DeVault. She has also explored how stay-at-home fathers construct their fatherhood identity and masculinity; this work has appeared in *Fathering* and *Michigan Family Review*.

Leslie E. Tower, PhD, is a professor at West Virginia University, holding a dual appointment in the School of Social Work and Department of Public Administration. Her scholarship focuses on women and work. She recently coauthored *Women and Public Service: Barriers, Challenges, and Opportunities*, published by M. E. Sharpe. She leads the policy development component of the WVU ADVANCE grant (HRD-100797). For the Council on Social Work Education (CSWE), the sole accrediting body of social work education, she is cochair of the Women's Council.

Amy Wendt, PhD, is a professor of electrical and computer engineering at the University of Wisconsin-Madison, and is codirector of WISELI. Her primary research area is ionized gases (plasmas) for materials processing applications. Dr. Wendt is also committed to improving the representation of women in engineering and other STEM fields. In addition to codirecting WISELI, she leads an NSF-funded project to infuse middle school science and math curricula with engineering content designed to increase the interest of women and minorities through an emphasis on societal challenges.